The Complete Idiot's Reference Card

Odds and Payoffs on a $2 Bet

1-9	$2.20	5-1	$12.00
1-5	$2.20	6-1	$14.00
2-5	$2.80	7-1	$16.00
1-2	$3.00	8-1	$18.00
Even (1-1)	$4.00	9-1	$20.00
7-5	$4.80	10-1	$22.00
2-1	$6.00	15-1	$32.00
5-2	$7.00	20-1	$42.00
3-1	$8.00	50-1	$102.00
7-2	$9.00	99-1	$200.00
4-1	$10.00		

This Horse Wins on a Wet Track

➤ He has wet-track form.

➤ He is bred for wet-track racing.

➤ He has big flat feet.

➤ He has early speed, which lasts longer in the mud.

➤ He has run well on the turf, wet, or otherwise.

➤ He has drawn an inside post position.

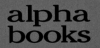

alpha
books

This Horse Wins a Sprint

➤ He breaks well from the gate. No Exceptions.

➤ He has early speed.

➤ He either runs on the lead or runs from just off the lead. If several horses show early speed, one who runs from off the pace is the likely winner.

This Horse Wins at Middle Distances and Routines

➤ He's light of body but has deep shoulders and wide chest.

➤ He has an inside post, but only if there's a short run to the first turn. Otherwise, post position doesn't matter.

➤ He has enough speed to stay in contact with the leaders (however, fast or slow they are), no matter how long the race.

➤ He's not required to carry more than a couple of pounds more than other horses, particularly if the race is a route.

The Super Combo System

➤ Add the number of each horse's finish in his last three races. If he finished second, fourth, and first, his number is 7.

➤ Count the number of days the horse has been away from the races. A horse who last started a week ago gets a 7.

➤ Add the number of lengths the horse finished behind the winner in his last three races. (A winner gets a zero.)

➤ Add the odds (to one) the horse started at in his last three races. 5-1, 3-2, and 2-1 equals 8 1/2.

➤ The horse with the lowest total gets your bet.

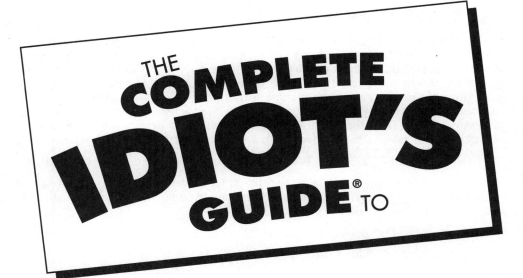

THE **COMPLETE IDIOT'S GUIDE**® TO

Betting on Horses

by Sharon B. Smith

alpha books

A Division of Macmillan General Reference
A Simon & Schuster Macmillan Company
1633 Broadway, New York, NY 10019-6785

Macmillan Publishing books may be purchased for business or sales promotional use. For information please write: Special Markets Department, Macmillan Publishing USA, 1633 Broadway, New York, NY 10019.

International Standard Book Number: 0-87605-328-2

Library of Congress Catalog Card Number: 98-29444

00 99 98   4   3   2   1

Interpretation of the printing code: The rightmost number of the first series of numbers is the year of the book's printing; the rightmost number of the second series of numbers is the number of the book's printing. For example, a printing code of 98-1 shows that the first printing occurred in 1998.

Printed in the United States of America

Photos and charts courtesy of the New York Racing Association, the United States Trotting Association, and Equibase.

Alpha Development Team

Publisher
Kathy Nebenhaus

Editorial Director
Gary M. Krebs

Managing Editor
Bob Shuman

Marketing Brand Manager
Felice Primeau

Senior Editor
Nancy Mikhail

Development Editor
Madelyn Larsen

Assistant Editor
Maureen Horn

Production Team

Production Editor
Mark Enochs

Copy Editor
Cliff Shubs

Cartoonist
Kevin Spear

Cover Designer
Mike Freeland

Photo Editor
Richard H. Fox

Designer
Glenn Larsen

Indexer
Angie Bess

Layout/Proofreading
Angela Calvert
Mary Hunt
Michelle R. Lee
Linda Quigley

Contents at a Glance

Contents

Foreword

Those privileged to inspect my college transcript are absolutely correct; I spent nearly as much time at Hazel Park Raceway as I did in the Bowling Green State University Library. While visiting the latter, I spent time searching in vain for the book you now hold in your hands.

In the decades since I left the academic world and wandered through a couple of brief careers on the way to my current post as a racing publicist, I have collected plenty of pseudo-scientific tomes about picking winners. Invariably they are awash in theories based on speed, breeding, track bias, the influence of celestial bodies, and quantum mechanics.

Garbage.

What's been missing in racing is a book such as this, cataloguing the basic elements of handicapping, a reference book to which you can return time and again to drill you in the fundamentals.

Of course advanced theories have their place, and as you begin to understand and enjoy racing, you will inevitably build your own base of knowledge, observing patterns of performance and noting their effect on the Daily Double and Trifecta. You'll also find those patterns sometimes gilded by fool's gold. Systems and theories always seem to crash and burn, but the fundamentals remain rock-solid. When the number of winners you pick starts to slide, it's time to again thumb through what I'm sure will become the well-worn pages of this book. Such a return to fundamentals renews any handicapper—and the handicapper's pocketbook.

I'm also convinced that much greater numbers of people might be attracted to the excitement and beauty of horse racing if the systems and snake oil they get from the "scientific" handicappers and "expert tipsters" could be replaced with an understanding of the fundamental principles governing why one horse should be favored over the others. That's exactly what lies between the covers here. I find no joy in consulting a tip sheet or newspaper selector; I want to stand or fall on my own knowledge and understanding.

If the novice doesn't understand the consistent and repeated truths about horse racing, all the mint juleps in the world aren't going to make the sport enjoyable. Arming yourself with a bit of basic knowledge is what will save the day.

Racing, whether among Thoroughbreds, Standardbreds, or Quarter Horses, is first and foremost built upon solid patterns of performance, and identifying and analyzing them. This is the key to success. There are plenty of good books about handicapping on the shelves where you picked this one out, but most go right to more advanced topics and bypass the list of simple, elegant truths found here in *The Complete Idiot's Guide to Betting on Horses*.

Even worse than books of obtuse theory, computer-handicapping programs bury these truths in machine code somewhere, replacing a little understanding with a lot of tapping on the keyboard. But, I have downloaded and used some of them on my PC— and you will too—but you'll be further ahead by understanding the basics Sharon Smith has neatly codified here.

I first became acquainted with Sharon when she worked on the broadcast team for the Breeders Crown series of championship harness races on ESPN. Her insight, wit, and recognition of the key factors that comprise any horse race were immediately apparent, and she's hit the winner's circle again with this book.

I know that I will refer to this book often, and every time I need to touch on the basics to give myself a handicapping refresher course, and you should, too.

I hope the publisher will also consider my suggestion to donate a copy to the Bowling Green State University Library so future generations need not wander in search of fundamentally sound information on playing the greatest game in the world— handicapping the horse races.

—John Pawlak, Director of Publicity and Public Relations
The United States Trotting Association

Introduction

Horse racing may be the world's oldest organized sport. We know the names of horses who won races more than 3,000 years ago, while all we know about other sports is that people kicked balls around. The sheer age of racing has created a mass of names, numbers, statistics, facts, and rumors that threaten to bury anybody who tries to make sense of them. But it's worth your time to figure out what's going on in racing because:

➤ It's among the most exciting spectacles you can see in this sedate modern world.

➤ It's an activity with a well-deserved reputation for appealing to the rich and famous. You can be poor and unknown and still rub shoulders with them.

➤ It's a sport with a long and rich history, one wrapped up in the history of North America.

➤ You can make a lot of money if you understand what's happening, and you know what to do with the information.

How to Use This Book

There are two major and two slightly minor forms of modern American horse racing. The two big ones are Thoroughbred and Standardbred (or harness) racing. Quarter Horse racing comes next, followed by steeplechasing. Most books you see take one of two approaches: They cover only one and ignore the rest altogether, or they concetrate on one and ghettoize the others into separate and much smaller sections. That's never been a good idea, and it's an even worse one today.

All forms of horse racing have always been more alike than different. A good-looking horse looks good, no matter what his breed. A good start is the first step to a victory, no matter how short or how long the race. Speed combined with stamina and strategy wins, whether the human is on the horse's back or in a vehicle behind him. A good betting system works, with slight variations, in each of the forms of racing. Nowadays, the different forms of horse racing are intimately entwined, thanks to television, satellites, and computers. At almost every racetrack or off-track betting facility, you need only to look up at the television screen to see races from distant tracks—races you're urged to bet on. Likely as not, these will be Thoroughbred races if you're at a harness track, and vice versa.

In this book, we treat horse racing as horse racing. It's true that there are differences between the sports, and these are noted as we go along, but most of the information here applies to each of the racing sports. Instead of separating the sports, we separate the facts you need into categories you can understand.

In Part 1, we look at the horses. No matter what some books might claim, nobody can talk to horses. Let me revise that. You can talk to them, but none have ever responded.

Their language skills are limited. You can, however, observe them, analyze them, and even come to understand them. That's the first level of understanding you need if you hope to win at the racetrack.

In Part 2, we'll move on to people. Racetrack people do talk, sometimes too much, and we'll take a look at what they say, as well as what they really mean when they say it. Racing people hold the reins, literally and figuratively, and it's necessary to know their roles, their intentions, and their skills to succeed at the betting windows.

The races themselves make up Part 3. The tracks and the competitions held on them form a fourth partner in the relationship of horse, horseman, and bettor, one that's silent in the normal sense but whose characteristics make the difference between winning and losing.

Finally, in Part 4, we examine the game—the process of betting on horse racing. Some people are perfectly happy just going to the racetrack or watching races on television, getting sufficient satisfaction from the beauty and excitement of the sport. But more of us like to be part of the spectacle. We love to predict who's likely to run well and guess who doesn't have a chance. We love to cheer when there's money and not just honor on the line. And most of all, we love to win, whether it's two dollars or a lot more than that. This book will help you to become an informed observer of racing, whether you watch for the sport and spectacle or whether you're hoping to earn back the price of your admission to the track.

Extra Help

These boxes give you ideas, tips, warnings, and interesting information that will help you understand what's going on at the racetrack.

For the Record

These boxes contain information you don't necessarily need to enjoy and bet on the races, but they'll make you a more knowledgeable race watcher. You won't discover who's going to win here, but you will find out about what happens to horses and people when they decide to race each other.

Inside Track

Here you'll find useful tips that will help you identify the possible winners before you lay out your money.

Bad Bet

Some horses don't deserve your money, and this box will help you to find and avoid them.

From the Horse's Mouth

If you learn the words in this box, you'll not only sound like you know your way around the racetrack, you'll understand tips, information, and facts that you overhear while watching the races.

Part 1
The Horses

Horses can be mysterious creatures, even to people intimately acquainted with them. Part of the mystery is based on the fact that they're simply not people. They don't think like people do, nor do they react like people do even when faced with identical stimuli. The mystery deepens when horses become athletes, and it takes even more twists and turns when people are invited to bet on them.

In Part 1, we'll look at the horse as racing athlete. The first couple of chapters examine how horse racing evolved into the sport it is today, and how old-time racehorses became the Thoroughbreds, Standardbreds, and Quarter Horses we trust our money to.

Every horse needs speed, soundness, and a little veterinary care to win, so we'll wind up this section with advice on how to assess each of these factors.

Chapter 1

Man, Meet Horse

In This Chapter

➤ The long, long history of man, horse, and racing

➤ Racing comes to America

➤ The three racing breeds and how they grew

Man first met horse at the end of a spear point. It was a momentous meeting for each species. In the horse's original home, North America, the meeting and subsequent overhunting by man contributed to the animal's eventual extinction on his native continent. In Asia, the refuge of the surviving horses, the encounter led to a relationship much more profitable for both.

After a few thousand years of munching on horseburgers, prehistoric man realized that he could have his horse and eat it, too. He could use the horse to haul his bearskins or his berries, and then eat his transportation once they got to the new homesite.

Eventually, of course, people found it was even more profitable to refrain from dining on too much horsemeat. In addition to being able to carry more weight than a human could, even the slowest horse was faster than the swiftest human. Some horses were faster than others, and people enjoyed watching and predicting what was going to happen when the horses met. The step from hauling to racing was short, inevitable, and lucrative for the humans who owned the quickest horses.

Racing Begins

There's no record of the world's first horse race—there weren't any chart callers in attendance—but it probably happened about 5,000 years ago somewhere in central Asia. We don't even know for sure whether the first racehorses were ridden or driven. Driven, probably, since most horses then were much smaller than they are today.

We do know when and where the first organized and recorded races occurred— somewhere in Greece before 1200 B.C. By the time of the Trojan Wars, racing was a well-established sport. Legend has it that the wars began over the kidnapping of the beautiful Helen of Troy, but Homer's Iliad gives the impression that the kidnapping of a couple of equally beautiful Trojan racing stallions helped keep it going. The Greek warrior Diomedes won an important chariot race, the first race to go down in the record books, with the stolen pair. Homer didn't mention the odds.

Four hundred years later, the very first Olympic Games featured mule chariot racing, followed a few Olympiads later by horse racing, both chariot and ridden. Here's where we first hear about *race fixing*, in which the nefarious tool was fermented mead. History neglects to say whether the mead was supposed to make the horses run faster or slower, but it does tell us that fixers were punished by having to build a statue to Zeus on Mount Olympus.

From the Horse's Mouth

The **chart caller** makes a simultaneous written record of how individual races are run and how each horse performs. Nowadays, videotape is available to bettors at some tracks, but race charts remain vital to successful handicapping.

When in Rome, You Take Your Racing Seriously

At least Greek cheats weren't crucified like race fixers in Rome often were. Romans took enthusiasm about horse racing to a level that hasn't been reached since. They watched, cheered, gambled, and occasionally began revolutions at the races.

Emperor Justinian celebrated the fifth anniversary of his reign with a racing program in which a dispute over a chariot race contributed to a revolution that killed 30,000 people.

Contrary to legend, Emperor Nero may not have fiddled while Rome burned. He may have been at the races instead. Earlier in his life, Nero's wife had made the mistake of scolding him for returning too late from the chariot races. He promptly killed her.

From the Horse's Mouth

On a **dark day**, the bane of the serious racing fan, no racing is conducted at a particular racetrack to give some rest and relaxation to both horses and racetrack workers. Today, thanks to computers, television, and satellites, there's no such thing as a dark day at many racing facilities. You can bet on horses you've never seen at places you've never been.

For the Record

You can still see organized chariot racing. The sport reemerged in the Rocky Mountain states in the late 1940s when horsemen in Utah and Idaho were looking for something to do with their Quarter Horses during the off season. Pairs of horses competed first with sled-like cutters, then with two-wheeled chariots made of aluminum and titanium alloy. Today, the sport features a modest winter-season schedule. You can't bet on most modern chariot racing, at least not legally, but you don't have to worry about getting caught up in revolutions.

The fall of the Roman Empire began the longest spell of dark days in the history of horse racing.

The Dark Days of the Dark Ages

After the Romans, organized racing disappears from history for more than 500 years, although people undoubtedly raced their horses informally. During the Dark Ages, too little money and too much religion conspired to suppress a sport that was already decried by the straight-laced as an expensive vice.

Two events vital to the future of racing did occur during the dark days of the post-Roman world. One was the invention of the stirrup, a device that allowed the rider to remain securely in the saddle while thinking about something other than gripping his mount's sides with his knees. The second was the development of the iron horseshoe, a piece of equipment that allowed a horse to cover many more miles carrying more weight than the barefoot horse. The shoe was immediately useful to pack horses, but it later became a tool that permitted horses to race long and often.

Medieval Racing

Racing reappeared in the 11th century in England. Horse sellers who brought their animals to the Smithfield livestock market near London raced their horses against each other to demonstrate

From the Horse's Mouth

The **stakes race** represents the highest level of horse racing. Horses are either invited by the track or staked to the race by a fee paid by their owners. The fees are added to the purse, so stakes are sometimes also called **added money races**.

strength and soundness. The spectators included both prospective buyers and interested observers, some of whom probably placed the occasional private bet.

The 12th century saw the first recorded stakes race. Several noblemen from the court of Richard II competed for 40 pieces of gold in a race over a three-mile course. The king himself was more interested in crusading than racing, but he didn't mind that his knights wanted to prove whose horse was fastest.

The Foundations of Modern Racing

Henry VIII loved racing so much that he required his dukes to maintain racing stables. His daughter Elizabeth also enjoyed racing, but it was first called the Sport of Kings during the reign of her heir, James I.

The horse-loving King James did two important things (beyond sponsoring a new version of the Bible, of course). First, he built a royal residence in the quiet country town of Newmarket and, by either great insight or sheer luck, drew attention and horses to one of the three or four best regions in the world to breed and raise horses.

For the Record

Some places, like Newmarket, raise better horses than others. Ireland, Normandy in France, and most of all—the Bluegrass region of central Kentucky, can boast more than their share of fine and fast horses. Temperate climate, rainfall, and the presence of good breeding stock contribute, but the fact that the soil lies over bone-building limestone is probably the reason for all the good horses. Should you bet on a horse from one of these regions? Yes, with all other factors being equal.

James I also encouraged British breeders to lighten up. He believed that the heavy English horses weren't as fast as they might be, and he himself imported a couple of Arab stallions for crossbreeding.

The Puritan rebel Oliver Cromwell did his best to suppress horse racing during his brief dictatorship during the 17th century, but the restoration of Charles II to the throne saw the restoration of racing, too. With Charles II, modern horse racing was off and running.

Every one of today's racehorses, whether Thoroughbred, Standardbred, Quarter Horse, or steeplechaser, descends in one line or another from one of three Middle Eastern stallions imported into England following the reign of Charles II. These three, the

Byerly Turk, the Darley Arabian, and the Godolphin Arabian, were the founding fathers of the Thoroughbred breed. The Thoroughbred, in turn, was the ancestor of all other racing breeds.

By the time the three great stallions arrived, the English mares they met were already more refined than their ancestors had been, thanks to earlier imports by James I and others. Since race times weren't kept, no one knows whether these English horses were faster or slower than the Middle Eastern imports, but everyone now knows that their combined genes produced the fastest horse in the history of the world.

For the Record

The Arabian today is not as fast over normal racing distances as the modern Thoroughbred, a fact that's helped prevent Arabian racing from becoming widely established as a betting sport. People apparently don't bet as enthusiastically on horses they see as being slower than others, even though the competition is as intense and the challenges of handicapping the same as in Thoroughbred racing. But Arabians do dominate one form of racing—endurance events of 50 and 100 miles. As an Olympic event, there's no betting, but if there were, the smart money in endurance races would always be on Arabians.

Horse racing in its modern form emerged during the 18th century in England, as did the Thoroughbred breed. The Jockey Club, not an organization of short riders but a governing body, was established in 1750 to formulate rules and policies for racing. In every country that conducts organized racing today, a Jockey Club or its equivalent controls the sport.

Racing also became a sport of young horses. Before the 18th century, horses never raced before the age of five. In 1730, the first four-year-old races were held. Within a few years, three-year-olds, then two-year-olds, were competing. Today, races for the very young pay the largest purses, although most races are for older horses.

Inside Track

In modern racing, two-year-olds compete within their own age group. Three-year-olds also stay in their division until summer, then most go into all-age races. The older horse, unless clearly geriatric, is usually the best bet.

English racing in the 18th century also saw racing's first superstar. Eclipse, unbeaten and unchallenged, won 26 races in a two-season career, but his greatest performance was in the breeding shed.

He fathered plenty of good racehorses, but he's best remembered today as the direct male ancestor of more than 95 percent of modern Thoroughbreds. Eclipse's birth in 1764 was the single most important event in racing history.

The Racehorse Sails West

Europeans discovered America to be a prime market for racehorses long before the establishment of the Jockey Club or the birth of Eclipse. There were, as yet, no Thoroughbreds when the first racehorses stepped off the ship onto the American continent.

They were unwelcome in the Puritan strongholds of Plymouth and Boston, but they were eagerly awaited elsewhere. The first racetrack in America was built in 1665 on Long Island, less than a year after the Dutch turned New York over to the English. Racing was conducted more informally in Virginia, but in both colonies it developed into a sport popular with the wealthy and the ordinary alike.

English horse breeders were happy to find America to be an excellent place to dispose of less-than-successful breeding stock in exchange for healthy crops of tobacco or timber.

The Founding Fathers of American Racing

Diomed, the first Epsom Derby winner, was a modest success in England during the first few years of his breeding career. By 1798, he was an elderly 21 and unwanted, except by American breeders. For ten years, Diomed repaid the country that gave him a second chance by fathering a dynasty of fine racehorses and excellent breeding animals. His great-grandson Lexington, the most influential Thoroughbred of the 19th century, appears in the pedigrees of almost every winner of stakes races in the world today.

In 1756, a little English Thoroughbred named *Janus* arrived in Virginia to be bred to local mares with the hopes of producing offspring capable of winning the four-mile races then popular. But Janus persisted in producing stocky little short-distance horses like himself, becoming the founding father of the entire Quarter Horse breed.

In 1788, a gray stallion named *Messenger* arrived from England, disembarking in Philadelphia. He had been a modestly successful racehorse in England but wasn't considered good enough to be used at stud in his native country. Messenger was plenty good enough for America, becoming the maternal grandsire of the continent's first racing star, American Eclipse, as well as the paternal grandsire of Rysdyk's Hambletonian, the founder of the Standardbred breed.

And Then They Evolved

Although their ancestry is similar, the three modern racing breeds began to diverge dramatically during the mid-19th century, leading to the racehorses and the racing sports we know today.

Thoroughbred

Thoroughbred racing began its final evolution into the modern sport during the second half of the 19th century, with the Civil War providing the catalyst for change.

The scorched earth of the postwar South could no longer supply the horses for the regional match races that had dominated the attention of the racing public before the war.

The war also minted hundreds of new millionaires in the North. Dozens of these new kings of industry believed themselves to fit right into the Sport of Kings. Horse breeding and ownership boomed.

More important to racing's future was the fact that there was plenty of money in the hands of ordinary people too, thanks to increased factory wages. The money quickly found its way into betting pools and bookmakers' pockets at the dozens of new racetracks that appeared across the continent. From just one modern-style Thoroughbred racetrack in regular operation at the end of the Civil War, there were more than 300 by the turn of the century.

At the same time, the structure of Thoroughbred racing became more appealing to spectators and bettors. Traditional heat racing was abandoned in favor of dash racing.

From the Horse's Mouth

In **heat racing**, the horses are required to win two or more individual races before being declared the winner of the event. In **dash racing**, one race decides the event.

The distances of the dashes varied, from 3/4 mile to more than two, making it more difficult to pick winners. But the new races weren't won by the last survivor, as heat events often were, and bettors loved the idea of pure speed conquering all. Since speed was what breeders had spent a hundred years perfecting in the Thoroughbred, it was the ideal match.

Standardbred

Harness racing began to take on its modern trappings even earlier. Its immediate English ancestor featured horses ridden at the trot over coaching roads, challenging the clock rather than other horses. Since a horse lasts longer at the trot than at the gallop, these races could be very long indeed, sometimes several heats of 20 to 50 miles each. Occasionally, the horses were timed while pulling various vehicles at the trot, but the ridden races were more popular in England.

The enthusiasm for ridden trotting races did not long survive the voyage across the Atlantic. Fast trotting remained popular, but ridden trotters did not. Although some ridden races were held, especially in the early years of the 19th century, trotting in America became almost exclusively a harness sport by mid-century.

For the Record

Today, 150 years later, there's a new interest in ridden races for Standardbreds. There aren't many events in the so-called Boots and Saddles series, but an increasing number of trotters and pacers are being trained to race under both harness and saddles.

It also became a sport of short, single-length events. By 1806, the fact that a horse named *Yankey* became famous for trotting a mile in less than three minutes established that distance as both goal and ideal for the sport. Whether against the clock or against other horses, whether under saddle or harness, trotting races became what they remain today—one mile competitions. Heat racing did persist in harness racing, though, and a few major events today are still contested in multiple heats.

Concentrated as it was in the North, trotting suffered little during the Civil War, even though a few Kentucky stallions became unwilling warriors when they were confiscated by Confederate raiders. As Thoroughbred racing did, the harness sport benefited from the post-war boom times. In fact, harness racing drew more spectators and produced more celebrated stars, both human and equine.

The harness-racing breed received its name and its identity in 1879 when an association of breeders established its "Standard of Admission to Registration," under which a horse who could trot a mile in two and a half minutes qualified as a member of the new harness racing breed.

Today, Standardbreds qualify by being born to other Standardbreds. The late 19th century also saw the emergence of a type of horse that eventually became more important than trotters in American harness racing. This is the pacer, and you'll hear more about him in Chapter 2.

Quarter Horse

Quarter Horse racing, in its organized incarnation, is a much newer sport because its governing body wasn't even formed until the 1940s. But short racing did exist in a mostly unstructured form, primarily in Texas and a couple of other Southwestern states much earlier. The animal widely considered the first of the modern Quarter Horses, the legendary *Steel Dust*, made his reputation in the Southwest just before the Civil War.

The Structure of Modern Racing

The late 19th century saw the emergence of the betting systems we still use in American racing, although the lack of computers and other electronics made the wagering process more cumbersome and more subject to manipulation. That, as well as the absence of almost any government regulation, made the late 19th century the Golden Age of race fixing.

Not that there wasn't skullduggery before, but the postwar influx of money into the sport made cheating both worthwhile and profitable.

Horses trained under false names, were entered under still other names, were slowed by jockeys, were interfered with during races. Other horses were drugged, poisoned, or kidnapped. Bookmakers themselves would enter horses with no chance of winning, then offer odds that would lure the unsuspecting to bet on them. Other bookmakers, while paying for accurate information from racing stables, would spread false information to bettors in order to improve their own chances of not having to pay out.

The excesses of the era led to demands on the part of both wealthy owners and less wealthy fans. Bettors wanted legitimate information, and in 1894 they got the Daily Racing Form. Owners wanted control, and that same year they got the American Jockey Club, which soon became the licensing board for all racing participants in New York. Government intervention came later, but the first steps to a regulated sport had been taken. By the turn of the century, American racing was essentially the sport it is today, and the equine participants were the animals we now know and love.

The Least You Need to Know

➤ Horse racing is as old as recorded history and is among the oldest organized sports.

➤ All American racehorses today, whether Thoroughbred, Standardbred, or Quarter Horse, descend from three Middle Eastern stallions imported into England during the 17th and 18th centuries.

➤ Modern racing established its roots in America during the 19th century, and today's racing is much like the sport of 100 years ago.

Who's Who

Racing people like to say that God made the horse, but Man made the Thoroughbred. True and quite a compliment to Man. To be fair, the same thing is true of all animal breeds. Where evolution leaves off, selective breeding begins, as people try to create animals that are bigger, handsomer, tastier, or—in the case of racehorses—faster than others of their species.

The first stage of selective breeding leads to a *type*, which is an animal more likely than others to look or perform in a particular way. That's not good enough for most human beings, who like the sound of "guaranteed" better than "more likely."

So people create breeds, in which pedigrees are authenticated and animals must be approved to qualify for membership. Sounds like a country club.

Even a highly controlled breed membership guarantees nothing about performance, but it does dramatically increase the likelihood that qualities such as speed and determination will appear in future generations. Breed requirements also protect financial investments since would-be participants must go to the owners of registered breeding stock to obtain their own animals.

These equine country clubs were established during the 19th century for Thoroughbreds and Standardbreds. Quarter Horse pedigree control is less absolute and more recent. We'll discuss that later. Now, let's look at each of the racing breeds and the characteristics you should know if you want to succeed at the racetrack and enjoy yourself while you're at it.

The Thoroughbred

Any modern Thoroughbred is a remarkably well-documented creature. Even the most determined human genealogist isn't likely to know the names of every one of his ancestors, plus all their brothers, sisters, aunts, uncles, children, and in-laws for more than 22 generations. English Thoroughbreds do (or their human owners do). American Thoroughbreds may have a few unidentified black sheep in their pedigrees, although none for at least a hundred years.

But if you go back 23 generations or so, you might have a little trouble figuring out just who contributed genes to the Thoroughbred. We know that the Arab-type horses imported into England 300 years ago supplied fine thin legs, light body structure, and elegant heads. We suspect that English horses of previous centuries offered size, muscle, and heavy bone. There were probably even a few pony ancestors.

What this genetic mix means is that today's Thoroughbred can vary in appearance and physique. Some variations matter when you bet on a horse, and some don't.

Color

Color is undoubtedly the least important physical characteristic of a racehorse, at least in terms of racing ability. Color helps you spot your choice on the far side of the racetrack, and sometimes it does a little more than that.

A Thoroughbred can be any solid color, although white and true black are so rare that they're almost nonexistent. Bay is the most common color among Thoroughbreds, followed by chestnut, gray, and roan, and the nearly black shade officially known as dark bay or brown. A Paint Horse—one with splotches of white and a solid color—is impossible in the Thoroughbred gene pool, so a paint can't be registered. The Jockey Club will assume that the stallion, mare, or the owner has been up to no good.

No color is automatically superior to any other color in terms of speed or stamina, although breeders, owners, trainers, and bettors each have their prejudices. However, there's one case where it really might matter (just a little, to be sure).

From the Horse's Mouth

A **bay** horse is red or brown with a black mane and tail, while a **chestnut** is reddish, a **gray** or **roan** has white hairs intermixed with a darker color. A **dark bay or brown** looks black to anyone with normal eyesight.

A horse who looks like a parent in build and color is somewhat more likely to run like that parent, and color is a factor to consider if you don't know much else about the horse. Make it part of your decision if you're thinking about betting on an unraced two-year-old, or you're trying to pick the Kentucky Derby winner out of a field of horses, none of whom has ever been asked to run a mile and a quarter.

A stallion is said to *stamp* his offspring when they look like him, and it is true that those who stamp tend to be the best stallions. Color is one of the aspects of stamping, although which color doesn't matter at all.

White on the lower leg also has no effect at all on racing ability, but some experts think that a white leg combined with a white hoof is a warning sign. White hoof walls are softer than dark ones, sometimes making nails more likely to pull loose. If that happens during a race, disaster can result. Other experts like to point out that great champions such as Nijinsky, Northern Dancer, and Secretariat each had more than one white hoof. Size and conformation characteristics are far more important than color, on the leg or elsewhere.

Height

Watch any field of Thoroughbreds heading to the starting gate, and you'll see a group of horses fairly similar in height and weight. Owners and trainers contribute to this consistency, believing that horses of average height are more athletic and agile than horses that are too tall or too short. Oddballs often don't even get to the races.

They're probably right. Most winning racehorses are of average height, 15.3 to 16.3 hands. Shorter and taller horses do sometimes make it to the races and a few become superstars, but most good horses fall into the middle range.

In some circumstances, being shorter or taller than average can be an advantage. In other cases, it can be limiting. Here are points to consider before betting on an unusually tall horse:

Bad Bet

Don't assume too much because of the tendency of horses who look like a parent to run like them. Big red Secretariat's best racing offspring was little gray Lady's Secret.

From the Horse's Mouth

Conformation refers to a horse's physical structure, both overall shape and individual body parts.

From the Horse's Mouth

A **hand** is four inches. Horse height is measured from the ground to the high point of the **withers**, the top of the shoulder just in front of the saddle. A horse who's 16.3 hands, for example, is 16 hands 3 inches, or 67 inches tall at the withers.

From the Horse's Mouth

A **furlong** is 1/8 of a mile. It's the primary unit of race measurement in North America and in Britain, although much of the rest of the racing world uses kilometers and meters.

➤ If the race is very short—under six furlongs—a tall horse may have trouble. Tall horses usually don't break out of the starting gate as quickly as smaller ones, and a short race gives him little time to make up for a poor start.

➤ A racetrack with sharp turns can be difficult for a tall horse. Watch out if your tall bet is running on a racetrack less than a mile around or one with a flattened oval shape.

➤ A tall horse usually has a long stride and can do well on a track that features wide, sweeping turns and a long stretch.

➤ Tall horses usually excel in steeplechasing or any other racing over fences. They dominate in events with wide or high fences.

As for short horses, there are more situations in which they enjoy an advantage.

➤ Their greater agility out of the starting gate gives them a big advantage in short races. The shorter the race, the more likely it is that a short horse will win.

➤ A race in which the first turn comes soon after the start is made to order for small horses, who can get themselves into full stride quickly.

➤ Surprisingly, small horses often have greater stamina than tall ones, even though you might assume that their shorter strides would make them have to work harder during a race. It's probably because their comparatively light body structure means less weight to haul around the racetrack. A short, stocky horse loses this advantage.

Thoroughbred Conformation

Body shape and structure affect both speed and stamina. We're not talking here about physical defects that make a horse too sore to run his best. Those are discussed in Chapter 4. In this section, we'll look at some of the characteristics that differentiate a slow horse from a fast one and a horse that can sail through a mile and a half from one who's gasping for breath after six furlongs.

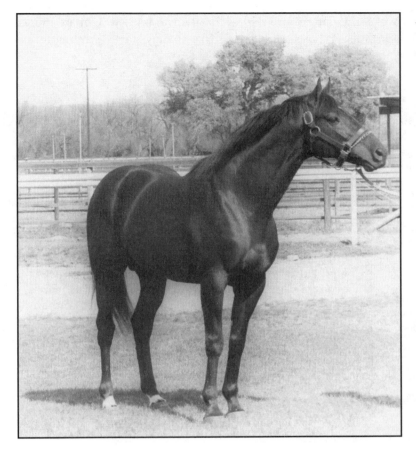

A Thoroughbred stallion whose body shape suggests speed.

Hindquarters

The horse's hindquarters make up his power train. They're the best indicator of speed potential.

While the hindquarters won't tell you anything about his health, determination, courage, or anything else that goes into making a racehorse, it will tell you whether he has the physical potential to run fast:

➤ Horses with wide hindquarters usually have more pure speed than horses with narrow ones.

➤ Their wider centers of balance also make them quicker and more secure out of the starting gate.

From the Horse's Mouth

Hindquarters are what we'd call the hips and buttocks in the human being.

➤ Horses with narrower hindquarters and the resulting lower body weight are more likely to excel at a distance. What's more, a less-than-snappy start won't matter if there's a long race ahead.

Head

The other end can also indicate speed. The head itself doesn't have much to do with it, no matter how some people—including supposedly expert horsemen—are convinced that a horse with piggy little eyes or clown-like floppy ears can't possibly run fast. They can, and they often do.

A horse whose head is much bigger or smaller than normal may have balance problems, but this is rare among Thoroughbreds.

How the horse carries his head does matter. A horse with a high head may look proud and impressive, but he probably won't be able to keep his speed up much beyond a sprint distance. Short breath and short stride that result from the high head carriage will see to that. There are exceptions, of course. Man O' War ran with remarkably high head and set distance records that have never been equaled, but you and I aren't likely to see any Man O'Wars on our visits to the track.

Chest

Drop your gaze a couple of feet to the horse's chest. From the front you want to see enough width of chest and rib cage to accommodate lung expansion. Lung capacity is more important for horses expected to run a distance, so a narrow-chested horse—while not desirable—may be a reasonable bet in a short race.

From a side view, you're looking for shoulder depth and slope rather than size. A long, sloping shoulder means a long stride—a necessity for any horse expected to run farther than six or seven furlongs.

If you have a good eye, you may be able to predict stride length at the gallop by watching the horse in the walking ring or the post parade.

Bad Bet

Watch out for the horse whose head carriage changes dramatically once the gate opens. The high-headed sprinter type becomes a low-headed distance runner. Note it for next time.

From the Horse's Mouth

The horses amble around the **walking ring** after being saddled and before moving onto the track, where they begin walking in front of the stands in the **post parade**.

At the walk, a horse who sets his back feet down in front of where his forefeet had been will probably have a long stride at the faster gaits, too.

Back

Judge the horse's back length by estimating the amount of back visible between the end of the saddle and the point at which the hindquarters start to rise up. The back, whether short or long, has little relationship to speed, but it can play a role in racing success:

➤ Short backs are usually stronger and less subject to injury than long ones. A short-backed horse can usually carry more weight without discomfort, making him a natural for races in which a lot of weight is assigned.

➤ But those races—especially steeplechases or other races over fences—also come with taller riders. Short-backed horses sometimes don't have space for tall riders, making them poor candidates for victory. What's more, short-backed horses often can't manage a decent arc over jumps and lose precious ground when racing over fences. So the key in steeplechases is this: short enough back to stay healthy; long enough back to accommodate the rider.

➤ In flat races, particularly in cases where the horse is expected to carry weight, shorter is better than longer.

Other Characteristics

Here's a sampler of other physical characteristics that contribute to speed and racing ability:

➤ **Thin is best for fashion models, chimney sweeps, and winning racehorses.** A horse whose bone structure is hidden under a layer of fat isn't in good enough condition to win.

➤ **Feet count.** Ideally, all racehorses should have hooves proportional in size to their bodies. Some very fast horses have very small feet, but distance horses, turf runners, and good performers in the mud almost never do. Big feet in mud and on turf; small feet in dirt-track sprints.

➤ **Noses matter, too.** Tiny nostrils make it difficult for a horse to take in air, while too-large ones can mean a breathing problem. Both faults are more noticeable over a longer distance.

The Standardbred

Standardbreds, although they have more Thoroughbred blood than anything else, wouldn't be racing at the trot and pace while pulling a vehicle if there weren't other genetic contributors as well.

The most important was the now-extinct Norfolk Trotter, an old English coaching breed that was never used for competitive racing. But the nature of people and horses being what they are, Norfolk Trotters were enthusiastically used in long road races against the clock.

As railroads displaced coaches in long-distance transportation, both the Norfolk Trotter and their 20- to 40-mile timed performances disappeared. But the horses left behind their racing legacy and their genes.

The Norfolk Trotter had a healthy dose of Thoroughbred blood himself, but he had heavier bone and more muscle. He also had physical characteristics that enabled him to trot smoothly and very rapidly.

American farmers and others interested in moving their goods and themselves as quickly as possible naturally wanted Norfolk Trotter blood, and they imported plenty of it. Some of it found its way into the Morgan breed, and Morgans—as well as more direct Norfolk Trotter descendants—combined with the Thoroughbred during the mid-19th century to provide most of the genes to the Standardbred pool.

For the Record

Some equine historians think the original Justin Morgan, who shared the name of his human owner, was actually a stocky, fast-trotting Thoroughbred. But he probably did have some unrelated trotting blood since he passed trotting rather than running speed to his many descendants.

To Trot or to Pace, That Is the Question

Genes other than Thoroughbred and Norfolk Trotter also found their way into the Standardbred mix—genes that have played a vital role in modern harness racing. As the trotting horse contingent evolved into the Standardbred, a smaller and less-popular group of harness racers were busy competing around North America. They were *pacers*—animals who looked pretty much like good trotters and pulled their vehicles as fast or even faster.

The pace has been around for thousands of years and, during the Middle Ages, was considered the more comfortable gait for lady riders. In the late 19th century, pacers began to be accepted as an alternative to trotting Standardbreds. Since many of the newly designated Standardbreds produced off-spring who preferred to pace, pacers became acceptable as a separate but equal variation of the breed.

A hundred years ago, most races were for trotters. Today the opposite is true, probably because pacing is a faster, more consistent gait.

What Makes a Standardbred?

Standardbreds, trotters or pacers, have a lot in common with each other in spite of their different gaits. Let's look first at similarities.

Size

Most Standardbreds, regardless of gait, tend to be shorter than Thoroughbreds but slightly heavier in body structure. Most successful Standardbreds are between 15 and 16 hands tall.

From the Horse's Mouth

The **trot**, a gait midway between the walk and the run, features legs on opposite corners moving together. It's the gait of most four-legged animals. The **pace**, performed by camels, a few breeds of dogs, and pacing horses, features legs on the same side moving backward and forward at the same time. Pacers are sometimes called *amblers* or *side-wheelers*.

Although harness horsemen, like most horsemen, believe that a good big horse beats a good little horse most of the time, history offers more examples of Standardbred champions who are smaller-than-average.

Color

Both trotters and pacers are usually bay, occasionally chestnut or brown, rarely gray, and never paint or pinto. Most have little white on their legs or faces. Some of this uniformity of color occurs because racing people believe they prefer it.

Temperament

Most Standardbreds are good-natured and easy to manage, partially because they get a lot of handling very early in their lives. In addition, the process of hooking a horse to a vehicle requires an animal who cooperates. Difficult horses have to be remarkably good to get a chance to race. They have to be even better to be bred because nobody in harness racing wants to perpetuate bad temper genes.

The Differences Between Trotters and Pacers

There are important differences between the two kinds of harness horses, besides the obvious one of their racing gaits. The pace has distinct physical requirements, and the two gaits are different enough that an astute observer can tell whether a horse is a trotter or pacer merely by watching him graze in the field.

A trotter with excellent conformation and gait.

A pacer with excellent conformation and gait.

Trotting Horse Characteristics

Although less than 20 percent of today's harness races in North America feature trotters, some of the most prestigious ones do, including the Hambletonian, the Dexter Cup, and the Kentucky Futurity. There are also plenty of lower-level trotting races, particularly for young horses.

Here are some of the physical characteristics to look for in your trotting candidate:

➤ Among trotters, there may be no great advantage to height, but body length does matter. The nature of the gait makes interference between front legs and hind legs possible as the horse reaches for more speed. While there are plenty of exceptions, most good trotters are at least as many inches long in the body as they are in height at the withers.

➤ A fast trot is best performed by a horse with large hindquarters since the gait is based on rear propulsion. You'll often see good trotters whose hindquarters are higher than their withers as viewed from the side. This horse is referred to as being built *downhill*. For a trotter, going downhill doesn't mean he's no longer the horse he used to be. It's a description of good trotter shape.

➤ People used to think that trotters needed a lot of bend in their rear legs to be fast, but this was probably because the great Hambletonian transmitted the characteristic to his offspring. They most likely won in spite of their rear leg conformation, not because of it. Some horses trot well with straight hind legs, some with dramatic bend. Don't worry about it.

➤ Do worry, though, if you're eyeing a trotter whose hind legs bow inward at the hocks as viewed from behind. These *cow hocks* (so named because every cow you meet, fast or slow, has them) cause a horse's rear hooves to rotate inward at a fast trot, often striking the opposite front foot. This interference makes a smooth, fast trot almost impossible for the horse to maintain.

From the Horse's Mouth

The **hock** is the rear leg equivalent of the knee.

Pacing Horse Characteristics

No matter what day you go to the harness races in North America, even Hambletonian Day at the Meadowlands, you'll see more races for pacers than trotters. So put most of your effort into identifying good pacing body type.

For the Record

The Meadowlands is the modern Mecca of harness racing. The New Jersey track features the highest level of Standardbred racing over the longest season. When you hear a driver referred to as a Meadowlands driver or a horse as a Meadowlands winner, it means they've reached the top rung of their sport.

➤ Unlike trotters, pacers don't need body length to assure that forelegs and hind legs on the same side don't interfere with each other. Instead, they need adequate body width. So good pacers tend to be blockier than trotters, with comparatively short bodies and wide chests. Narrow-chested pacers can move as fast as others, but they often crossfire, causing injury to themselves or causing them to be slowed by the equipment that prevents the injury.

From the Horse's Mouth

Crossfiring occurs when one hoof strikes the hoof or leg on the other side. The left hind foot, for example, raps the right front hoof.

➤ The pace is powered almost as much from the shoulders as the hindquarters, so you'll see good pacers with narrower hindquarters and more pronounced shoulders than trotters. Pacers with withers higher than their hindquarters are said to be built *uphill*, and that doesn't mean that they have more work ahead of them when they race. For a pacer, it can be an advantage.

➤ Cow hocks present few problems to pacers, unless they're so severe that the horse can't keep his balance. It's not true that a pacer is better off with cow hocks. He's just not at as much of a disadvantage as other horses.

Quarter Racing Horses

Note the name of the section. Although they're members of the same breed, Quarter Horses and Quarter Racing Horses are not exactly the same thing.

Nowadays, Quarter Horses who race are more like Thoroughbreds than they are like roping horses, cutting horses, steer-wrestling horses, or any other members of their own breed. Once you've learned to pick a Thoroughbred who should perform well in short races, you can pick a Quarter Horse with the potential to win in his own sport.

It's not just because of the similarities in the demands of the two sports. Genetically, there's very little difference between today's Quarter Horse and Thoroughbred, and— among Quarter Racing Horses—the difference is shrinking rapidly.

There are two reasons for all those Thoroughbred genes. The American Quarter Horse Association, the breed's registry, wasn't established until 1940. Before then, owners of quick little western horses who wanted more size and elegance bred their animals to Thoroughbreds. After 1940, the new registration rules conveniently permitted these habits to continue.

It's the owners of Quarter Racing Horses who've taken greatest advantage of the rule that permits the offspring of a Quarter Horse and a Thoroughbred to be registered as a Quarter Horse. Each decade that passes sees the Quarter Horses used in racing become more and more Thoroughbred. But there are still a few differences between the breeds, although the differences may be just a matter of degree. Quarter Horse races are shorter than normal Thoroughbred sprints; the standard distances range from 220 to 400 yards. So a Quarter Horse with the potential to win should be like his sprinting Thoroughbred cousin, only more so.

There are a few special characteristics to look for in a Quarter Racing Horse.

Size

For every horse generation that passes, the Quarter Racing Horse becomes taller. He's still shorter than the average Thoroughbred (14.3 to 15.3 hands) because height is not an advantage, and breeders aren't attracted to tall stallions even if they want more Thoroughbred blood.

In fact, too much height is a disadvantage since longer legs and a lengthier stride go along with it. The long-striding horse can rarely get himself into top gear before a Quarter Horse race is over.

Quarter Horses are likely to be heavier than Thoroughbreds of similar size since they need solid bone to take the stress of sudden acceleration. They also need plenty of heavy muscle, particularly in the rear end.

Hindquarters

A Quarter Horse without substantial hindquarters isn't going to have the power to get out of the starting gate quickly and will fail at racing. There are almost no exceptions to this rule. No rear, no horse.

Body Length

Quarter Racing Horses should be short-bodied and stocky, at least compared to Thoroughbreds, because this is the body type that can survive the pounding of the short, all-out stride necessary in a race of a quarter mile or less. It's an inflexible body type, but that doesn't matter. Standard length Quarter Horse races are run on the straightaway, and turns play no role at all.

Head and Neck

The Quarter Racing Horse needs to carry his head and neck higher than the Thoroughbred since he's going to have to be able to break out of the starting gate completely alert. Some good horses carry their heads low at the walk, and then bring them up at the gallop. Others never get them up and always lose ground at the start.

A Word of Warning

While it's challenging and often helpful to try to pick out possible winners by their physical characteristics, it's most useful with young horses who've never started or with horses trying a new kind of race.

Once a horse has a racing record, his past performances are far more important than his physique. Winner's circles see their share of rangy sprinting Thoroughbreds, long-bodied pacers, and tall Quarter Horses.

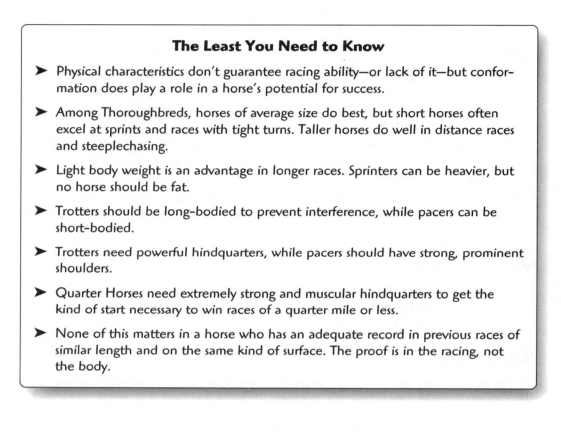

The Least You Need to Know

➤ Physical characteristics don't guarantee racing ability—or lack of it—but conformation does play a role in a horse's potential for success.

➤ Among Thoroughbreds, horses of average size do best, but short horses often excel at sprints and races with tight turns. Taller horses do well in distance races and steeplechasing.

➤ Light body weight is an advantage in longer races. Sprinters can be heavier, but no horse should be fat.

➤ Trotters should be long-bodied to prevent interference, while pacers can be short-bodied.

➤ Trotters need powerful hindquarters, while pacers should have strong, prominent shoulders.

➤ Quarter Horses need extremely strong and muscular hindquarters to get the kind of start necessary to win races of a quarter mile or less.

➤ None of this matters in a horse who has an adequate record in previous races of similar length and on the same kind of surface. The proof is in the racing, not the body.

Chapter 3

The Race Goes to the Swift...

In This Chapter

➤ Breeding and speed

➤ The different kinds of speed

➤ Spotting speed in training

Horse racing isn't a skill sport, at least not for the equine participants. Races are almost always won by the fastest horse. Unfortunately for the speedballs, other factors play a part in every race, and the fastest horse one day may not be fastest next week. That's why they take bets.

Assessing the relationship between speed and the other factors that affect a race's outcome is *handicapping*, and we'll talk about that in Part 4. Here, we're concerned with speed itself—where it comes from, how you identify it, and what it means in a particular race.

Breeding

Pure speed is one of the horse's most consistently transmitted talents—more than jumping aptitude, polo-playing ability, or the tendency to do cute tricks. On the surface, it should be pretty easy to find the speediest horse. Just identify the fastest parents, bet on the offspring, and collect your money at the betting window.

It's not that easy, of course, and there are two primary complications. First, you don't get to bet on baby horses galloping across their pasture. By the time they parade in front of you at the racetrack, they've been influenced by trainers, riders, grooms, and injury. Second, while speed is often passed down, sometimes it's not—for no discernible reason.

But you can still look at breeding to try to identify the naturally fast horse. This is particularly useful when you're betting on young horses, especially first-time starters.

The Battle of the Sexes

Sire and dam are equally responsible for the quality of the offspring—genetically speaking, at least. However, because the mare has four months after the birth to teach her baby how to use his legs and then to compete with him in pasture races, there's evidence that the mare is more responsible for his future success on the racetrack.

From the Horse's Mouth

The **sire** is females the father, the **dam** is the mother, and the **foal** is the baby. Other words to know: A **stallion** is an adult male horse; a **mare** is an adult female.

Inside Track

There's no point in looking much beyond the second generation in the pedigree. Slow parents with fast grandparents might produce a fast horse, but slow parents who had slow grandparents will produce a slow horse.

But even the busiest mare rarely has more than five or six foals reach the racetrack during her lifetime, while a successful stallion will have hundreds. This may change as wider use of embryo transfer techniques allow good mares to pass on their genes without actually carrying the foal, but at present, a mare's production is limited. Thoroughbred and Standardbred racing do not permit embryo-transfer horses, but Quarter Horse racing does.

While you can learn about the speed and racing quality of mares, you have a much better chance of identifying natural speed by looking at the sire and the two grandsires, simply because more information will be available. But it's still not easy.

You'll find it hard to pick winners strictly based on the winning records of their sires. Almost all stallions used in breeding were winning racehorses.

It's a matter of biology and numbers. It doesn't take very many stallions to produce plenty of future racehorses. Even Thoroughbred stallions, who are required to be bred naturally, normally sire no more than 50 or 60 foals a year, although a few extremely busy ones are bred to over a hundred mares. Some Standardbred and Quarter Horse stallions, whose registries permit artificial insemination, have been known to sire more than 200 offspring a year.

Occasionally, a very well-bred stallion who never won or never even raced will get a chance, but it rarely happens and even more rarely succeeds. In general, only good racehorses are used as stallions.

So if they're all winners, how do you pick the stallions that transmit speed? You look for certain kinds of winners.

Skip the Hard Knockers

Some winning racehorses aren't particularly fast. While it's fine to bet on them, they generally don't produce fast foals. You're looking instead for stallions who won because of speed, not because they were brave or determined or long-lasting. The so-called *hard knockers* are worthy of respect and represent most of what's good about Thoroughbreds, but their admirable characteristics are transmitted less consistently than speed.

Don't look just for big names in the lines reserved for sire and grandsire. Look for fast horses. How do you tell the difference?

From the Horse's Mouth

Artificial insemination is accomplished by fooling the stallion into believing that a stuffed sawhorse and a big test tube are the mare. It's safer and more lucrative than natural breeding, and the mare doesn't even have to see the stallion. Nobody said they were particularly smart.

For the Record

Almost all of the programs you buy at the racetrack have the sire and dam listed just below the horse's name. Some also have the dam's sire to help you identify her general level of quality. Cigar's basic breeding line: Palace Music–Solar Slew, by Seattle Slew. Palace Music is the sire, Solar Slew the dam, and Seattle Slew the maternal grandsire. Some past-performance publications help by adding the sire's sire to the line—Palace Music (The Minstrel).

The Good, the Fast, and the Young

In all the racing breeds, success at two and three years of age is the best indicator of natural speed. By following this guideline, you'll eliminate a few fast horses who were slow to mature, but you'll also eliminate most of the winners who succeeded because of qualities other than speed.

Stallions who raced well themselves while young are the most successful in breeding, but those who only raced while young may have had short careers because of problems with health and soundness. These problems are often transmitted too, but they usually don't affect individual races. (Consult Chapter 4 for information on this subject.)

Since speed is often but not always transmitted, you will be looking at stallions who not only raced well themselves while very young but also sire foals who race well at two and three. Quarter Horse racing concentrates so heavily on the racing of very young horses that you can assume that almost all of the sires were effective at two or three. In the other two categories, here are a few names to look for:

Thoroughbreds	Standardbreds
Capote	Artsplace
Deputy Minister	Beach Towel
Forty Niner	Die Laughing
Storm Cat	Sierra Kosmos
Mr. Prospector	Supergill
	Valley Victory

From the Horse's Mouth

The word **get** means to win or be competitive at a particular distance. A Kentucky Derby winner can *get* a mile and a quarter. Just to confuse you, the word also means the collective offspring of a stallion: Secretariat's *get* have not quite matched his talent on the racetrack and sometimes can't *get* the longer distances.

Sprinters Rule at Stud

This is important in Thoroughbred racing, where race distance is part of the betting equation. In Standardbred and Quarter Horse racing, where distances are more uniform, it doesn't apply.

To be entirely accurate, stallions who excelled at the longer sprint distances tend to sire the fastest offspring. They produce foals with the best combination of natural speed and the other qualities that make a good racehorse. A pure sprinter—one who wins at five or six furlongs but no longer—can sometimes sire successful babies, but they tend to struggle to get the six furlongs.

The horse who sparkled at seven furlongs or a mile often produces foals who win at short distances and long. To some observers, this well-established fact is a mystery, but it really proves that pure speed is the most important ingredient in winning, whatever the distance.

Stallion Information

Some tracks provide a little help by printing the stud fees of the sires of two-year-old starters. A high stud fee is usually based on the proof (or the strong belief) that a stallion will produce a high percentage of fast offspring. Breeders can be wrong, certainly, but high stud fees aren't paid for stallions who don't produce winners, at least not after their first foals are two years old. The breeding line on the program might read Deputy Minister ($75,000)–Mitterand, by Hold Your Peace. Unfortunately, some of the very best stallions don't have published stud fees, and you might see nothing.

What is a high stud fee? Among Thoroughbreds, anything over $5,000 means the stallion has sired his share of winners. Anything over $50,000 probably means he's sired a champion or two. Standardbred and Quarter Horse stud fees tend to be much lower because of artificial insemination.

If you want to know more about the stallions in a racehorse's pedigree, you'll have to do a little research.

➤ The *Daily Racing Form* (available on newsstands near racetracks) carries charts of stallion standings on a regular basis, as does Thoroughbred racing's primary breeding journal, the *Blood-Horse,* and some other past-performance publications.

➤ In Standardbred racing, the United States Trotting Association is the primary repository of breeding statistics. Write the USTA at 750 Michigan Avenue, Columbus, Ohio, 43215 for a list of their available publications.

➤ Quarter Horse racing is governed by the American Quarter Horse Association, which produces several publications that include breeding statistics. Write for information on AQHA publications to P.O. Box 32470, Amarillo, Texas, 79120.

From the Horse's Mouth

The **stud fee** is the amount the mare's owner pays to breed to the stallion. It's usually payable only if she produces a live foal.

All Speed Is Not Created Equal

In Thoroughbred racing, fast horses rarely run equally fast from the starting gate to the finish line. There are variations on the speed theme, some admirable and some undesirable.

Cheap Speed

A horse with the breeding and conformation to run fast may be described as having *cheap speed*. The description usually comes from a disappointed bettor, and he's not unhappy because he got a fast horse at a reasonable price.

Cheap speed is speed that fades before it should. Possessors of cheap speed dash out of the starting gate or, occasionally, out of a pack of horses while the race is underway, getting themselves to or near the lead. Then they proceed to slow down and lose.

Nobody wants to ride, train, or bet on a horse with cheap speed because the finish line always seems to come too late, no matter how short the race. This means that disappointment is coupled with frustration and annoyance.

Horses who have it are usually thought to have no guts, although they generally have the same problems that plague other losers in every kind of racing:

➤ They hurt, and the pain starts after a short distance of racing.

➤ They don't have much talent to begin with.

➤ They may not be well trained.

➤ They don't understand what racing really requires.

Most horses with cheap speed also possess a characteristic shared by almost all race-horses, fast, slow, or in between. They can make one effort, and only one, to run fast during a race.

The One-Run Thoroughbred

Among Thoroughbreds, it's the rare horse who can run fast, slow down, then run fast again. Most racehorses have only one run to call on, and the difference between horses is when the run comes and how long it lasts. With cheap speed, the run never lasts long enough. With more admirable horses, the run can last long enough to win, whether it comes early or late.

Early Speed

Horses with early speed break out of the gate quickly, challenge for the lead immediately, then run as fast as possible as long as possible. Most horses can't run at anything resembling top speed for more than six furlongs, but this is enough to win the majority of races run in North America. Brilliant early speed is a fine thing to have, provided your ambition isn't to win a Triple Crown race.

Just how long early speed can hold and whether it can last as long as or longer than six furlongs depends on a lot of factors other than the horse who possesses it, including track design, racing surface, post position, and the characteristics of the rest of the field. We'll look into these factors in Part 3, and we'll talk about identifying horses with good early speed in Part 4.

Late speed wins races, provided the horse has clear sailing to the finish line.

Late Speed

In order to have any shot at winning, a horse has to be running at the end. Horses who save their one run for late in the race are just as admirable as horses with early speed, but the results of their races are more affected by outside influences. Other horses running faster or slower than expected, bulky fields that give them nowhere to make their one-runs, accidents in front of them—the late runner can be devastated by all these unforeseen events.

Horses with late speed have been known to make suckers of bettors. A horse who's always running fast and well at the end, making up yardage with every stride, gaining on the leaders as the finish line approaches, convinces a lot of people that he'll win it all next time, provided the race is just a little longer.

Sometimes that's true, but some horses never seem to get there, no matter how long the race. Late speed in a long race is not necessarily a formula for success.

For the Record

The rules are a little different with Quarter Horses. There's only one kind of speed in Quarter Horse racing—all out. The races are just too short to make any run that doesn't start at the gate and end at the finish line. Some horses start better than they finish, and some come on toward the end; but there's no real differentiation between cheap, early, and late speed.

Standardbred Speed

Early and late speed exist in harness racing, but they often result more from human strategy than equine preference. All Standardbreds are bred to compete at the standard one-mile distance. Some do have more natural speed and some do have more stamina, but the variations aren't as pronounced as they are in Thoroughbred racing.

Early speed is most important in races on harness tracks a half mile in circumference because a horse who doesn't get himself into contention early probably finds it impossible to pass horses on the short straightaways and the four sharp turns. Late speed is required on the one-mile tracks and those 5/8-mile tracks that feature wide, sweeping turns.

We'll talk about how to identify the horses best suited for those tracks in Parts 3 and 4.

Workouts and Speed

While his performance in previous races is the most important key to a horse's likelihood of winning, his performance in workouts can be used to identify his natural speed. Workouts can also provide information about current condition, but since most workouts are shorter than actual races, you're likely to learn more about speed than readiness.

In Thoroughbred racing, morning gallops are the workouts that provide the information. In Standardbred racing, you'll be looking mostly at qualifying races since harness works are usually not conducted in the public, and the results are not published. In Quarter Horse racing, horses are worked in the morning, but meaningful workouts are both less frequent and less public than in Thoroughbred racing. If you do hear numbers, you may take them into consideration, particularly with first-time starters at well-organized racetracks.

Is It a Workout or Is It Just Exercise?

While most racehorses come out of their stalls every morning for exercise, not all of these expeditions qualify as workouts. Sometimes, the horses are simply led around the barns; on other days, they're asked to do a slow jog on the track.

Occasionally—once or twice a week for good-quality, lightly raced Thoroughbreds or only occasionally for heavily raced animals—they work. You can also call the activity a workout, and under either name it consists of a gallop under a rider on the main racetrack or on a training track.

Even formal workouts vary. Here are the kinds of workouts you are most likely to read or hear about, along with their commonly accepted definitions.

From the Horse's Mouth

Around the racetrack, most people use the word **barn** when talking about the structure in which the horses are housed, even though the buildings are really stables or sheds.

From the Horse's Mouth

In harness racing, you'll often hear the word **train** instead of *work* for the serious exercise that includes performing at close to racing speed.

➤ Breezing (noted by the symbol "b" in lists or charts) means that the horse galloped without serious urging by his rider.

➤ Handily (noted by "h") means the rider urged the horse for more speed.

➤ Driving (noted by a capital "D") means the horse was asked for racing speed. This is an uncommon occurrence in workouts.

➤ Other notes you may see: a "g" means the horse worked out of the starting gate. A small "d" means that dogs were up on the track. No, the horse didn't have to dodge yelping canines, but he did have to run a little wide, since barriers were placed on the track to keep the working horses away from the rail. Both a "g" and a "d" means you have to subtract at least 1/2 second from the horse's time to compare it with other workouts on the same day at the same distance.

Public versus Private

You have to spend time figuring out all these symbols only if the workout was done in public. Most Thoroughbreds train at the racetrack, but some are kept at private training centers. You'll never hear about many of these workouts, except in rumor or gossip.

Some trainers who don't have access to private training tracks hold their public workouts in private by sending their horses out before the sun rises. There are a couple of things you can conclude about horses who are worked secretly:

➤ They have trainers who are willing to risk life and limb.

➤ They may have speed that their connections hope to keep secret before race time.

➤ They may have soundness problems that their trainer wants to sneak past the track veterinarian who approves entered horses.

It's true that some trainers with no nefarious purpose like to send their horses out very early so that they get first crack at a pristine track surface, and others just don't like the idea of other people assessing their horses' readiness.

In Thoroughbred racing, respectable public workouts are conducted in daylight under the control and direction of racetrack personnel. They're the only kind that provide useful information to the average racegoer, although, as you'll soon see, the quality of the information is occasionally suspect.

Some racing jurisdictions require horses to show up for at least one public timed workout before they are permitted to race. But remember that a horse forced to work for official clockers provides the most suspect information of all. He probably won't be asked for much of an effort by his exercise rider.

From the Horse's Mouth

Connections are the human beings involved with a racehorse, primarily the owner and trainer. Sometimes, the grooms, breeder, and regular jockey are included in the group.

Bad Bet

Never read anything into the fact that harness horses aren't worked in public. That's the tradition, even among the horses who are stabled at the racetrack.

The Hand That Holds the Stopwatch

Workout times are only as good as the people who control the stopwatches. In a perfect racing world, workouts would be meticulously and electronically timed as races are, but since most working horses don't break out of the starting gate, their starting points have to be noted a little randomly.

The human timers, known at the track as *clockers*, vary in their talents. There's also the potential for variation in their honesty. After all, a crooked clocker who has timed a brilliantly fast unraced horse might record the time a couple of seconds slower than it was, then rush to the betting windows when the horse makes his racing debut.

Does this happen? Probably. But it's rare at good racetracks, especially for stakes-quality horses and horses whose trainers are known to run their own stopwatches. Rumors of repeated mistimings will cost a clocker his job.

The greater danger for bettors is putting too much reliance on fractional differences between horses. Human hands and eyes are neither quick nor accurate enough to make a meaningful differentiation between fractions of seconds.

Where Is All This Information?

Some clockers work for racetracks, while others work for the *Daily Racing Form* and other suppliers of racetrack data. We'll have more in Part 4 on how to find and read past performance information, but note here that a workout line, usually at the bottom of the list of the horse's previous races, will read something like this:

Latest Workout Jul 7 Bel 4f fst 49 2/5 h *3/21*

It means that the horse worked at Belmont Park on July 7th, going 4 furlongs on a fast track handily (under urging) in 49 2/5 seconds. He was third fastest of 21 horses who worked that distance on July 7th.

There's another useful source of workout information in past performance publications, including the *Form*, but it requires that you clip or remember figures that might not be useful for weeks. This is the *daily workout tabulation*, which lists all workouts for each day at a given racetrack. They're published with the horses' names in alphabetical order, and they sometimes include interesting tidbits at the bottom that highlight a handful of individual horses.

From the Horse's Mouth

The **bullet** work is the fastest of the day, symbolized by a big black dot to the left of the horse's name.

Tabulations allow you to judge the quality of an individual horse's workout, enabling you to determine exactly how much speed he actually showed. In comparison, the past performance workout line includes the bullet workout symbol as well as the horse's standing for the day, but it doesn't let you judge how the workout compares. Third fastest might just be a fraction faster than 21st fastest, or it might be seconds faster.

To judge speed, you need to know how fast other horses were running on the morning of the workout. You might see a figure that suggests brilliant speed, but the tabulation might tell you that the horse was faster than only three of fifty horses who worked that day. The speed was in the racetrack.

What's Fast and What's Not

This is the big question, one to which there's no simple answer since track surface and weather both affect how fast a horse runs. We'll cover that in Part 3, but you can use these figures to assess Thoroughbred workouts. In general, at a top-level racetrack in New York, California, or Florida during the winter season, you are permitted to be impressed with handy four furlong workouts of 47 3/5 seconds, five furlong workouts of 1:00, and six furlong workouts of 1:12 4/5. In the case of two-year-olds, you'll be looking for signs that the horse can run three furlongs in less than 36 seconds, either breezing or handily. Those babies have some speed.

For the Record

In times of more than one minute, the first figure represents the number of minutes, followed by a colon, followed by the number of seconds. The fractions of seconds are printed either as fractions or as decimals. 1:12 4/5 becomes 1:12.4. Note that some tracks use a decimal notation, and the 1:12 4/5 will appear as 1:12.8.

Standardbred Works

Workouts are different for Standardbreds, who tend to race much more often than Thoroughbreds. A healthy harness horse, even a top stakes contender, may race once a week during the height of his season. He keeps himself healthy and sharp by racing.

He's likely to train in private once or twice a week in addition to racing, but he won't be asked for real racing speed in those workouts. What's more, you're not going to hear about them. But there is one kind of race training that you can use to assess the speed of the horses you're considering.

In most places, Standardbreds are required to successfully compete in *qualifying races*, also known as *qualifiers*, before they are allowed to race in betting events. Some experienced horses are also required to requalify, but those horses have problems that we'll talk about later.

Standardbreds rarely train in public, so less information is available to you.

Young horses and horses new to a particular area have to prove several things in these nonbetting, no-purse races:

➤ They can line up behind the starting gate.

➤ They can start evenly.

➤ They can trot or pace a mile without breaking stride or interfering with other horses.

➤ They have enough speed to compete in the kind of racing conducted in the area.

The results of qualifying races appear in the past-performance charts that you find in racing programs at harness tracks and in handicapping publications such as *Sports Eye*. They're reported the same way as other races except that you'll see a "Q" or a "Qua" next to the information about the race. There are a couple of things to pay attention to when you're trying to find signs of real speed in a qualifying race:

➤ Qualifiers are rarely as fast as betting races since trainers and owners don't want their horses to be worked too hard when there's no money to be won or bets to be cashed.

➤ Fast quarter times tell you about a horse's pure speed.

➤ Fast final times tell you if he's ready to win immediately.

From the Horse's Mouth

The **purse** is the prize money in a horse race. Almost all tracks pay prize money for the first four places; some pay a small amount to the fifth place finisher.

Bad Bet

Just before each race, some horses are *scored*, or asked to trot or pace at top speed for a few hundred yards. It's a lung-opener, not a demonstration of speed. Don't bother trying to time it.

Compare the horse's speed in the qualifier to what other horses have been doing on the same racetrack, allowing for the fact that the horse probably will not have been pushed too hard.

The Least You Need to Know

➤ The fastest horse almost always wins. Who's fastest on a given day may change, but speed is the cornerstone of racing success.

➤ Speed is one of the most consistently inherited characteristics of horses.

➤ Breeding helps determine speed. Because of the influences of training, injury, and racing circumstances, breeding is best used to predict speed in young, untried horses.

➤ Although the dam may be the more important influence, sheer numbers of offspring make the sire the more useful predictor of speed.

➤ Look for sires who were good racers at the ages of two and three and who sire offspring who are good at two and three. Also, look for sires who excelled at short distances.

➤ Morning workouts can show speed, provided you can find public and accurately timed performances. They're most useful in identifying speed in lightly raced, young horses.

➤ In harness racing, horses have to qualify before they can be entered in a betting race. These qualifiers, while slower than betting races, can show you fast 1/4 miles, which indicate natural speed.

Chapter 4

...But Also to the Sound

The fastest horse in the world will never win a race if he's not healthy enough to go into training, to be entered into races, and then to finish those races with some degree of comfort. In the horse world, a healthy horse is called *sound*, and racing requires the highest level of soundness of all the equine sports.

Soundness is so important to racing success that it's on par with speed. A sound horse won't necessarily be fast enough to win, but a fast one who's unsound may not last long enough in either his career or an individual race to win either. A winner needs both.

How Soundness Affects Results

Unsoundness can change the outcome of races in several ways:

➤ It can turn a fast horse into a slow one. If it hurts to run fast, most horses slow down.

➤ Unsoundness can assure that a horse won't get beyond a sprint distance, even though he's bred to run farther.

➤ It can cause a horse to bear out on turns or in the stretch, losing yardage just when he should be making up ground.

➤ It is the cause, direct or indirect, of almost all breakdowns, in which a horse is injured so badly that he can't finish a race. Worst of all, unsoundness can lead to catastrophic injury, a disastrous accident to one or more legs from which only the most valuable horses are even given a chance to recover.

Where's It All Coming From?

The problem lies equally with the sport and the animal. The nature of the activity and the way the horse has been bred to compete in it each contribute to the epidemic of unsoundness in the modern racehorse. Understanding the role of each culprit will help you identify specific cases of unsoundness and decide how much it matters in a particular race.

Inside Track

Steeplechasing is a separate case. There's less force involved in the galloping since the horses are asked for slower speeds and less acceleration. But there's great force exerted on the forelegs as the horse comes down from the jump. Unsound horses can't race over fences, although sometimes they're trained to steeplechase by people who don't know what else to do with them. Beware of first-time starters over fences.

The Stress of Racing

The first and most significant barrier to soundness in the racehorse is the fact that the sport is physically stressful. The galloping horse uses a four-beat gait. This means that at the various points of the stride, the horse's entire weight is carried on each leg individually. That's half a ton or more of body weight balanced on a single thin leg. The trot and pace are two-beat gaits, with two legs carrying all the weight alternately, but that's still a quarter ton per leg. Add to that one of the basic laws of physics ($F = M \times A$; *force* equals *mass* times *acceleration*) and you get an extraordinary amount of force exerted on a delicate structure of bone and soft tissue. Breeders could create horses that reduce the mass aspect of the equation by breeding lighter horses, but there remains the belief that we talked about in Chapter 2—that bigger horses are faster. It's probably wrong, but it's ingrained.

The Racetrack

The racetrack—the playing field of the sport—may also contribute to unsoundness. In Thoroughbred racing, horses go around one to four turns, depending on the length of the race and the size of the track. In harness racing, they complete two, three, or four turns in a standard length race, again depending on the track. Quarter Horses are lucky enough to face no turns, unless they're entered in the rare half-mile races.

Left to their own devices, horses slow down when they need to gallop or trot around turns in order to take pressure off joints and bones being asked to bend unnaturally. Following that famous law of physics, they reduce force by reducing acceleration.

In racing, horses may be allowed to take it easy at the first turn but rarely at the final one since the finish line is just around the corner. The stress on the bones and joints reaches a dangerous level around turns.

The racing surface also contributes to unsoundness. Hard surfaces jar bones and joints more than soft ones, but soft surfaces can cause tendons and ligaments to stretch and pull. As you'll see in Part 3, racetracks put a lot of time and effort into striking a balance, some with more success than others in keeping horses sound.

The Horses

Even though soundness and racing success go hand-in-hand, soundness and speed often do not. Breeders, in an effort to get more and more speed in their product, contribute to soundness problems by perpetuating characteristics that make horses unsound. A brilliantly fast horse will get a chance to be bred—provided he lives long enough—even though he himself was chronically unsound.

Sometimes this works well for breeders, owners, and the sport itself. Several of the greatest Thoroughbred stallions of the past fifty years, including Raise a Native, Mr. Prospector, and Danzig, were fast but unsound racehorses. At stud, they transmitted their speed and more soundness than they enjoyed themselves. Others are not so lucky.

As a bettor, all you can do is realize that some horses, including some very fast and good ones, have a potential breakdown lurking like a suicide bomber within their legs. Whether any given day will be the one depends, in part, on the other factors you see in the horse and in the circumstances of the race.

Problems You Can See

Some unsoundness remains the secret of the trainer until the day the horse slows down and pulls up limping after the finish line, or until he breaks down during the race. Everybody suspects unsoundness after they see a horse euthanized on the racetrack.

But everybody can see or assume some potential problems in advance. They join the other factors you consider as you decide how to place your bets.

Bucked Shins

Bucked shins are minor injuries to the foreleg, consisting either of microfractures along the front of the cannon bone or simpler inflammation of the tissue covering the bone. They're common in Thoroughbreds and Quarter Horses but rare in Standardbreds. They're caused by placing force on bone not quite ready to withstand it. The Standardbred's gait limits the force enough to protect him.

Bucked shins cause pain and swelling along the front of the leg, and most horses slow down because of them. A horse may not limp if both shins are equally sore. Bucked shins happen once in a horse's lifetime and can cause a good horse to lose unexpectedly or an average one to run even worse.

You can't see existing bucked shins, and you certainly can't tell by looking if shins are about to buck. Here's the profile of a horse most likely to develop bucked shins, one who may not be a good object for big bets:

➤ He's a two-year-old, although three-year-olds buck if they start training late.

➤ He's started a couple of races or shows fast workouts in his past performance line.

➤ He's been racing or training regularly with no break for a month or two. If you spot a gap in training, he may have already bucked.

➤ He's a racehorse. Almost all Thoroughbreds and Quarter Horses buck their shins at some point. A few lucky ones are so gently and carefully trained that nobody except the horse ever notices that he ever bucked.

Tendon Injuries

All the racing breeds suffer tendon injuries, many of which you won't be able to see as the horse goes to the post. Most tendon injuries result from too much pull on the tendons at the back of the legs, although some can be caused by a blow.

You can't see minor tendon pulls, but you certainly can see bowed tendons. Bows are a sign of past, present, and future problems for a racehorse. In Thoroughbreds and Quarter Horses, look at the front legs. In the harness horse, bows can appear in front and hind legs equally.

A classic bowed tendon looks like a thickening that runs the length of the back of the lower leg. Other kinds of bows look like big bumps on the back of the cannon bone, either just below the knee, in the middle of the leg, or just above the ankle.

Once bowed, a tendon almost never returns to a normal appearance, so you'll be able to see it unless it's covered by bandages. More on that later. There are two things you need to know about bowed tendons. First, a horse with long, sloping pasterns is most likely to suffer tendon injury of any kind and much more likely to suffer a bow.

Second, horses can race again after suffering a bowed tendon, so you're likely to see them on the racetrack.

If you do and want to bet on them, remember these two additional facts. A healed bowed tendon is never again as elastic as is was before the injury, and a horse who has already bowed is 50 percent more likely than the average horse to bow again. Second, a horse with a bowed tendon can be brought back into a condition to race again, but he will almost certainly not race at his previous level.

If you see a horse who used to be a major track stakes horse running in low-level events at a small track, take a look at his legs. They may show you why he's a risky bet even against much lower quality horses.

Bad Hocks

The hock, the rear leg equivalent of the knee, is the site of several soundness problems, especially for Standardbreds. You'll often hear any kind of hock pain or injury referred to as *bone spavin*, although there are non-spavin hock problems, most much less serious, that affect racehorses.

Early bone spavin, actually a form of arthritis, shows up as slight lameness only when the horse is cold. After he warms up, he seems just fine. You'll often see horses going to the post who seem very stiff in their hind legs, but they may do very well and be fine for a bet once the gate opens.

Unfortunately, the disease eventually progresses to permanent stiffness in the hock joint, forcing the horse to raise his hips abnormally to maintain his gait. At that point, he won't be able to win anything. Watch carefully as the horses warm up. Don't necessarily reject one who is stiff at first, but if he's still stiff after several minutes of movement, bet on somebody else. Curbed hocks also need a close look. A *curb* is a slight thickening of a ligament that connects the hock to the back of the rear cannon bone. (A curb usually creates a much smaller bump than a bow.) A *cap* is a bump on the back of the hock.

From the Horse's Mouth

A **spavin** is a lump or thickening in the hock area.

Neither a curb nor a cap is particularly serious since they're usually caused by a slight kick or a knock against something hard. A recently acquired curb is painful and will cause the horse to limp until it heals. You're unlikely to see one in the post parade because it will be obvious to even the most desperate trainer that a horse with a painful curb won't beat anybody.

If the injury that caused the curb was severe enough, scar tissue will form, and the bump will become permanent. This will limit the number of people who admire the horse's good looks, but it will not limit his racing ability.

Equipment that Shouts Unsoundness

Indications of unsoundness can also be applied to the horse along with the saddle or harness. Some you can see. Others are not so visible, and racetracks help you with these by posting, either on a chalkboard or on the tote board, information about special equipment.

From the Horse's Mouth

The **tote** or **totalisator board** displays betting, time, entry, and other important information, usually in the infield of the track.

From the Horse's Mouth

The **fetlock** is the rear ankle joint.

Some tracks don't post equipment information but do announce it over the loudspeaker system. It's important, so pay attention to the announcements.

Bandages

This equipment you can see. Here's the rule in Thoroughbred and Quarter Horse racing: Bandages on the rear legs may or may not mean soundness problems, but bandages on the front legs almost always do. The rear bandages that you don't have to worry about at all are those that cover the fetlock and continue a few inches up the cannon bone.

These small, light bandages are called *run-downs* and serve to protect the skin of the fetlock from irritation from the racetrack that occurs as the hind feet dig into the surface. At tracks with deep surfaces, all the horses going to the post may be wearing run-downs.

Bandages that continue up the rear cannon bone may be there to give support to the ligaments and tendons surrounding that bone. If so, somebody (such as the trainer) has some serious doubts about the horse's soundness.

Front bandages of any kind are almost never used on a completely sound horse for a race. They are regularly used for protection against bumps and knocks during training gallops.

Front bandages being used for the first time in a race are a sure indication that the horse has problems with bones or tendons (or the trainer thinks he's about to have them). Horses with front bandages often run well and sometimes win, but they're not fully sound when they do it. They run with a risk attached.

Some past performance charts include bandage information about previous races. If a horse has worn bandages in his previous races, you can assume he's going to in the one you're considering. You won't have to wait until he parades onto the track to find out.

Bar Shoes

Most Thoroughbred and Quarter Horse tracks post or announce information about bar shoes. These shoes also suggest that the horse using them has shortcomings in the soundness department.

Bar shoes are used to give extra protection to sore hoofs by spreading the concussion over a larger surface. Bar shoes, although they allow some horses to race when they otherwise couldn't, can be dangerous: to you, if he races away with your money because he's still too uncomfortable to win; and to him because one sore foot may cause him to put extra weight on his good feet. The excess stress on one leg causes many catastrophic breakdowns.

From the Horse's Mouth

A **bar shoe** looks like a regular horseshoe, except there's an extra segment of steel or aluminum connecting the two ends.

Standardbred Equipment

Harness trainers tend to employ so much equipment to make their horses trot or pace better and faster that it's much more difficult to try to figure out which items mean unsoundness and which are merely experiments. The racing trot and pace are unnaturally extended, and even well-conformed horses can occasionally interfere with themselves, with rear feet striking forelegs, and vice versa. Harness horses often carry an entire tack shop's worth of boots, cups, and bandages designed to prevent themselves from cutting or bruising their own bodies.

From the Horse's Mouth

Tack is the equipment used on a horse for riding or driving. Driving equipment is also called *rigging*.

All this equipment does not necessarily mean that the horse is unsound, although it may. He may merely have a creative or desperate trainer. Too much unneeded equipment is probably distracting for a horse, and one of the most admired competitors in harness racing is a horse who races well with a minimum of add-ons.

Predicting a Breakdown

There's nothing much worse than seeing a horse you've bet on break down during a race—except, of course, for seeing a horse you own or like break down. Here are some of the situations and characteristics that lead to breakdowns:

➤ Horses four and older break down more often. Computer analysis turned this fact up, surprising a lot of racetrack people who thought that untried young ones were more vulnerable. Not so.

➤ Among Thoroughbreds, horses who break down are much more likely to have raced within the previous two weeks. This is not the case among Standardbreds and Quarter Horses.

➤ Horses who suffer soft-tissue breakdowns—tendon and ligament injury—are likely to have been scratched from another race during the previous couple of months.

➤ Most breakdowns occur on fast racetracks, whether dirt or turf.

The length of the race and weather conditions don't seem to play a part, although some experienced racetrack people are convinced that muddy tracks are more dangerous. Others point out that mud cushions sore legs. Remember that plenty of six-year-old horses who've started within two weeks, who've been scratched previously, still don't break down on fast racetracks. Their risk is just a little greater.

The Vet Check

All licensed racetracks have a veterinarian who checks horses before they race. The vets have the authority to order a horse scratched if they feel his condition makes racing unsafe for his rider, himself, or other horses. A horse who's too unhealthy to give his bettors a fair shake may also be scratched.

The vets may all be skilled enough to detect an unsound horse, but they vary tremendously in their inclination to order scratches. It's probably because of the policy of their racetracks rather than any preference of their own. At lower level racetracks that offer small purses, most horses have questionable soundness, and only one with a very severe problem is going to be ordered scratched.

At a good track, every horse is checked by the vet the morning he's scheduled to be raced. His legs are felt, he is walked in front of the vet, and he may have his temperature and heart checked. Later, he is observed as he warms up, and he's given a visual check as he approaches the starting gate. The vet can order him scratched at any point in the process.

From the Horse's Mouth

A **scratch** is the withdrawal of a horse from a race after he has been announced as an entry.

The gate scratch often infuriates bettors, since their bets are automatically transferred to the starting favorite—who usually features much lower odds. Don't be annoyed if it happens to you. A horse who's so unsound that the vet scratches him at the gate is not going to win anything anyway.

Now, after hearing about all these unsound horses, take a look at a sound one:

Sunday Silence won the 1989 Kentucky Derby in early May, raced much of the year, then won the 1989 Breeder's Cup Classic in November.

The Least You Need to Know

➤ Unsoundness is nearly as important as speed to racing success.

➤ The force exerted on equine legs during races is the primary cause of unsoundness, although some problems are perpetuated by breeders.

➤ Almost all young Thoroughbreds and Quarter Horses suffer bucked shins, and one about to buck is usually a bad bet.

➤ An older horse with a bowed tendon can race, but he'll never be as good as he used to be, and he's more likely to suffer the same injury again.

➤ Healed curbed hocks are usually no barrier to racing success.

➤ Rear bandages may or may not mean unsoundness, but front ones almost always do. The first use of front bandages is a particularly worrisome clue.

➤ Older, overraced horses running on fast tracks are more likely to break down than other horses.

Chapter 5

The Pharmaceutically Correct Horse

In This Chapter

➤ The three different categories of medication

➤ Lasix and bute: what they do for horses and bettors

➤ Testing for drugs, illegal and otherwise

There is no more complex, confusing, or contentious issue in horse racing than the question of drugs. The industry prefers to call it medication, but a pharmaceutical by any other name is just as difficult to figure.

Whatever name you give the substance, it's difficult for the bettor to determine just what drug the horse has been given legally, what he might have been given illegally, and whether any of it makes a difference to the outcome of the race.

There are two additional complications that everybody involved in racing faces:

➤ Drug rules vary, sometimes dramatically, between racing jurisdictions. What's legal in one state can get you disqualified, fined, or suspended in another. Since racing is a legal betting sport, state governments have been reluctant to give up their rulemaking to an outside body, and there is, at the moment, no uniform drug policy.

➤ Science has been more effective in coming up with new drugs to use on horses than in developing new tests to uncover their illegal use. The states' control of drug rules also plays a role in testing since each state conducts its own. Some are better at it than others.

If you want to win at the races, whether you're an owner, trainer, or bettor, you've got to try to understand what's going on with drugs.

The Three Categories

Drugs used on racehorses can be grouped into three general categories, although the same drug can fit into all three, depending on the circumstances and the intentions of the person who administers it.

➤ Some are intended to cure ailments or alleviate pain. They are believed to have no effect on performance and are permitted as race-day medications, although the quantity the horse may receive is regulated in most states.

➤ Others are therapeutic, but they have side effects that could alter the outcome of races. These are likely to be used for horses in training, but they are not permitted, except in trace amounts, in horses when they race.

➤ Others have no legitimate use in horses other than to alter race results and are illegal if they're detected in any horse scheduled to race. A few of these are illegal whether the horse is scheduled to race or not. Post-race tests, for example, occasionally turn up positive for cocaine. The horse isn't arrested, but he's disqualified and his people are investigated.

Scientists, horsemen, and bettors are constantly adjusting and readjusting their ideas about which side effects exist and which don't, and which matter to the outcome of a race. Racing authorities also adjust, although rarely as quickly as the other interested parties.

The Big Two

Most important to racing are the medications known as the Big Two. They are phenylbutazone and furosemide, better known by their most widely distributed brand names, *Butazolodin* and *Lasix*. These medications are permitted in most of North America, usually in controlled doses.

They are not legal as race-day medications in most other countries, where the racing authorities (if not horse owners and trainers) believe that a horse who's not sound enough to race without medication is not sound enough to race, period.

The Big Two have been accepted as widely as they are because of the belief that, while they work on horse ailments, they don't really affect the results of a race. That's nonsense on its face. If a horse doesn't run as well without a drug, the presence of the drug clearly has an effect on the race.

But it's a little more complicated than that. Let's look at each of the two drugs, beginning with the first one to become widespread in the racing business.

Bute

Everybody calls it *bute*, even though its proper and generic name is phenylbutazone. This drug is legal for race-day use in all but a handful of states and Canada. Bute has been used in animals and humans since the late 1950s, primarily as a painkiller for those suffering from orthopedic injuries. Twist your knee playing tennis, and you may leave the doctor's office with a prescription for bute.

For the Record

Proponents of bute describe it as nothing more than an aspirin-like analgesic, designed to ease minor aches and pains. In reality, it's a little more than that. Bute *is* an anti-inflammatory drug, reducing pain-causing inflammation rather than the pain itself.

Bute has been accepted by racing authorities because it has no effect on the central nervous system and doesn't make a horse run faster or slower than his physical structure, training, or mental inclination permits him to do. Bute, the authorities think, doesn't make a horse run like anyone but himself.

The primary side effect is a risk of stomach ulcers, a condition that doesn't affect the results of individual races either. But anything that allows an injured horse to race carries some baggage along with it.

Here's a possible scenario. A horse has a sore knee or hock. The best solution for the horse, although not for his connections who pay the bills, is for him to stay in his barn. But the trainer needs a paycheck, so the horse gets his bute, his swollen joint doesn't hurt quite so much, and he races.

Unfortunately, he doesn't get the cue from his body to ease up the pressure on his sore leg, and he suffers a catastrophic breakdown. He carries himself, his jockey, other horses, and possibly your money into disaster with him.

Of course, most horses who race on bute don't break down, partly through luck and partly because most racing jurisdictions limit the amount that can be used on race day. With a little good fortune, the horse about to break down will still get a few faint cues and ease himself up. The bottom line is that bute is usually a safe, effective drug. It's so cheap—only about $10 a dose—that you'll see races where every starter has been given the drug.

Inside Track

You look for the letter "B" to identify a horse who's been given bute. It will be next to his name in the program or in the past performance charts.

Where it's legal, the use of bute is so widespread that you can't assume much one way or another if a horse is using it. You might think that a horse who needs an anti-inflammatory has soundness problems, so you put a black mark or two next to his name. But the drug is so cheap and so widely accepted that some trainers use it even on sound horses, believing that it's good insurance against the pulls and strains that are inevitable in a horse in training.

On the other hand, a horse not on bute is very likely to be sound, and you can give him a point or two for that. This is especially important if the horse comes from the barn of a good trainer (see Chapter 8). You can be moderately confident that the horse is ready to race to the level of his talent, to finish the race on four legs, and to give you a run for your money.

He won't necessarily be fast enough, but he should be sound. All other things being equal, the non-bute horse is a good bet.

For the Record

Bute made headlines in 1968 when Dancer's Image became the first Kentucky Derby winner to be disqualified when the drug was discovered in his post-race test. Bute had been legal in Kentucky before 1962 and again became legal in 1970. Several winners since have raced on it.

Lasix

The second of the Big Two is called Lasix, even though its generic name is furosemide. It is at the same time more controversial and more uniformly permitted than bute.

It's permitted because it helps treat one of the most common health problems of racehorses, and it's controversial because there's now good evidence that it does more for a racehorse than treat that medical condition.

Lasix debuted on the pharmaceutical stage in the late 1960s as a diuretic for humans. It increases the volume of urine produced by the kidneys, reduces blood pressure, and causes excess fluid in the tissues to decrease. As with most successful human medicines, Lasix was soon used on horses. It proved to be useful for the treatment of animals who retained fluid in the lungs after a bout with respiratory disease. But Lasix had a couple of side effects that made racing officials worry about its potential abuse:

➤ Since it increased urine flow, there was the danger that Lasix might mask the presence of other drugs in post-race tests.

➤ Since it appeared to improve lung capacity in sick horses, there was the danger that it might improve healthy horses, too. Lung capacity is part of the physical package that makes a good racehorse.

But Lasix proved to have one side effect that far outweighs everything else for racing people. It appears to reduce the incidence of bleeding from the lungs, the great scourge of the modern Thoroughbred racehorse.

Bleeding

Bleeding—its proper name is *exercise-induced pulmonary hemorrhage* (EIPH)—worries all horse people. Bleeding involves the rupture of tiny blood vessels in the lungs, and it's extraordinarily common. Some horsemen believe that most Thoroughbreds would show evidence of blood in the lungs or trachea after every race if they were all examined internally.

Most incidents of bleeding are minor, with no blood visible to the casual observer and often no apparent effect on the horse's performance. But sometimes it's severe, with blood flowing from the nose, and the horse so impaired that he can't finish the race.

Bleeding is prompted by strenuous exercise, particularly at high speed. These horses are often affected:

➤ Quarter Horses, particularly those older than two or three.

➤ Thoroughbreds, particularly sprinters and middle-distance horses.

Inside Track

If you hear a horse called a bleeder, he's one who suffers so badly that blood is visible and his performance is clearly affected. His past performance line may show that he stopped suddenly, followed by the word "bled."

Less affected:

➤ Steeplechasers, although their work is clearly strenuous. The speed demanded of them is less than what's required for racing on the flat.

➤ Standardbreds, although there is some bleeding among horses who race under harness. As the harness record for the mile comes closer to the running record, we may be seeing more bleeding, but at the moment it's primarily a condition of short-running Thoroughbreds and their close relatives.

It's not entirely clear why there's so much EIPH among Thoroughbreds and Quarter Horses. It may be in the nature of horses, or it may be that asking horses to run fast in the presence of air pollution has created the problem. No specific genetic flaw has been found in bleeders, but it's an area of extensive research. However, it is clear what seems to help: Lasix. No one is sure why it helps, but it's probably because a reduction in blood pressure decreases the pressure on the blood vessels, making them less likely to burst.

It doesn't help completely, and it may not always help. Severe bleeders can bleed right through it. But horsemen believe it's a valuable treatment anyway.

Some racing jurisdictions require horses to bleed in the presence of a veterinarian before they can use Lasix. Others allow the drug for a horse whose bleeding has never been seen by anyone. At racetracks in those states, you may see every horse in the race with an "L" next to his name. Trainers even find it worthwhile to ship a nonvisible bleeder to a permissive state to establish a Lasix history.

Just why is Lasix so popular? It's twice as expensive as bute, and it doesn't always work, especially among serious bleeders. Here's a fact that used to be a well-whispered secret among trainers and bettors: Lasix appears to make almost all horses run a little faster.

Several recent studies have shown that horses, whether or not they've ever shown signs of bleeding, run better on Lasix. The studies haven't yet shown why even non-bleeders may improve on the drug. The possibilities:

➤ The horse may enjoy reduced body weight because of the diuretic effect of Lasix.

➤ The drug may allow the horse to take more oxygen into his bloodstream, leading to greater athletic capacity.

➤ The drug may protect the tiny blood vessels subject to rupture under stress even in healthy lungs.

Bad Bet

Remember that a horse who's been put on Lasix because of a serious bleeding incident in a race or workout is more likely than most other horses to bleed badly again. He won't be a good bet, no matter what drug he's given.

The effect is greatest the first time a horse races with Lasix, although some improvement continues in later races. The importance of first time Lasix use is so great that entry lists almost always include, in addition to the L for Lasix, a special notation for first time users. This will usually be the symbol L1. An L1 horse is worth serious consideration because of the likelihood of improvement.

Most racing jurisdictions require that a horse who bleeds visibly go into temporary retirement. If the bleeding occurs in public, he will be placed on the *vet's list* and prevented from starting for a period ranging from four days to several weeks, depending on the jurisdiction. A second bleeding incident may see him banned for a year.

Serious bleeders will be hard for you to spot. If there's no notation of bleeding in the past performance charts, you have to search out the vet's list. Racing publications occasionally print the list, along with various people suspended for various infractions, but the list mentioning a horse entered in today's races would have been printed weeks ago. The information is normally not included in programs or entries, although handicappers' comments sometimes note that a horse is just coming off the vet's list.

Lasix is believed to have no side effects likely to injure the horses who receive it. They don't get ulcers, and they are no more likely than other horses to break down. But some opponents of the drug believe that Lasix may have a negative effect on the Thoroughbred breed as a whole by permitting bleeders to run and win, and then be bred to produce offspring who also bleed.

Most racing people, though, are content to let future racing people worry about that. They appreciate the drug, as did well-informed bettors—until everybody started using it. You still sometimes spot a first-time-out Lasix horse, who becomes a horse worthy of consideration because of it.

From the Horse's Mouth

The **vet's list** is made up of horses ordered out of action by the track vet for physical reasons. They have to be checked before they are eligible to start again.

From the Horse's Mouth

An **out** is a start.

Other Drugs for Bleeders

Some states permit hormones to be used on bleeders, particularly estrogens, and these don't seem to have much role in betting decisions. Other bleeders are given special vitamin concoctions, and still others get inhalation therapy. These treatments aren't reported publicly, but you'll sometimes hear about them from newspaper handicappers and other tipsters. They undoubtedly help some horses, but the jury is still out on whether they are important enough to become a factor in betting decisions.

Therapeutic Drugs

There are hundreds of perfectly fine, legal, effective, and safe drugs given to treat the ills of racehorses. The only reason racegoers need to worry about them is that some of them are not permitted to be in the horse's system at race time.

Drugs legal for equine use but not legal on race day fit into six general categories:

➤ Sedatives that make a horse drowsy

➤ Tranquilizers that make him dull

➤ Stimulants that make him more lively

➤ Bronchodilators that make him breathe better

➤ Anesthetics that hide pain

➤ Masking agents that do him neither good or harm, but do hide the presence of other drugs

Side effects put some important drugs into these categories. Horses have plenty of allergies and use a lot of antihistamines, many of which have a sedative effect. These drugs can be used legitimately and still cause a disqualification if they are administered too close to race time.

While most racing jurisdictions allow trace amounts of legal drugs and publish dosage guidelines, horses differ in their reactions to drugs. Sometimes the effects linger a little too long.

Occasionally, a drug intended for one horse gets into the feed tub of another. Racing jurisdictions take care of this excuse by making the trainer personally responsible for whatever happens to his horses, regardless of whether he fed, treated, or watched them himself. This is the *absolute insurer* rule.

Talk to any group of trainers, and you'll hear a lot of complaining about the policy, and you'll occasionally hear about a drug disqualification being overturned because the trainer proved accidental administration. But no better idea has yet appeared than the absolute insurer rule, and it probably prevents a fair amount of sloppy care or downright cheating

For the Record

Every now and then a drug traced to an improbable drug source appears in a post-race test. In 1986, an English stakes winner was disqualified when the stimulant theobromine showed up in his sample. It turned out that the horse had snitched a Mars candy bar from his groom.

Illegal Drugging

Some trainers do deliberately try to improve their horse's performances with drugs that are either specifically illegal or so new that they are not yet listed by the authorities. These trainers may bet on their horses, but they are usually not trying to create a specific order of finish for betting purposes.

They just want their horses (and themselves) to have an extra advantage. They would never describe themselves as race fixers. Nor, probably, would most track officials. But the authorities are just as eager to catch them as anybody else trying to alter the outcome of a race.

Trainer-administered illegal drugs are most likely to be stimulants. Those few cases where an outsider is involved probably involve sedatives or tranquilizers. After all, it's easier to make a horse lose than to make him win. All the bronchodilators in the world won't help a horse who's unsound, or slow, or not inclined to make an effort.

For the Record

Drugging by someone other than the horse's handler is rare everywhere, but it's more likely to happen at small tracks than big ones. Still, there have been incidents with very big horses. In 1974, Kentucky Derby winner Riva Ridge tested positive for a tranquilizer after running an unexpected fourth in a race in New Jersey. Who got to him was never discovered. Nowadays, top horses have guards.

In general, race fixing by drug is not something to worry about. But if you're planning to bet on a Thoroughbred at a small track and see him ignore the backfire of the starting gate tractor as he parades past it and stagger along as if he's carrying another horse on his back, think twice. That's not normal behavior for a horse ready to race.

Are They Drugs or Are They Treatments?

There are a few other treatments that may or may not help horses run faster. Some are illegal, some are frowned upon, and some don't show up in current tests, making regulation difficult. Here are the two most common:

➤ *Jugs* are injections of a solution of substances into a horse's jugular vein just before the race. Jugs usually include vitamins, amino acids, minerals, and possibly a trainer's secret substance. It's believed that the jug has more effect than the same substance fed to the horse since it goes immediately to the bloodstream. A lot of trainers and tipsters swear by jugs, but there's no real proof yet.

➤ *Milk shakes* are also used, illegally in some areas, to improve racing performance. No, they're not the beverage you use to wash down your hamburger, but rather a sodium bicarbonate solution not much different from the antacid you take after you eat that hamburger. The logic is this: Sodium bicarbonate is supposed to neutralize the lactic acid that builds up in muscles, causing fatigue and muscle pain. The lactic acid buildup is most intense in high-speed, mid-distance races. Milk shakes became especially popular in one-mile Standardbred racing, at least until racing authorities noticed.

Testing

There's a pervasive belief among racing skeptics that the testing laboratories are far behind the chemists creating new drugs and even farther behind people willing to use the drugs unethically. They point to the fact that less than one percent of the samples tested nationwide each year come back positive.

The truth is this: The labs are behind, and scientists admit that there are several dozen equine drugs that simply don't show up in current tests. An industry-wide effort is underway to catch up to modern chemistry. There's also the very practical trend to save for future tests blood and urine samples from suspicious cases that don't show anything under current testing procedures.

How Testing Is Done

The procedures vary from state to state, but usually the winner (or all placed horses) are required to give post-race urine samples. Beaten favorites are also tested, as is any horse whose performance stood out as too good or too bad to be true. Random finishers are also selected for testing.

For the Record

Drug testing used to be done with saliva, but urine is more accurate. Still, many racing people still call the testing locale the "spit barn." It's supposed to be a well-guarded facility, but the quality of the security varies widely.

Most jurisdictions split the samples, saving some for retesting should the first test come up positive. Others do two tests on every sample. Some split only a few randomly chosen samples, while others do blind testing for quality assurance.

When a positive to an identifiable illegal drug is discovered, the information is relayed to the racetrack, usually a few days after the race. The horse is disqualified, the purse is redistributed, and the trainer usually gets suspended. The length of the suspension depends on the drug, with long penalties imposed for the discovery of one of the drugs with no known therapeutic value.

The betting results are not changed, and this invariably infuriates the holders of tickets on losing horses. Disgruntled bettors have taken their cases to court, but so far, there's been no change in this policy.

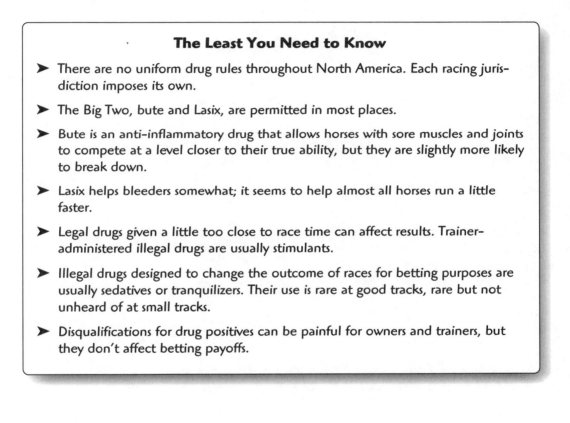

The Least You Need to Know

➤ There are no uniform drug rules throughout North America. Each racing jurisdiction imposes its own.

➤ The Big Two, bute and Lasix, are permitted in most places.

➤ Bute is an anti-inflammatory drug that allows horses with sore muscles and joints to compete at a level closer to their true ability, but they are slightly more likely to break down.

➤ Lasix helps bleeders somewhat; it seems to help almost all horses run a little faster.

➤ Legal drugs given a little too close to race time can affect results. Trainer-administered illegal drugs are usually stimulants.

➤ Illegal drugs designed to change the outcome of races for betting purposes are usually sedatives or tranquilizers. Their use is rare at good tracks, rare but not unheard of at small tracks.

➤ Disqualifications for drug positives can be painful for owners and trainers, but they don't affect betting payoffs.

Chapter 6

Age, Sex, and Other Ways to Discriminate

In This Chapter

➤ Why older is usually better among racehorses

➤ The equine battle of the sexes

➤ Brains versus brawn among racehorses

➤ The angry or nervous horse

If speed and soundness were the only things that mattered, the horse most likely to win would be easy to pick out. While the circumstances of the specific race might alter the outcome, you could be pretty sure about how your horse was going to perform.

But speed and good health aren't all there is to a racehorse. Several other characteristics also contribute to a horse's success, and you should keep them in mind if you hope to succeed yourself.

Age

You might think that age would be a straightforward element of race analysis. You read the horse's age as it's printed in the program, think about what it could mean to the race, then make your decision about his chances. Unfortunately, it's not always quite so clear, and the confusion starts early.

The Birthday

No need to keep a calendar: All racehorses have the same birthday even though it's possible for a horse to be born any day of the year.

Left to their own devices, most horses will breed so that the resulting foals are born between early spring and late summer—from March to August in most areas. Occasionally, fall and winter foals appear. In order to prevent confusion for breeders, race planners, and bettors, January 1 has been selected as the official birthday of all racehorses.

On New Year's Day, every horse born during the previous year celebrates its first birthday, whether he's 10 months, six months, or one day old. The next January 1, he becomes a two-year-old, and so on. The difference between the official birthday and the real one is important in all two-year-old racing and in three-year-old racing at least until September.

This foal will be a year old next January 1, regardless of how many months he's been alive.

Some Two-Year-Olds Are Yearlings

Breeders do their best to make sure their foals are born as soon after January 1 as possible (a December 31 foal is a disaster), but luck and scheduling sometimes sees foals born in June or even July. A two-year-old race scheduled before June is likely to include one or more yearlings.

Many past performance publications and track programs help you identify the chronological yearlings in two-year-old races by printing the month of birth after each horse's breeding line. This is also occasionally done for three-year-old races so you can pick out the chronological two-year-olds there.

It matters to betting decisions, but just a little. The actual birth month isn't a magical dividing line. A horse too young to race well the day before his real birthday isn't going to be automatically mature enough the day after. Consider the birth months of two-year-olds a loose guideline.

A very late birthdate—especially if this race is scheduled early in the year—should be considered a mark against the horse as you make your betting decisions. Conversely, an early birthdate gives a horse an advantage in physical and mental development.

Do remember that each horse matures at a slightly different rate. Some very young horses, even chronological yearlings, are ready to race, while horses several months older are not. But, in general, older is better for two- and three-year-olds. Throughout those years, horses grow in height, gain more bone density, and develop bigger muscles.

From the Horse's Mouth

A **yearling** is a one-year-old horse.

Inside Track

Among horses as well as people, females mature a little earlier. Two-year-old females tend to be more ready to race than males of the same age.

What's in a Name

Some birthdays give a horse a whole new name. What you call them depends on age, sex, and sport.

➤ In all racing breeds, two- and three-year-old males are *colts*, while two- and three-year-old females are *fillies*, although you'll occasionally come across old-timers who don't use the word *filly*. To them, all females are *mares*.

➤ With Standardbreds and Quarter Horses, four-year-old males become *stallions* and four-year-old females become mares, and they retain these names for the rest of their lives.

From the Horse's Mouth

Geldings are castrated male horses. They usually undergo the operation as yearlings or two-year-olds, but it can be done at any time. Gelded males usually concentrate on their racing careers better than stallions, so the operation is almost always done on young male horses who are not likely to be in demand as stallions.

➤ At four, Thoroughbreds are still colts, becoming stallions at the age of five. Fillies are fillies at four, becoming mares at the age of five.

➤ Standardbreds and Quarter Horses of both sexes are officially described as *aged* after their three-year-old seasons, although they are still also stallions and mares.

➤ Thoroughbreds are never officially aged, but you may use that word to refer to a really elderly horse.

➤ In all three breeds, geldings are called geldings from the day of their surgery. They are no longer colts, even if they are babies.

When Age Matters

In racing, age matters most when horses are very young or very old. What's old is relative. In most other horse sports, a horse under the age of six is a mere baby, far too young to excel. But he can be competitive into his late teens.

Not so in racing where most horses are at their best from the second half of their three-year-old season through their five-year-old year. But they do race long before and after that two-and-a-half-year period, and you should try to understand what age means to the not-quite-prime competitors.

Inside Track

Young horses ready to race come in all sizes and shapes, but compact ones—small but muscular—seem to be earliest to mature in all the racing breeds. Rangy, long-legged horses have rarely learned to operate their bodies properly as young two-year-olds.

Two-Year-Olds

Some bettors avoid two-year-old racing as if they might be turned to a pillar of salt if they as much as watch it. Others love the Three P's of baby racing: *promise, potential,* and *possibility.*

You never know if you might be watching a Man O' War or a Niatross when you see the gate open for the first time on a horse.

The word "possibility" is the key to either side in the debate over betting on two-year-olds. He might be Man O' War, or he might be a horse who doesn't know which direction to go and isn't about to let anybody show him. Two-year-olds can be erratic, physically and mentally.

There is an aspect of two-year-old racing that makes it easier for bettors, at least those wagering on Thoroughbreds and Quarter Horses. Two-year-olds race shorter distances than most other horses, especially early in the year. You don't have to fit stamina into the equation. Speed is all.

In Thoroughbred racing, two-year-olds race at 4 and 5 furlongs early in the year, stretching to 6 to 7 furlongs as summer progresses. In the fall, there are a few mile and 1 1/16 mile races for two-year-olds at the bigger racetracks.

In Quarter Horse racing, two-year-olds start at 220 yards early in the year, never going more than 440. Standardbred two-year-olds race at one mile, like older horses.

If you want to bet two-year-old races, follow the guidelines in Chapter 3 to identify speed. Then keep in mind the following facts about two-year-olds:

➤ **They have to learn how to race.** Workouts, even in company with other horses, can't simulate the cavalry-charge nature of real racing. Some horses become frightened, while others are thrilled by the competition. Each kind makes mistakes, running too fast, slowing up, ducking in, drifting out.

➤ **Experience counts.** Horses with even a little experience are more likely to win than first-time starters, but even they will experience things in your race that they've never seen before. They probably will be a little quicker to adjust than a first-time starter, but not necessarily.

The Older Horse

At the other end of the age spectrum are the older horses. Racehorses are a little like supermodels. They're branded as too old just as they are reaching full maturity.

In racing, it's not just prejudice. Because of the physical stress caused by pounding on racetracks, horses' legs age much more quickly than the rest of them. By the time they reach the age of six, most racehorses have old legs. Just how old depends on how many times a horse has started, the kind of surface he's been racing on, and how fast he runs. Turf horses tend to last a little longer, as do distance runners and Standardbreds.

Occasionally, a horse who is extremely sound to begin with can win at sprint distances on hard dirt tracks when he's well past the age of six. He should be worshipped as well as bet on.

From the Horse's Mouth

Turf horses race over grass courses rather than dirt tracks. Some horses do both, but most are better on one than the other.

Sex

Most races are segregated by sex. Fillies and mares are permitted to run in most races, but other races are scheduled exclusively for them. There is a widely held belief among most people involved in racing that female horses aren't quite as good at racing as males. Sometimes they are and sometimes they aren't.

What they are is different. Even in their own races, fillies and mares require a little extra analysis before you bet on them.

The Battle of the Sexes

Most observers believe that female horses can run or trot as fast as male horses of similar class (pacing is different). What the females often lack are some of the other qualities that contribute to winning, primarily consistency. The lack of consistency can be between races or even within a single race. The villain is hormones.

Hormones

Stallions are affected by hormones too, but a surge of testosterone seems to help a stallion run better, bulling his way to the lead, fighting off the opposition. This is true, provided the stallion doesn't kick the trainer's head off as he's being saddled. But female hormones cause a different reaction—a desire to be somewhere else other than the racetrack. Here are the factors to consider when betting on fillies and mares, some hormonal, some structural.

Time of the Year

Heat periods (internal, not meteorological) are what you have to watch for. Fillies start coming into heat in the spring of their two-year-old years, and most continue with heat periods until they die. A few mares have heat periods year-round, but most only cycle from late winter to late summer. Many fillies and mares run their best races during the cold weather of fall and winter.

For the Record

The scientific name for heat is **estrus**, but around the racetrack you'll hear it called season, horsing, or filly trouble.

Time of the Month

Heats come as often as every two weeks and can last three to five days. During these spells, female horses might pay more attention to the siren song of their hormones than anything else in their lives. This causes the inconsistency on the racetrack, a characteristic most pronounced if there are male horses on the track. Even geldings become attractive to a mare in heat. Some mares run fast as ever during their heats, while others can't outrace their own shadows. They are probably hoping their shadows have turned male. Some trainers give their mares a drug with the trade name Regumate™ during the spring and summer to suppress heat periods. These mares should run normally, but the drug isn't reported, and you will have no way of knowing about it.

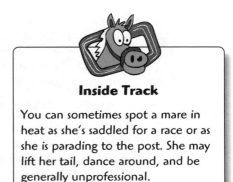

Inside Track

You can sometimes spot a mare in heat as she's saddled for a race or as she is parading to the post. She may lift her tail, dance around, and be generally unprofessional.

➤ **Age.** Two-year-olds are more competitive with males than other fillies and mares are, possibly because their heats are both less intense and don't come quite so often. It may also be because females mature more quickly than males.

➤ **Distance.** Among running horses, females are most competitive with males over sprint distances, probably because of the advantage of wider hips in sprinting. They are also very competitive over distances of a mile and a half and up, probably because they have less body weight to haul around the racetrack.

➤ **Gait.** Among Standardbreds, trotting females are probably equal to males. It's hard to know for sure because good ones are kept in female-only races. Among pacers, males are clearly superior to females of similar class. The wider hips of fillies and mares are an advantage at the trot and a disadvantage at the pace.

Courage

Courage is the most admired quality in a racehorse, although it's certainly less useful than speed and soundness. But courage can make a difference in individual races, and it can surely make you enjoy watching your horse run if he displays it.

Webster's defines courage as the mental or moral strength to persevere. Change the word *moral* to *physical*, and you have a good description of courage in the racehorse.

Racehorse courage usually comes in the form of willingness to make an effort in spite of pain, whether the pain comes from the lungs at the end of a long, demanding race, or whether it comes from legs hurting from injury, age, or too much racing.

Some horses show incredible courage, often with little common sense to go along with it. Black

From the Horse's Mouth

You'll often hear a brave racehorse referred to as **game**.

Gold, who won the Kentucky Derby in 1924, broke a leg racing in New Orleans a few years later. He won the race and is buried in the infield of the racetrack. As recently as 1985, the champion Thoroughbred Roving Boy won a race in California in spite of having fractured both hind legs during the stretch run. More common (and safer) kinds of racehorse courage might show up like this:

➤ A horse who holds on to his position in spite of challenges from fresher or even faster horses.

➤ A horse who allows himself to be urged into an opening between horses that's a little narrower than he is.

➤ Every horse who is competitive and runs a respectable race, even though his legs and muscles feel the wear and tear of too much racing.

You identify these horses in the past performance charts. In Part 4, you'll find help on how to identify horses who hold on when challenged, as well as those who keep coming in spite of rough going.

Intelligence

Equine intelligence is a hotly debated topic both among people who work with horses every day and those whose contact is more casual—people like bettors. In each group, you find people who think racehorses are bright and others who think they are among God's stupidest creatures. The truth is, as most truths are, somewhere in between.

What's Smart and What's Not

Intelligence in animals is usually determined by their ability to learn tasks and to remember what they've learned. Horses don't learn very quickly compared to dogs and cats and several other animals, but they have memories that put elephants to shame.

Does this mean that horses are intelligent? Let's put it this way. They are intelligent enough to train and race, where the skill level is low and the importance of routine is high.

For the Record

One of the favorite stories racing people tell involves an old groom who was asked if horses really are stupid. His paraphrased answer, "They're not so stupid. I never saw any horses lining up to bet on any people."

A truly stupid horse is a bad racehorse, even if he happens to be fast.

➤ He may forget how he's supposed to behave in the starting gate.

➤ He won't remember that a horse coming up on his outside isn't a predator.

➤ He won't know that being saddled or harnessed is supposed to be a mental cue to get ready to race.

On the other hand, a very intelligent horse can sometimes get himself into trouble.

➤ He may have figured out that he's supposed to be in the lead at the finish and translate that into a desire to be in the lead at all times—not good strategy in long races with other early speed horses.

➤ He may observe that once he's in the lead in the stretch, he is pulled up by his rider or driver. Not understanding that this happens after the finish line, he may do it himself several yards too soon.

➤ He may realize that he's going to get fed and brushed no matter how he performs and will opt out of making an effort.

A horse who shows a number of inexplicable acts in previous races you've seen may be too smart or too stupid for his own good. In the hands of a really good rider or driver, this may not matter. In the hands of a human on the low end of the intelligence scale, it may.

Temperament

Bad-tempered horses are dangerous to the people who work with them, as well as to other horses. If they're not so temperamental that they can't be forced to follow racing procedures, they can give good accountings of themselves on the racetracks.

For the Record

At most running tracks, saddling takes place in public view. At harness tracks, harnessing may be done in public, or it may be finished before you first see the horses. If you can watch the horses being prepared, do so. You can learn a lot about the horse's temperament and condition.

Watch saddling or harnessing if you can.

Here's how you spot the bad actors:

➤ They fight and kick when they're saddled or harnessed.

➤ After the rider or driver is up, they fight human control.

➤ They have to be isolated from other horses to prevent possible injury from kicking or biting.

➤ They are difficult to load into the starting gate, or they refuse to line up behind it if they are Standardbreds.

From the Horse's Mouth

The **stewards** are the policemen, judge, and jury of the racetrack, enforcing rules and making decisions about eligibility and results. They can order bad actors off the track until they learn to behave.

Most horses, even temperamental ones, begin to behave once the gate opens. The excitement of racing distracts them from their annoyance with their people, the other horses, and the world in general. The few who would rather bite the competition than beat it won't win, and they won't be allowed to race again until their manners improve.

Some horses are nervous rather than angry, but they too can expend so much energy before the start that they don't have enough left to race effectively. Avoid the following:

➤ Horses who work themselves into a sweaty lather of tension, unless the day is so hot that every horse is sweating.

➤ Horses so upset by the sights around the track that they jump and hop their way through the post parade.

➤ Horses who seem afraid of the crowd.

Horses who work themselves into a lather long before the start use up precious energy.

You may miss some perfectly good bets by avoiding the angry and the nervous. Some bad-tempered horses do perform brilliantly. The turf champion Halo and the trotter Nevele Pride alternated magnificent victories with biting their handlers. But a lot of people think each would have been even better if they had been able to control their tempers.

The Least You Need to Know

➤ Speed and soundness matter most, but other qualities play a role in winning and losing.

➤ Most racehorses are at their peak between the ages of three and a half and five.

➤ Two-year-olds tend to be erratic on the racetrack, but compact early foals with at least one previous race make the best betting prospects.

➤ Racehorse legs age faster than the rest of the body, so an older horse who has raced on less stressful turf, in longer and slower races, and under harness lasts longer than sprinters on dirt tracks.

➤ Fillies and mares race best when they are not in heat, usually in the fall and winter.

➤ Females are most competitive with males at the age of two, at very short or very long distances, or if they're trotters.

➤ Courage is not the most important quality of a racehorse, but it's probably the most admired. It often makes a difference in individual races.

➤ The best racehorse can't be stupid, but some horses are a little too smart for their own good.

➤ Bad-tempered and nervous horses often use up their chances, wasting energy with prerace antics.

Chapter 7

The Well-Equipped Horse

Greek charioteers were probably the first to spend the off-season experimenting with equipment to make their horses run faster. Greek bettors were probably the first to spend the next summer trying to figure out what the new equipment meant to the outcome of the races.

Today, after more than 3,000 years of experiments with equipment, there isn't much that somebody somewhere hasn't tried before. The few entirely new inventions are slow to be approved by racing's governing bodies anyway.

What the bettor must deal with is the racehorse trainer's apparently limitless desire to tinker with existing equipment—adding, subtracting, combining, altering, and otherwise adjusting what goes onto the horse.

Feet First

As important as they are to racing success, there is a limit to what even the most inventive trainer can do with a horse's feet. Running horses don't wear anything other than horseshoes. The Standardbred wears boots as well as shoes, but the fancy footwear usually protects him from himself rather than makes him faster.

From the Horse's Mouth

Horse **boots** consist of cups, pads, wraps, and other devices that are placed on and around a horse's leg. They aren't pulled up over his feet.

From the Horse's Mouth

An **off track** is one that isn't dry and fast. It can range from slightly damp to brown soup.

Inside Track

Always bring binoculars to the racetrack so you can examine things like footing and equipment. If you're at a simulcast facility, get as close as you can to the screen.

Shoes

Thoroughbreds and Quarter Horses normally race in extremely light all-aluminum horseshoes called *racing plates*. Most are plain, but some trainers experiment with shoes intended to increase support or traction for horses who seem a little too tentative in their strides. These shoes are not reported to the public and cannot be figured into race analysis.

But a shoe designed specifically for racing on muddy tracks does have to be reported at almost every race-track. Its use is important to watch for when it rains.

The shoe is the *mud caulk*, better known around the racetrack as the *sticker*. Whether or not to use it keeps trainers awake when they hear rain pattering on the roof. Mud caulks are only used on off tracks, but they don't fit all off tracks.

Stickers are shaped like normal horseshoes, except that studs or other components that protrude from the shoe surface are added to the bottom. The studs dig into the muddy track, helping to prevent skidding as the horse's hoof strikes the ground. Why don't all trainers use stickers when it rains?

➤ Skid is normal and desirable. It allows the tendons and ligaments to absorb and distribute some of the stress and shock of the ground strike. If the hoof sticks too much, nothing gives and catastrophic injury can result.

➤ Mud caulks are heavier than flat racing plates, and every ounce counts for the running horse.

➤ The decision to use them usually has to be made the day of the race and that means reshoeing shortly before race time. Nails have to be pulled and reinserted, creating the risk of chipping the horny part of the hoof or pricking living tissue. Either can cause temporary lameness and defeat.

To bet on off-track races, you must mirror the trainer's decision-making process, except that you have one advantage. You can watch a race or two over the track, including the race right before the one you're interested in. The trainer usually can't wait quite so long to make his decision.

If you have a sharp eye, you can assess how the horses are reacting to an off track:

➤ You can see some horses show their insecurity with the footing by shortening their strides.

➤ You can see some horses appear to climb with their front legs.

➤ You can see some jockeys make their moves to the inside or outside more tentatively than they do on a dry track.

If you do see this evidence of slippery footing, the horses with mud caulks may well have a big advantage. If the footing seems normal in spite of the mud, the horses who have been reshod with stickers may be at a disadvantage to the horses wearing the light racing plates.

Mud caulk information is posted by racetrack officials prior to the races. Don't bother looking in the program or the past performance charts since they're usually printed too soon to include it. Instead, watch the tote board or a chalkboard posted near the betting windows. At simulcast facilities, the information is usually relayed via the screen. You'll have to watch closely to see it because it may be shown only once or twice during the session.

The use of bar shoes is also reported at some tracks. In Thoroughbred and Quarter Horse racing, they almost always mean that the horse is at least a little unsound. See Chapter 4 for further information.

From the Horse's Mouth

Simulcasting is the broadcasting of live races to another location for betting purposes. It's like watching the races at home, with a betting window instead of a kitchen for your trips away from the screen.

Standardbreds and Shoes

Shoeing is a little different for harness racing because the choice of shoe affects gait as well as traction. Shoes with small projections, known as *grabs,* are used even on dry tracks when a trainer thinks his horse's gait will become smoother or faster if his feet don't slide quite so much. Trainers are less likely to be concerned about traction on off tracks since harness tracks have less cushion and don't get nearly as muddy as running tracks do. We'll talk about track surface and what it means to the outcome of races in Chapter 12.

Standardbred trainers also worry about the weight of their horses' shoes since an ounce or two more or less in any one of the four shoes can change a horse's stride. Heavier shoes, particularly in front, make some harness horses stride out more, extending their gaits. A heavier shoe on one foot can balance an uneven gait.

Standardbred trainers do a great deal of experimenting with shoeing, far more than trainers in any other equine sport. You'll hear about very little of it unless you have a contact at the stable. But Standardbreds race often—sometimes once a week—and you occasionally can spot a horse whose trainer has discovered the right shoeing combination. He may be the one who shows a sudden improvement over his last race.

Horse Headwear

A horse may race with his legs, lungs, and heart, but his head carries a greater variety of equipment than any of the more critical parts. Most of the items are used to calm and control tense competitors. We'll look first at the equipment worn by running horses.

Blinkers

The first course of treatment for a horse whose mental efforts fall short is a pair of blinkers. Blinkers are used on these animals:

➤ Horses who are distracted by other horses.

➤ Horses who become nervous at the sight of spectators.

➤ Horses who are inclined to see ghosts.

Being outfitted with blinkers is the racehorse's equivalent of having your seat changed by the teacher so you don't pass notes to your classmates during English class.

Thoroughbred and Quarter Horse blinkers consist of a light cotton or synthetic hood that's placed over the horse's head and fastened under his jowls with Velcro, snaps, or buckles. Holes are cut out for the ears and eyes.

A plastic or leather cup is fastened to the back edge of each eye hole, restricting the wearer's peripheral vision. The cup may be less than an inch wide, limiting the horse's view only slightly, or it may be two inches or more, allowing the horse to see only directly in front of him. The cup may almost completely cover the eye, but it may have a slit cut out in back so the horse can see behind but not see what's directly next to him. You will also see blinkers in which the cups differ on each side.

The variations in cup design are supposed to match up to the different causes of a horse's nervousness. They allow the trainer to find a combination that blocks out distractions while still permitting the horse to see and respond to the competition.

Changes involving blinkers are made public before a race, and it's done for good reason. Some horses behave even worse with them than without. The first use of blinkers is always an experiment, and the horse should be bet with caution.

Bad Bet

Blinkers with big, closed cups can lose a race for a horse who doesn't notice another horse coming up alongside in deep stretch. By the time he sees the competition, it's past him.

The best approach to blinkers is to examine the past performances of a horse you're interested in, looking for good races with the blinker arrangement he's using for the current race.

But remember that you may also want to consider a horse who seems to have been racing in a distracted manner without blinkers. He may be ripe for a change and could be a good bet if his trainer has decided to make the change in the current race.

For the Record

In Thoroughbred racing, most of the top stakes horses don't wear blinkers. There are plenty of exceptions, Secretariat included, but the best horses usually concentrate just fine on their own. In Quarter Horse racing, most horses at all levels wear blinkers, probably because half a second of lapsed concentration can lose a race.

A horse with blinkers and shadow roll shouldn't see much to make him nervous.

Shadow Rolls

A large, soft roll of sheepskin or synthetic material over the noseband of the bridle also helps prevent distraction. It's called a shadow roll and was developed to discourage horses from thinking that their own shadows are barriers that require a jump or a zig-zag.

Shadow rolls are especially useful in night racing since the lighting comes from several directions and creates unfamiliar shadows. But some trainers use shadow rolls even on cloudy days, believing that racehorses are more likely to pay attention to their jockeys and respond to their urging when they can't look down under their own feet.

The rolls don't work on all horses. Some horses trust only their own judgment about footing and won't run confidently if they can't get a good look at what's underneath their feet. As with blinkers, there's always an element of experimentation the first few times shadow rolls are used.

The use isn't reported to the public, so you have to rely on your own powers of observation. If you notice a horse without a shadow roll jump or move suddenly right or left for no reason, watch to see if a shadow roll is added next time he starts. The little piece of sheepskin may be enough to turn a loser into a winner.

For the Record

John Henry made shadow rolls famous by winning several million dollars in comparative old age while wearing one. John Henry, who was still a top stakes horse at the age of ten in 1985, probably wouldn't have been distracted from his duties if the Grand Canyon opened under his feet, but his shadow roll looked great in winner's circle photos.

The Bridle

Most horses race in a simple snaffle bit consisting of a metal bar that goes through the mouth, connected to the straps of the bridle by round or D-shaped rings on each side of the face. The bar is jointed in the middle, a design that lessens the pressure on the sides of the mouth that occurs when the jockey steers.

The snaffle is a mild bit, but some horses need more control. Rather than making the bit more severe and risking injury to the horse's mouth, the trainer of a difficult horse is likely to try a bridle with straps that cross over each other in the middle of the nose.

Racing people call this arrangement a figure-8. It helps prevent a strong horse from pulling, evading the bit, or otherwise ignoring his jockey's orders.

For the Record

Some very good horses are pullers, probably because they want to get along with winning, not waiting until the jockey decides it's time to go. Seattle Slew won a Triple Crown wearing a figure-8 bridle.

Like the shadow roll, the figure-8's use isn't reported to the public, but its presence is obvious to anyone who looks. If you spot a horse with a regular straight noseband (or no noseband at all) and notice that pulling or fighting seems to contribute to his defeat, watch him next time. If he's sporting a figure-8, it may make the difference.

Tongue Ties

Some racehorses allow their tongues to slip back in their mouths, partially blocking their air passages. A horse who does this is said to swallow his tongue, although he's really just allowing loose flesh to clogs up the works. The tongue stays in the mouth.

Swallowing the tongue rarely does more than slow the horse down, but occasionally a horse collapses on the track because of it. Not every horse does it, but almost every Thoroughbred wears a tongue tie, a stretchy white ribbon that ties the tongue to the lower jaw so it can't slip back.

Horses don't seem to mind tongue ties, and trainers would rather be safe than sorry. They are now so common that they don't figure into betting decisions.

The Saddle

The modern racing saddle appeared around the turn of the century after American jockey Tod Sloan revolutionized race riding. Prior to Sloan, jockeys rode like all 19th-century horsemen, with long stirrups, weight in the center of the horse's back, and in an upright position.

Sloan shortened his stirrups and moved his body over the horse's shoulders, freeing the animal's back and hindquarters. Horses ran faster and stayed sounder. This is called the *racing seat*. It's not going to change, but there's been little experimentation in saddle design.

For the Record

European jockeys use a more upright position, but their weight is still forward over the shoulders. It may look different, but it's still a classic racing seat. There's no real evidence that either the crouched or upright position gives a horse an advantage.

The changes don't involve saddle shape but rather the weight that's added to make up the difference between jockey and weight assignments. Every horse who starts in the Kentucky Derby, for example, will most likely carry some of his assigned 126 pounds in the form of added weight. Even more ordinary horses are likely to carry added weight if they're ridden by lightweight jockeys.

Traditionally, bars of lead have been used, either inserted in slots in the saddle or in pads under the saddle. The weights are uncomfortable since there's no way to prevent inflexible lead from pressing somewhere on the horse's back or sides.

Some equipment designers and jockeys are experimenting with new weight designs, including one that consists of flexible pads that are weighted themselves. They don't press as much and they don't shift awkwardly. The great Cigar had his own personal set.

A bettor can't know whether a horse is carrying comfortable pads or unpleasant lead bars, but it's a good bet that the pads will become the rule rather than the exception in the future. Assigned weight may then become less of a burden.

Harness Racing Equipment

Standardbreds carry considerably more equipment than running horses. It offers plenty of opportunity for trainers to experiment.

Sulky

The most dramatic and visible change in harness racing during the 20th century has been in the vehicle pulled by the horse. It's the *sulky,* also known as a *racebike.* Look at Currier and Ives harness racing prints from the mid-19th century and you'll see ponderous, high-wheeled carts.

The modern modified sulky places the driver's weight behind rather than over the wheels.

The wheels began to shrink late in the century, evolving into a small, light design with bicycle-style wheels. The traditional sulky dominated the sport until the late 1960s, when a modified vehicle appeared. The new sulky placed the driver's weight behind the wheels rather than over them, allowing the horse to move more freely. The modified sulky was clearly faster than the old sulky and became the vehicle of choice.

But design experimentation continued. Among the new sulkies that appeared was one that featured bent shafts, and it appeared to almost everyone to be faster than the now-conventional modified vehicle.

From the Horse's Mouth

The **shafts** are the poles that attach the sulky to the horse's harness.

But racing officials decided that the bent-shaft sulky is potentially unsafe, and it was banned from most racetracks. That ban has been in the courts for several years, so the bent-shaft sulky may not have disappeared forever from all tracks. If it's used at a track you attend, note that some experts are convinced that it leads to substantially faster times for the horses who pull it.

For the Record

If you're interested in seeing old-time sulkies and other harness equipment, visit the Harness Racing Museum and Hall of Fame, 240 Main Street, Goshen, New York.

From the Horse's Mouth

The **gallop** is the horse's fastest gait. A good gallop is cherished in Thoroughbreds and Quarter Horses and dreaded in a Standardbred because he has to be pulled out of contention if he breaks into one.

From the Horse's Mouth

A trotter who stays **flat** keeps trotting rather than breaking into a gallop.

Equipment for Gaiting

Almost all pacers wear *hopples*, sometimes called *hobbles*, to help them maintain their gait. These plastic loops make it easier for a horse to go into the pace from a walk and help prevent him from breaking into a gallop from the pace.

If you go to the harness track enough times, you may someday see a free-legged pacer. Figure him this way: If his trainer thinks the horse can stay on gait without hopples, he probably can.

Trotters, who are more likely to break out of stride anyway, don't get as much help from equipment. There are half hopples that go around only the front legs, and some new four-legged trotting hopples, but the jury is still out on whether they help to keep a horse flat.

Some trainers and drivers think that *head poles* or *gaiting poles*, which run alongside the horse's shoulder and neck, help some horses to stay on stride. They force the horse to keep his body straight, and a horse usually has to bend a little to break into a gallop.

A blind bridle and ear-muffs keep this horse's mind on his business.

Harness

At its simplest, the harness is nothing more than a device to attach the sulky to the horse, but it also provides the framework to add or subtract other items of equipment, most of which are designed to improve the balance and ease of the stride. Among the equipment you may see:

➤ A strap that attaches the head to another strap that goes around his chest, keeping the horse from raising his head. This is a *martingale*.

➤ A strap that attaches his head to the top of his back, preventing him from lowering his head. This is an *overcheck* or a *checkrein*.

➤ Boots and bandages, all designed to protect his flesh from being struck by his own feet. These include bell boots on his hoofs, knee boots, elbow boots, and protective bandages on any or all cannon bones. A horse who wears boots probably needs them, but boots distract and probably slow horses down at least a little.

A horse who races well with little equipment is a joy to behold and an even greater joy to bet on.

Standardbreds use blinkers and shadow rolls for the same reasons running horses do. They also commonly use blind or closed bridles, which include leather or plastic flaps next to the eye. A few are equipped with earmuffs if the sound of the crowd distracts them. Occasionally, you'll see Thoroughbreds with ear coverings, but they're primarily used on harness horses.

Probably fewer than half of all Standardbreds race with open bridles and no shadow rolls, even though they tend to concentrate better and behave more calmly than Thoroughbreds. Conventional wisdom says that driving horses fear the sight of their own vehicles behind them, so the widespread use of closed bridles may be as much a remnant of tradition as a concern about distractions.

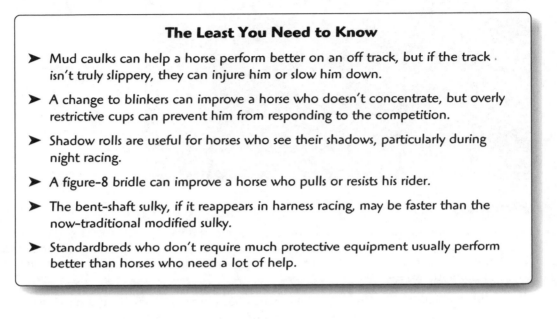

The Least You Need to Know

➤ Mud caulks can help a horse perform better on an off track, but if the track isn't truly slippery, they can injure him or slow him down.

➤ A change to blinkers can improve a horse who doesn't concentrate, but overly restrictive cups can prevent him from responding to the competition.

➤ Shadow rolls are useful for horses who see their shadows, particularly during night racing.

➤ A figure-8 bridle can improve a horse who pulls or resists his rider.

➤ The bent-shaft sulky, if it reappears in harness racing, may be faster than the now-traditional modified sulky.

➤ Standardbreds who don't require much protective equipment usually perform better than horses who need a lot of help.

Part 2
The People

People may not be quite as important as horses in racing, but you still won't see a single race without them. Actually, that's not quite true. A few years ago, an entrepreneur tried to get approval for a racing circuit that featured ponies ridden by remote controlled dummies. It didn't fly.

In the real world of racing, you'll find trainers, jockeys, drivers, track officials, and an army of other people whose sole objective is to put on the racing show. Does it really matter who's training, riding, driving, or scheduling races? How much difference do these people make in the outcome of a race? The answers: yes and maybe not quite as much as you think.

After you read the following chapters, you'll begin to understand, appreciate, and judge the people who get the horses onto the racetrack. What's more, you'll be able to decide just how much weight you should give their contributions when you make your betting decisions.

Chapter 8

The Rulers of the Racetrack: The Trainers

In This Chapter

➤ Early training

➤ Breaking to race

➤ The roles of the racetrack trainer: conditioning, athletic development, and placement

Even though the horses do the running, trainers are the real kings of the racetrack. Each trainer rules his own little country located in the long, narrow barns of the backstretch.

Trainers do have to rely on owners to provide the horses and pay the bills. They need jockeys and drivers to ride and drive, and they require racing officials to schedule the races. But the trainers send the horses out to race, and so they rule the racetrack.

Early Training

Racetrack training is actually the last step of the training process. There are other less celebrated and less powerful trainers who put their stamps on the horses before they come under the control of the kings of the backstretch.

On the Farm

Many horses receive their first lessons in how to be racehorses before they leave the farm where they were born. The work begins for the Thoroughbred and Quarter Horse at about 18 months of age. Standardbreds may start a month or two earlier since their work is a little less stressful to growing bones and joints.

Horses learn very little about athletic performance during early farm training, but they do learn the basics of starting, stopping, steering, and responding in general to the requests of handlers, and then to those of riders and drivers. You can't make a horse into a winner at this point in his life, but you can make him into a loser. If he learns evasion or fear, or bad behavior in general, he will probably be a troubled racehorse forever. He can also suffer permanent injury if he's asked to do too much too soon.

It's difficult for anyone who wasn't there to know what went on in early training, and it's even more difficult for a racegoer to figure out if the horse's first trainer did anything that's going to affect his current racing ability. Some horses are four-legged angels in spite of terrible early handling. Others receive the best basic training and still bedevil their racetrack trainers, battling themselves more effectively than they fight the competition. Still others are trained carefully, behave badly, and race well anyway because of breeding, talent, or later training.

All you can do is to try to judge how the horse's current behavior might affect his performance and make your betting decision accordingly.

From the Horse's Mouth

The **backstretch** is the barn area of the racetrack. It's also called the **backside**. Just to confuse you, the *backstretch* is also the long straightaway on the far side of the racetrack.

Preparation for Racing

Most Thoroughbreds begin their race training at 20 to 22 months. Standardbreds and Quarter Horses usually begin a couple of months sooner because racing debuts come a little earlier in those breeds.

For the Record

Every now and then you'll see a race for Thoroughbred two-year-olds in late March, but they are becoming extremely rare. Standardbred and Quarter Horse two-year-olds do race that early, weather permitting.

Basic race training rarely takes place at an operating racetrack since officials don't want precious stall space occupied by horses not ready and able to race. They are even more reluctant to see their morning workout hours clogged up by young horses who don't know which way to gallop and don't listen to their riders when told.

Some horses learn the basics of racing on the same farm where they learned to carry a rider, but other young racehorses begin their preliminary race training at private training centers under the direction of a person who might be called a yearling trainer, a breaker, or a farm trainer. Some racetracks do turn themselves into training centers during their off seasons, but most racetrack trainers don't get involved at this level of training. Some do, especially in Standardbred racing, but owners are more likely to hire somebody else to teach a young horse his basic racing lessons.

At each kind of training facility the horse learns what he needs to be permitted onto a real racetrack. Thoroughbreds and Quarter Horses are taught by their trainer to gallop under riders, to be rated by those riders, and perhaps to break out of a starting gate.

If they haven't already been taught this at their home farm, Standardbreds learn to pull a sturdy, small-wheeled jog cart. Unlike the running horses who are ridden by lightweight exercise riders, young Standardbreds are driven by a trainer, even their ultimate racetrack trainer during these early sessions. A horse can pull considerably more weight than he can carry, so the trainers don't even have to be particularly light. The trainer-drivers work to balance the trot or pace of the young horse and may teach him to keep up his gait in the company of other horses.

From the Horse's Mouth

A horse is **rated** when his speed is controlled by the rider or driver.

Many training centers are so much like quiet, low-pressure racetracks that they conduct racing, complete with published entry lists. They don't take bets, and the races are usually shorter than those at real racetracks, but they do provide the young horses and their trainers with a chance to experience some of the sights and sounds of racing.

In Standardbred racing, young horses are required to compete in qualifying races before they are eligible to start at real racetracks. This is an effort to assure that bettors aren't going to put money on a crazy young horse who can't pace and is going to turn cartwheels with his sulky. Some Standardbred training centers conduct qualifying races, but most trainees are going to have to qualify at a real track, too.

Early Training at the Racetrack

Some horses—mostly Standardbred but some Thoroughbred and Quarter Horse—remain at training centers for their active race training. Most young Thoroughbreds, however, meet their racetrack trainers for the first time when the horse trailer pulls up at their barns on the backstretch of a racetrack.

They are still not ready to race. The trainer is going to have to put some finishing touches on their racing skills before they begin athletic conditioning. Thoroughbreds and Quarter Horses don't go through qualifying races, but most racetracks will require them to show that they know how to break out of a starting gate.

For the Record

Starting is a vital skill that's difficult to learn for both running and harness horses. Thoroughbreds and Quarter Horses break out of stationary stalls, while Standardbreds line up behind a mobile gate that allows them to reach racing speed before it opens. The easiest start of all is the one enjoyed by some steeplechasers who line up as well as they can behind an imaginary line and start when told to. It's also the most random, and steeplechases conducted at regular betting racetracks use the standard stall starting gate.

The Racetrack Trainer

The downside of being the king of the backstretch is the fact that you have to be all things to all horses. Only a small part of the job is physical development and instruction in racing skills. It doesn't even come first on the list of duties.

Health Care Worker

Most trainers will tell you that keeping a horse healthy and sound is the most difficult, most important, and most time-consuming part of the training process. The physical stress of racing makes health care for horses more challenging than it is for most people.

Successful trainers are the ones who best meet that challenge. It's an endless job. The trainer must:

➤ Work out the feed and supplement combination that gives the horses the energy to train and race.

➤ Keep track of vaccinations to prevent the communicable diseases that run through every racing barn, particularly in the winter.

➤ Develop a sanitary and cleaning routine that keeps the horses healthy without costing too much in labor.

➤ Know how to identify injuries, know when to rest the horse who has them, and know when a horse can perform adequately in spite of them.

You can spot the names of the trainers best at keeping horses sound on the lists of trainers whose horses make a lot of starts.

The biggest money-winning trainers aren't necessarily the ones who keep their horses sound. Big purses are won by fast horses, and the trainer (as you'll see later) can't always control the talent of the horses delivered to their barns in horse trailers. Look instead for number of starts, plus percentage of placings. If a trainer gets horses to the track and most of them bring back a check in most of their races, the trainer is skilled at horse health care.

There's are two other ways to spot trainers who know about healthy horses. Look for:

➤ Horses who don't look fat but who don't look too thin (but remember that all fit racehorses are invariably thinner than other healthy horses).

➤ Horses with dappled coats. Health dapples aren't the same as the gray and white spots sported by some gray horses. They are areas of light and dark shine that you can often spot on the backs and hindquarters of mature horses in good health. If someone tells you that a horse is nicely dappled out, you know his trainer has him in excellent health.

Inside Track

Past performance publications and many track programs include lists of trainers' starts, including first-, second-, and third-place finishes.

Athletic Development

Although less important than health maintenance (if they're sick or sore they can't race, much less win), athletic conditioning is still high up on the list of trainers' duties. Racing isn't a skill sport, but there's still a great deal a trainer can do to improve on the natural talents that a horse carries onto the racetrack.

For some horses, training is a natural extension of health care. If the horse is basically sound, much of his athletic training becomes conditioning. In fact, you'll often hear trainers referred to as conditioners, particularly at the Thoroughbred racetracks. Trainers with good horses spend more time conditioning and less time nursing. Those burdened with cheap horses often do no conditioning at all. Fragile legs are good for a limited number of miles, like cheap automobile tires, and most trainers would rather use up those miles racing than training.

But most horses are conditioned with workouts. Trainers have dramatically different ideas about workouts for horses in full training. In Thoroughbred racing, most trainers give their horses occasional workouts at distances slightly shorter and at speeds slightly slower than they will face in a race.

Recently, some trainers have become enamored of two dramatically different variations from this norm:

➤ In interval training, the horses are sent out in the mornings to complete very short, very fast workouts with intervals of rest in between. The trainers believe that if horses are asked in the morning for a greater effort of legs, lungs, and heart than they'll need in the afternoon, they will have more than they'll ever need in an actual race.

➤ In LSD, they're asked for the opposite. No, it's not that kind of LSD. It wouldn't get past the drug tests, although the horse might think he was indeed flying. *L*ong, *s*low, *d*istance workouts are supposed to improve the overall fitness level of the horse so that when he races his normal six or seven furlongs, he won't think about getting tired.

Either new philosophy can produce a good racehorse, as can the traditional fairly short, pretty fast workouts that produced Man O' War, Seabiscuit, Citation, Count Fleet, Native Dancer, and just about every great Thoroughbred racehorse who performed before trainers started dreaming up new approaches.

Standardbred trainers also use versions of both interval and LSD training. Most trainers jog their horses three or four untimed miles most days, with rapid miles known as training done only once or twice a week.

For the bettor, it probably doesn't much matter which approach the trainer follows, provided it makes the horse fit enough to race or train seriously every couple of weeks. You discover that by examining the past performance charts.

Equipment Adjuster

Trainers usually make the decisions about shoeing and other equipment that we talked about in Chapter 7. They may listen to suggestions from riders or drivers, but the final decision is theirs.

They also have responsibility for following the rules about equipment (yes, it is possible to use illegal horseshoes). They also must declare certain equipment changes so that bettors are aware of them.

Trainers usually buy the equipment themselves, then use it on appropriate horses. Owners are often billed for the equipment costs, although special bits, bandages, blinkers, or other items seldom go with the horse when he leaves the barn.

Finder of Spots

Once a trainer has come up with a horse who's healthy enough to race and fit enough to perform well, he must find a stage for that performance. His job then becomes locating races the horse is both eligible for and good enough to enter. The process is called *finding spots*.

The trainer who finds the right spots for his horses finds himself in the winner's circle.

At each racetrack, the racing secretary (more on him in Chapter 11) plans each day's race card.

The racing secretary issues condition books at least two weeks in advance, with occasional overnight additions. As soon as the books are published, trainers begin scouring them for races suited for their own horses.

Trainers are rarely happy with the conditions the secretaries set for the races. They complain that the races seem to be written for other trainers' horses, not their own.

95

From the Horse's Mouth

The **race card** is the daily schedule of races. Scheduling races is *carding* them or *writing* them.

From the Horse's Mouth

Condition books contain the scheduled races, with the conditions required for entry in each one.

Bad Bet

Differentiate between trainers who lead money lists because of one big horse and those who are up there because they win a little with a lot of different horses. The trainer with the one big horse may be as much lucky as he is good.

In reality, secretaries write races for the horses stabled at the track. They want full fields of horses entered in each race because fans don't like small fields. If a track has a lot of older male sprinters in the barns, you'll see plenty of six-furlong races for three-year-olds and up. If those horses are not very good, the secretary might add a condition such as this: for non-winners of two races since June.

In harness racing, the secretary is forced, with rare exceptions, to stay with the one-mile distance, but he will add conditions for number of races won, for amount of money won, and for age and sex.

Trainers of Thoroughbreds and Quarter Horses can look beyond the condition books to find good spots for their horses. They talk regularly to jockey's agents. The agents, hoping to find mounts for their clients, are happy to offer information about which races are coming up soft. More on jockey's agents in the next chapter.

A trainer who is particularly good at finding spots will make money for himself and the people who bet on his horses. The names of these trainers will be high on lists of money won, usually published alongside or instead of lists of winning percentages.

Locator of Prospects

Trainers vary greatly in how involved they become in finding the horses they train. A few work exclusively for private owners who breed their own racing stock. These trainers have nothing much to say about which horses get off the trailer at the racetrack.

Others work for anyone who'll provide them with a horse. These trainers are satisfied if the horse who climbs off the trailer has four legs.

Most trainers do have some say in what they train. Some, such as D. Wayne Lukas in the Thoroughbred world, have had a virtual blank check to go shopping at the elite yearling sales. Lukas has spent tens of millions of dollars for his clients over the years, buying the bluest Kentucky blood available.

Most trainers are a little less lucky. Rather than truckloads of money, they are given the chance to offer opinions, which may or may not be heeded by owners. There is every other variation between blank checks and deaf ears, each to be worked out by individual trainers and owners.

There is one area of racehorse buying that's almost exclusively the province of trainers. This is the rough-and-tumble arena of claiming races, where almost all claims are entered by trainers.

We'll have more on claiming races, the most common kind of race in North America, in Chapter 14, but there's one point on claiming races and trainers to note. The majority of trainers below the very top echelon try to make themselves expert in claiming races, not so much to win the individual race as to improve, replenish, and protect their own racing stables.

From the Horse's Mouth

In **claiming races**, all horses are available for purchase at a set price. Horses who run in these races are known as *claimers*.

If you hear somebody say that a certain trainer "really knows how to play the claiming game," remember that he's not playing the game for you. He may have a horse in the race you're handicapping, but his attention may be occupied with trying to take somebody else's horse or protect his own. Eventually, he'll have to try to win with the horses he claims, but some trainers of claimers have been known to put a horse where he can't win so nobody will claim him next time out.

Claiming races are popular with trainers because they offer an opportunity for success beyond winning one race. They're also popular with bettors who enjoy trying to work the claiming price and the trainers' intentions into the beting equation.

The Trainer/Owner

A few people both own and train horses. The most common scenario finds the professional trainer in possession of a horse or two that he may have bought with a client in mind, only to have the horse rejected. He may have been given or bequeathed the horse by a grateful owner, like Jimmy Croll and his million-dollar Horse of the Year, Holy Bull. Or he may have bred the horse himself. The trainer is traditionally given the right to breed one mare a year to a stallion he trained. Most sell the rights, but some breed their own mares, then train the offspring.

Trainer-owned horses are usually well cared for and competitive since ego and money are both on the line for the trainer. That's not necessarily the case with the second trainer/owner situation.

This involves owners who decide to train. Some may have a genuine calling for training and develop skills as they pass the test to get a trainer's license. But others find themselves training because they can't get along with anyone who trains for them.

An owner-trained horse is probably not a very good bet until there is past performance proof that he can perform with his owner calling all the shots.

Delvin Miller was among the best of the trainer/ drivers. Here he's with his brilliant trotter Arndon.

The Trainer/Driver

The trainer who drives his own horses used to be the rule in harness racing. Today, it's the exception, particularly at the major tracks with big-time racing.

Almost all trainers still drive their own horses during training hours, and most warm up their horses prior to races. Only by driving, they rightly believe, can they really assess how the horse is doing.

From the Horse's Mouth

A **catch driver** is a professional driver who doesn't train. As fewer trainers drive, the word *catch* is being phased out. A driver is now a driver.

But most Standardbred trainers have come to realize that training and race driving are separate skills, and being good at one doesn't make you equally good at the other. There have been trainers who were every bit as good at driving as the best catch drivers, including some of the big names in the history of the sport, Bill Haughton, Del Miller, and Stanley Dancer.

Although trainers still drive, you'll see fewer each year. When you look at a race consisting of trainer/drivers and catch drivers, you first judge all drivers by the same standards. More on that in Chapter 10. Then modify your assessment of driving skills with a few extra considerations. Trainer/drivers may have poorer statistics than their driving skills deserve:

➤ They don't get as many drives as catch drivers.

➤ They don't get to pick and choose among the stock of several trainers.

➤ They often have to drive horses who aren't quite ready to win but need the race to develop fitness.

The Assistant Trainer Question

Any trainer who has more than a handful of horses in his care probably employs one or more assistant trainers. In some cases, assistant trainers have little authority. In others, the assistant makes most of the important decisions about every aspect of the horse's care and training.

The problem for those of us without access to the backstretch is that we won't know about the specific situation with the horses we plan to bet on. In Thoroughbred racing, the name on the program almost always is that of the official trainer, the person who accepts the monthly fees from the owner, even if he rarely visits the racetrack and his assistant does all the work.

Some tracks help the bettor by printing the name of the official trainer, followed by the name of the person who actually saddles the horse, usually the assistant. At other tracks, the assistant's name is printed nowhere, leaving the bettor to think that training decisions have been made by a hotshot trainer rather than an inexperienced assistant.

In harness racing, there's a different situation. At many racetracks, the trainer named in the program may be the assistant, with the official trainer unnamed, even if he's the one who made all the training decisions. The harness racing industry is aware that there's something evasive about the practice, and there's a movement to require the person who takes the monthly training fees to publicize his name. Until honesty in program listings becomes the rule, bettors have to be careful when figuring trainers into handicapping decisions.

The Business of Training

Most trainers operate so-called public stables, accepting horses from a number of owners. The owners are charged a set fee per horse and are billed for special expenses. The trainer takes 10 percent of the purse money won by the horse in addition to the monthly fee.

Private trainers work for one owner or one racing stable. They usually receive salaries plus expenses, and they, too, usually receive 10 percent of the purse money.

Public trainers always hire and pay their own stable help. Private trainers may choose their own workers, but they may be paid by the stable.

Private trainers are more secure in the short run because they know exactly how much salary and operating money is coming in each month. In the long run, they're about as secure as baseball managers. If they win enough, they keep the job. If they lose a few too many races, they open public stables.

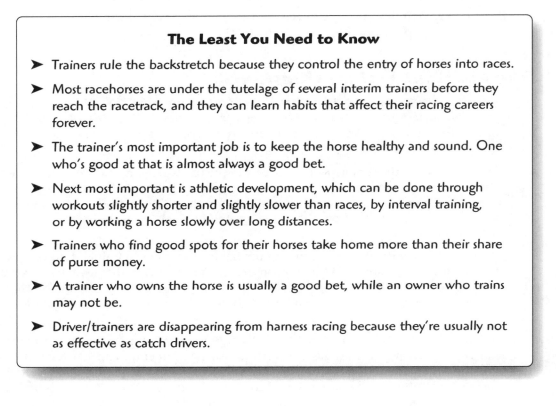

The Least You Need to Know

➤ Trainers rule the backstretch because they control the entry of horses into races.

➤ Most racehorses are under the tutelage of several interim trainers before they reach the racetrack, and they can learn habits that affect their racing careers forever.

➤ The trainer's most important job is to keep the horse healthy and sound. One who's good at that is almost always a good bet.

➤ Next most important is athletic development, which can be done through workouts slightly shorter and slightly slower than races, by interval training, or by working a horse slowly over long distances.

➤ Trainers who find good spots for their horses take home more than their share of purse money.

➤ A trainer who owns the horse is usually a good bet, while an owner who trains may not be.

➤ Driver/trainers are disappearing from harness racing because they're usually not as effective as catch drivers.

Chapter 9

The Hands That Hold the Reins: The Jockeys

In This Chapter

➤ Height, weight, and strength

➤ Female jockeys

➤ Apprentice jockeys and weight allowances

➤ The business of being a jockey

There's no doubt that a rider can make a winner into a loser. He can also make a loser into a winner, although it's a little more difficult. In the vast majority of races, however, the pilot's impact on the outcome is only minor. The horse makes the difference, not the human.

It's true that a superb horseman, or a terrible one, plays a greater role in the result than a rider of average ability, particularly in races where unusual situations develop. But most people are average, and most races develop along predictable lines.

While the hands that hold the reins are less significant than many casual racing observers believe, they can't be ignored if you're serious about picking winners. A mistake that causes a delay of a fraction of a second makes the difference between a winning ticket and one that the custodian sweeps up after the ninth race. So just who's holding those reins, and what does it mean to the race?

Who Are the Little Big Men?

There's an inherent contradiction in every jockey, a contradiction so profound that it seems surprising that jockeys can exist at all. Riders of racehorses have to be very light

From the Horse's Mouth

A **flat race** is one without jumps.

and very strong at the same time, a combination remarkably difficult to find in the same person. To be able to ride in most flat races, a jockey can't weigh much more than 110 pounds (steeplechase riders can be heavier, perhaps 140 pounds).

At 110 pounds, he or she can carry a couple pounds' worth of saddle and still come in at the assigned weight for the average horse in the average race. That's not much body weight for an adult male who has to be in good enough health to perform a difficult, demanding athletic task.

At the same time that he has to be light, the jockey has to have considerable upper body strength. A Thoroughbred or Quarter Horse usually weighs at least half a ton, is young and energetic, and is only minimally trained to stop and steer. Some racehorses respond to gentle cues and finesse, but others need pure power to keep them where they are supposed to be.

Jockeys need muscles, something that contributes mightily to body weight, so jockeys make up for that extra weight by being short, sometimes very short. You'll rarely see a male jockey taller than about 5 feet 4 inches.

Julie Krone rides with the best, but few other women do.

Female Jockeys

When the first female jockeys were licensed in the late 1960s, some people believed that they would come to dominate the profession. They thought that women light enough and short enough to ride would be easier to find than men of similar body size. What was abnormally small for a man would be common and average for a woman.

Naysayers said that female jockeys would never succeed in any great numbers because most lack upper body strength. Thirty years later, the second group seems to be right, although comparative upper body strength is only part of the reason.

Among female jockeys, only Julie Krone reached and stayed in the very top echelon of riders. There are more women who inhabit the upper-middle range and make a very good living at race riding, but very few women ride in the big stakes races, the Triple Crown and the Breeder's Cup, possibly because the trainers fear lack of strength.

The shortage of rides limits the amount of experience that female jockeys can get, prompting even more trainers to avoid them. A bettor doesn't have to avoid a female jockey, but her experience and strength should be considered if they appear to play a role in a particular race.

If she doesn't get many rides, consider her like any other inexperienced jockey. Here are the situations that might matter:

➤ A horse who drifts, ducks, bears out, bolts (or does anything else that requires experienced hands on the reins) needs a rider who has seen a lot of starting gates.

➤ A horse who's difficult to control in the post parade, one who grabs his bit in his teeth and pulls, is not a good choice in the hands of a rider who doesn't seem to be strong enough to control him.

Of course, a horse who behaves badly in races or really acts up in the post parade is often a poor bet in anybody's hands since he uses up so much energy doing something other than race.

Weight

Every jockey's most relentless rival has neither four legs nor two. It sits on a solid steel base right outside the dressing room door. Actually, most jockeys have personal acquaintance with at least four scales every day.

The one at home tells him what he can eat that day. A second, inside the jockey's room, tells him if he needs to do penance in the hot box.

The third scale is the most important, the one every jockey faces before each race. He's allowed to be heavier than his assigned weight, but he can't be lighter. If he is, he has to make up the difference with lead weights in a saddle pad.

From the Horse's Mouth

The **hot box** is a small steam room or sauna that every track of any size supplies to the jockeys.

Inside Track

An announced overweight horse can sometimes be a very good bet. The fact that the trainer didn't switch to another jockey shows that he has enough confidence in both horse and jockey not to make a change to get the extra help of a little less weight.

From the Horse's Mouth

Apprentice jockeys are sometimes called **bug boys** even if they're girls. The phrase refers to the asterisk often used next to their names.

Finally, the jockeys have to reweigh after the race in an enclosure near the dismounting area. Again, the rider can be a little heavier than assigned. He usually is, if the track is muddy, but he can't be more than a fraction lighter (no ditching of the lead weights on the far side of the track is permitted).

There may be a male jockey somewhere who doesn't have to worry about his weight, but nobody has yet met him. Women usually have it a little easier, but even they have to be careful if they want to be eligible to ride every horse they may be asked to ride. Nobody wants to turn down a horse because they weigh a few too many pounds.

Thoroughbred racing tradition gives weight allowances to certain horses in certain races to help them be more competitive. In Chapter 14, we'll talk more about weight assignments, handicap races, weight-for-age scales, and what they all mean to bettors. For jockeys, generous weight allowances mean dieting, suffering in the hot box, and a career that may end because of weight rather than age or injury.

If the scheduled jockey can't make the assigned weight for a particular race, the trainer may dump him for a lighter one, or he may go ahead with the original rider. In that case, the horse will be announced as being "two pounds overweight" or whatever the excess happens to be.

The Apprentice Jockey

Weight and riding success are most closely entwined during the first year of a jockey's career. For that year, the jockey is considered an apprentice, a kind of working student. Given the competitiveness of racing, the young jockey would get almost no chance to race if he or she weren't given a special break.

Trainers are encouraged to use apprentice jockeys by being given a weight break for their horses. The weight allowance is scaled to give the greatest break to the most inexperienced jockeys. There are variations in different racing jurisdictions, but here's a typical scale chart:

Apprentice Allowances

Jockey's wins	Weight off assigned impost
0-5	10 pounds
6-35	7 pounds
For 1 year after 5th win	5 pounds

The allowance guarantees that some trainers will use apprentice jockeys on horses who need a low weight to have a chance, and it almost guarantees that an apprentice with natural talent will win a lot of races in spite of inexperience.

New jockeys with less talent don't win very often. Their weight advantage and skill disadvantage seem to balance each other out.

For the racegoer, a poor-to-average apprentice is not usually much of a bet, unless he's been given a horse with excellent credentials (unlikely, unless the horse really needs a weight break). But a horse with an apprentice who has won dozens of races can be judged like any other horse-rider combination. The weight will be a plus, while the rider's experience level will be a slight (but just a slight) negative.

Inside Track

Apprentices don't get the weight break in stakes races. If they get the mount anyway, it means the trainer really thinks the rider suits the horse. That's a plus.

For the Record

Jockey statistics appear in past performance publications and most track programs. You can identify both the number of rides and the percentage of rides in which the horse places in the top three. A high percentage is good (anything over 15 percent wins or 50 percent placings) but a high number of starts is just about as good. It means the trainers have confidence in the rider.

Jockeys and Morning Workouts

Even the most self-impressed jockeys' agents admit that most jockeys do important work in finding themselves good mounts. Just like trainers, jockeys study condition books, entry lists, and past performance charts. Just like agents, they negotiate with trainers to get the best horses in individual races. Unlike agents, they can demonstrate their skill and rapport with particular horses.

Most jockeys ride morning workouts to encourage trainers to use them in the afternoon. Some collect the standard exercise rider's fee of $20 or so, while others do it for free. Even the world's most successful jockeys often make themselves available for workouts when they want to make sure of keeping the mount on a specific horse.

Inside Track

If you see that a famous jockey has worked an unraced or lightly raced horse, you can be sure that he thinks the horse is worth his time. It's a horse to watch and maybe bet on.

It's a little like the star of a Broadway play not staying home when he has the flu for fear that the understudy might be so impressive that he takes over the role. The jockey, like the star, doesn't want another rider to come along and impress everyone. When a well-known jockey rides a noteworthy horse in a morning workout, the fact is often noted in the workout tabulations (see Chapter 3).

Jockeys also ride morning workouts if they want to be used in races by a trainer with a reputation of sending out a lot of winners.

The First Call Dilemma

Many top jockeys ride first call for certain trainers. That means the trainer can count on the jockey to ride his horse rather than any other in a particular race.

The arrangement isn't written in stone. It's subject to change by either party at any time and usually includes no special payment (although the owners of a successful horse may give a bonus to the stable's first call jockey). Some trainers enforce first call with great determination, never again using a jockey who violates it. Others are more understanding and will allow their first-call rider to take the mount on somebody else's horse with a future.

First-call riding gives a great deal of security to trainer and rider, and it gives a little security to the bettor. A horse ridden by a first-call rider will have a familiar pilot, one who has a vested interest in treating the horse well and getting the most out of him. But a first-call rider may be on the horse because he has to please the trainer, not because he thinks the horse has a snowball's chance in Hades.

Having a first-call jockey aboard is a bonus for a horse who has other good credentials, but a horse without past performance or workout indications of talent isn't going to become a contender just because he's carrying his stable's primary jockey.

Riding Skills

Jockeys must bring a few basic skills to the race. They have to stay aboard, and they have to be able to steer. You can safely assume that a jockey who's made a number of starts will do both adequately. Trainers wouldn't use him otherwise.

Other skills aren't as widely distributed in the jockey colony. If you can learn who's good at what, you can pick out the horse/rider combination that should be effective in each race.

Some of the skills are important in both Thoroughbred and Quarter Horse racing. Others are needed only at Thoroughbred tracks.

From the Horse's Mouth

The jockeys who ride at a particular racetrack comprise its **jockey's colony**. There's no imperialism involved.

A jockey must break well to succeed in his profession. So-so isn't good enough.

The Start

The break from the starting gate is the single most important event in a Quarter Horse race as well as in any Thoroughbred race at six furlongs or less. In short races, there isn't enough time or yardage to make up for a bad start. There's hardly enough to make up for a so-so start, even with a clearly superior horse. Its importance decreases as distance increases, but there's no race, including a three-mile steeplechase, in which the start isn't important.

A jockey who gets the jump on other riders is alert, not psychic. He doesn't so much anticipate the start as have himself and his horse ready the very second the starter chooses to open the gate.

Most horses are tense in the starting gate since they're imprisoned in a space only a few inches larger than their own bodies. So a good gate jockey has to exert a calming influence on the horse as well as being alert. Like the need to be light and strong, the need to be both relaxed and alert often don't exist in the same person.

There are no charts that list jockeys who break well from the gate, but you can often identify them on the past performance charts. These charts, as you'll see in Chapter 18, show the horse's position at various points in the race. First call (not the same as a jockey's first call for a ride) tells you the horse's position at the first time it's noted for the chart. This usually tells you how well the horse (and the jockey aboard him) broke from the gate.

For the Record

The first call differs for different length races. In sprint races, the first notation is for the start. In races longer than six furlongs, first call comes at a quarter mile.

The results charts from the previous day's racing will also report how the horses broke from the gate. Obviously, using yesterday's results won't tell you how today's horses are going to break, but you can use them to identify the riders who break effectively.

As you examine both sets of charts, you'll find the names of some riders who always seem to be in the first three or four out of the gate. The presence of one of these jockeys will be a big plus for a horse in a short race, and it certainly won't hurt one in a longer event.

Timing

A sense of timing is second in importance only to the start for a Thoroughbred jockey. It's not nearly as important in Quarter Horse racing, where there's one pace—all out. In Thoroughbred racing, even in very short events, you'll find that horses differ in where they like to run.

Some prefer to be in front from the start, while others would rather make their runs from behind. The jockey has to control how fast the horse is permitted to run while in front or when he should start his run from off the pace. Horses who run too fast on the lead don't last, and those who make their moves too late never get there.

Good timing can be hard to identify. It shows up primarily in the form of a high winning percentage. Even then, it's difficult to know if a horse wins because of its own superiority or because the jockey was good at judging the pace of the race.

Some observers believe that a rider who finishes second and third often but rarely wins has the physical skills to be a good jockey but lacks a sense of timing. He may actually be an outstanding jockey, if those second- and third-place horses finish as close as they do because he gets the most out of them.

If you think that raw results don't tell you enough, you can also examine past performance and results charts to assess riders' timing. Look for signs that a jockey, once he has allowed his horse to take the

From the Horse's Mouth

The **pace** is the speed of the horse or horses in the lead.

lead, manages to keep him near the front all the way to the finish. Or you want to see that a rider coming from behind makes his move at a point where the horse neither runs out of racetrack nor energy before the finish. He doesn't have to win, but you want to see him in contention at the finish line.

Turf Racing

Outstanding jockeys are usually outstanding regardless of the surface they race on, whether it's hard and dry or soft and muddy. Most of them are also good on turf, but certain jockeys really seem to shine in turf racing.

We'll have more on grass racing in Chapter 12, but note now why some jockeys are particularly good on the turf and what it means to people betting on them.

➤ Turf courses are usually smaller and have sharper turns than their adjacent dirt tracks. Jockeys who understand the need to get out of the gate quickly and to be well placed by the first turn excel on the turf, even in longer races where they don't need an early lead.

➤ Early speed usually doesn't hold up quite so well on the turf as it does on the dirt, so jockeys with a good sense of timing and pace when coming from behind are often very effective on the turf.

From the Horse's Mouth

Turf races take place on grass courses, usually located inside the main dirt track in North America. In Europe, almost all races take place on grass.

➤ Turf courses can't be groomed as easily as dirt tracks and are more inclined to develop bad spots. Jockeys who are good at placing horses where they want them to be rather than allowing others to dictate do well on the turf.

How do you identify these turf experts? The same way you identify jockeys with other important skills. You study past performance charts and daily results. With turf racing, you have additional tools.

Some track programs and most racing publications tabulate turf statistics separately, so you'll see the names of the jockeys who perform well on turf. If no turf tabulation is available, look at past performance charts to locate turf results. You'll identify them by the circled T on the race's line (see Chapter 18). Study them and you'll find the jockeys who perform well on the turf. Dirt track results are useful, too. In them you can find jockeys who ride well from off the pace.

The Business of Being a Jockey

Jockeys are self-employed, independent contractors who have to find their own work. It's a competitive field, and they have to work hard at getting rides if they hope to succeed.

Agents

At the big tracks, all jockeys employ agents to get them mounts. An agent will represent no more than two jockeys, one an apprentice and the other a journeyman.

Most agents receive 25 percent of what the jockey earns, although each jockey-agent relationship is different. Unless his clients are successful enough to ride most races on the day's card, an agent is likely to be a part-timer. He may book rides in the morning, then work in another capacity in the afternoon.

From the Horse's Mouth

A **journeyman jockey** is one who has completed his apprentice year.

A good agent is worth his weight in wins to a jockey. As skilled, knowledgeable, and personable as a jockey might be, he won't be able to do the negotiating among trainers that an effective agent can. An agent can bad-mouth other jockeys while tooting his own jockey's horn, something that's difficult for the jockey himself to do.

From the grandstand, you will have no way of knowing who represents whom, but you will be able to spot which relationships are working.

> ➤ Jockeys who always manage to be on contenders are probably good riders, but it's just as likely they are in possession of effective agents.

> ➤ While an agent can't always put a jockey on a winner, he can make sure the jockey is always in a position to bring home some money. Jockeys who reach the top of the money-winning charts usually have good relationships with their agents.

How Jockeys Are Paid

Jockeys have a strong financial motivation to win. They get little money for riding a loser, even a close-up loser, but they get a substantial paycheck if they win.

Jockey pay scales are set by individual racing jurisdictions or racetracks, sometimes in consultation with local jockeys' organizations, so there's some variation between tracks. One thing doesn't vary. All pay scales give the winning jockey 10 percent of the winner's purse. Here's a typical pay scale for the other finishers.

Pay Scale for Losing Rides

Total Race Purse	2nd Place	3rd Place	Other Finishers
Under $10,000	$70	$55	$45
10 to 20,000	$85	$70	$50
20 to 30,000	$100	$85	$60
30 to 50,000	$150	$100	$70
50 to 100,000	$300	$200	$80
Over 100,000	$400	$250	$90

Jockeys' organizations would prefer to see jockeys win either 10 percent of all purses or the scale rate, whichever is higher, and a movement to that effect is underway in several areas. The Jockeys Guild, the main nationwide organization, would like to become a recognized labor union, and that may happen soon. When it does, the pay arrangements may change. In the meantime, jockeys have a powerful incentive to win, not just race well, a situation that racing officials like just fine.

The Least You Need to Know

➤ While the jockey can certainly affect the outcome of a race, the average jockey in the average race is usually a minor factor in handicapping.

➤ The weight allowance given to apprentice jockeys is usually balanced by their lack of experience, but the unusually talented apprentice can use the weight break to win more than his share of races.

➤ Jockeys are employed on a race-by-race basis by trainers. A top trainer will never use a poor jockey, but a top jockey may occasionally find himself on a poor horse, just to please the trainer.

➤ Jockeys who know how to break well will dominate races of six furlongs or less.

➤ Jockeys who judge pace effectively will excel in Thoroughbred races, particularly in races longer than six furlongs.

➤ Some jockeys excel in turf races because they are good at positioning horses and at timing runs from off the pace.

Chapter 10

The Other Hands That Hold the Reins: The Drivers

In This Chapter

➤ Driving skills

➤ Identifying the good driver

➤ The disappearing trainer/driver

You may hear it called the Art of Race Driving, or you may hear it called the Science of Race Driving. If you're listening to a bettor who can't quite figure out why he lost, you may hear it called the Mystery of Race Driving.

All the titles point up one fact. The driver of a Standardbred racehorse is more important and plays a bigger role in the outcome of the race than does the rider of a Thoroughbred or a Quarter Horse. Ironically, he's more important, at least in part, because it's easier.

Most Standardbreds are calm, quiet, and well-behaved. Most flat runners are not. Drivers, not having to concentrate on staying aboard while getting the horse into the gate, out of the gate, and into a more or less straight line, can usually focus on strategy and tactics throughout the race. Jockeys are more often along for the ride.

Some jockeys do make tactical decisions and some drivers just go along with the flow, but the comparative importance of the human participant is different in each sport. You'll hear different estimates of the relative contributions.

In flat racing, you'll find consensus somewhere around 90 to 95 percent horse, 5 to 10 percent human. The figures are a little closer in harness racing, but you'll be hard pressed to find anybody who thinks the horse is less than 75 to 80 percent responsible for whether he wins or loses. In both sports, the horse is still most of the race, but you can't ignore the hands on the reins in either sport.

Driving Skills

Identifying the drivers with the most important skills helps you to share in their wins. Here's what's important.

Leaving the gate effectively is the single most important thing a good driver does.

Leaving

In the old days, harness racing was a little like NBA basketball. All the effort went into the final quarter. That has changed, and today the first quarter is almost as important as the last one. Drivers used to be able to take it easy for most of the race, worrying only about staying out of trouble. After three quarters, they'd then race to the wire.

Nowadays, the increased speed of racing in general, the strategy employed by almost all drivers, and even the rules of the sport mean that everybody races hard from the start. Racing quickly from the start is called *leaving*, and the driver who does it well is going to be both admired and successful. Everybody leaves now, but not everybody does it equally well.

Figure the odds. If everybody leaves, hoping to get to or near the front, most are going to lose out. The loser will

From the Horse's Mouth

The **wire** is the finish line, even though there's rarely either a wire or a line. Instead, it's a marker on a judge's stand in the infield of the track. You're supposed to imagine the line.

be the driver who hasn't adequately assessed his horse's early speed, who hasn't gotten his horse sufficiently alert, or who lacks the aggressiveness to stake a claim on track position and hold onto it no matter what.

By the first turn, a driver good at leaving usually manages to get his horse to the rail, or just one horse out, without finding himself behind a wall of horses. Leaving well is more important on the 1/2-mile and 5/8-mile tracks than on the one-mile tracks. We'll get into track size more in Chapter 12.

Timing the Move

Bad Bet

Leaving can be dangerous when it turns into the aborted leave, where the horse gets moving quickly but has to be taken back suddenly because there's no space for him. He wastes energy and loses position at the same time.

Except perhaps for the superstars who set their own rules, no horse can maintain top speed on the lead for an entire race. A good driver knows when to ask for speed and when to ease off.

A driver can actually be too good at this. Some drivers understand pace so well that they used to ask their horses to leave, then settled back on the lead at such a slow pace that the field of horses would seem to be crawling around the track. The leading driver, whose horse retained plenty of energy, would then ask for speed in the final quarter. Nobody could catch him.

The smart strategists prospered, as did people who bet on them, but fans (including those who bet on the other horses) despised the technique.

The so-called *slow quarter rule* now prohibits this practice. It's the harness racing equivalent of a shot clock, eliminating any deliberate slowdowns. The horse can be disqualified and the driver suspended if he's guilty of racing any quarter too slowly. The rule has affected race driving:

➤ It's helped create a more aggressive driving style. No more leisurely three quarters.

➤ It's helped horses who come off the pace, but not too far off. The leaders may tire, but the distant trailers can't get through traffic.

➤ It's rewarded subtle strategists. They can still slow their horses on the lead, as long as it isn't too obvious.

➤ It's made great drivers excel even more. A driver who understands both strategy and pace can place his horse on or off the lead, assess the speed of the leader, and make his move accordingly to take advantage of his own horse's energy level, as well as that of the other horses. Somehow, good drivers seem even better when a slow quarter rule is in effect and is enforced.

For the Record

Some drivers carry stopwatches to judge time and pace. Others have the biological equivalent of clocks in their heads, and they can tell you to the fraction how fast the previous quarter went. Drivers may also get a glimpse of the tote board or hear the track announcer call fractional times, but the posting may come a couple of seconds too late for the driver to make strategic decisions.

Avoiding trouble is a vital talent.

Avoiding Trouble

Good drivers seem to be able to keep themselves and their horses out of situations that lose races. Foremost is the ability to avoid being *parked*.

No, being parked doesn't involved stopping and standing. In fact, if you're parked you have to work even harder than you would if you avoided this catastrophe. Being parked is being forced wide. It's undesirable in any racing sport, but in harness racing it can be a disaster. Sharp turns and the extra width of the sulky make being parked a very difficult obstacle to overcome in any race. A driver who usually manages to avoid it is worth following and often betting on.

Trouble also comes when a driver is forced to take evasive action because a horse directly in front of him suddenly slows down. This happens often since racing directly behind another horse is actually good strategy. It's called *racing under cover*, and it allows a horse to move quickly without expending much energy. Racing under cover follows the same principle as slipstreaming in auto racing.

A good driver knows if the horse he's racing behind is likely to slow suddenly, while a not-so-good driver is happily oblivious, until he unhappily has to pull his horse up to avoid an accident.

Inside Track

An occasional horse races well parked, even preferring it, possibly because he doesn't like horses on his right side. But he usually isn't a good bet since his driver will not want to be embarrassed by racing parked. He'll probably force the horse near to the rail, where he will lose.

Good Hands

Good drivers have good hands, which—in the horse world—means gentle and sensitive ones. Bad hands pull, causing the horse to pull back in response. It's not a situation conducive to winning.

A heavy-handed driver isn't always easy to spot, but you may see a horse pull against the restraint of the bit, toss his head, or simply have the look of wanting to fight his driver.

Measures of Success

Track programs and racing publications give you different lists of successful drivers. You may find lists of drivers whose horses:

➤ Have won the most money.

➤ Have won the most dashes (individual races).

➤ Have won the most races in less than two minutes or less than 1:55.

➤ Have finished in the first three most often.

More useful than any list is an effective tool dreamed up by the harness sport. It's the *Universal Driver Rating System*, commonly called the *UDR*, a statistic designed to identify the drivers most likely to give you a run (or rather a trot or pace) for your money.

The UDR looks like a batting average, but it's more elaborate than a simple placing percentage. The rating gives the most weight to a win, next most to a second-place finish, and a little credit for a third. Unplaced finishes, even close ones, get no statistical consideration.

Any UDR above .300 is good, with a couple of caveats. A UDR based on only a few starts, perhaps at the start of a year or the early days of a race meet, is statistically invalid. A great driver may have goose eggs and a poor one may be batting a thousand.

In some situations, other lists come into play. A driver like John Campbell, who's won around 2,000 races in less than 1:55, will be right at home driving a very fast horse in the Hambletonian or Little Brown Jug. A driver high on the money lists will be the same. A driver with a high UDR, but one that was earned at small tracks, might be overmatched in the big ones.

For the Record

The Hambletonian, for three-year-old trotters, and the Little Brown Jug, for three-year-old pacers, are the Kentucky Derby, the Super Bowl, and the Indy 500 of harness racing. They're the sport's most publicized and prestigious events.

Some people believe that the UDR is too complex. Just look at the winning percentage, they say. Anything above 15 percent wins from starts signifies a good driver. True, but it doesn't give enough credit to the driver who manages to get every horse into contention, win or lose. Look at all the lists to pick good drivers.

Also look at past performance and results charts for the drivers whose horses are in good position after a quarter, whose performance lines rarely show that they are parked, and who hold their positions or improve in the final quarter.

Newcomers

Racing programs inform you if a driver is less than fully experienced. The letter P in a circle appears next to his or her name, the sign of a provisional driver.

From the Horse's Mouth

A **provisional driver** is one who has raced less than a year and has had fewer than 25 starts in betting races.

You'll occasionally see an A for amateur or F for a driver licensed to race only at fair meets. All of these symbols count against the horse when you're trying to pick a winner.

Sometimes this strike against the horse doesn't make any difference. Amateur driver Mal Burroughs drove his horse Malabar Man to victory in the 1997 Hambletonian. Burroughs' amateur status didn't affect the outcome, and it didn't even affect betting since Malabar Man was the heavy favorite. No professional could have driven the horse any better.

Catch Driver Versus Trainer/Driver

At any major track today, the horse you bet on is probably handled by a person who neither trains nor owns the horse he's driving. Fifteen years ago, you would have seen a 50-50 balance between horses driven by their own trainers and horses driven by driving specialists, the *catch drivers*. Thirty years ago, the catch driver would be the oddity.

The trend toward catch driving has raised the standards of driving in general. It's inevitable that somebody who specializes in an activity gets better. Does this make the catch driver a better bet? Not necessarily. The trainer/driver may be better in certain situations:

➤ Trainers do know their horses better than anyone else, even the most sensitive catch driver.

➤ They stand to profit more than any catch driver if the horse wins and may have the stronger motivation.

If the trainer is a competent driver (and some of them are more than competent) he may be the better bet.

Good trainer/drivers are more difficult to identify than good catch drivers. They usually make far fewer starts, so they rarely show up on lists of top dash winners. If they have one or more very successful horses, you may find their names on the lists of top money winners. But they may not be highly placed on the UDR lists or the percentage lists either, even if they are extremely good drivers. Here's why.

➤ They may be more likely than good catch drivers to drive first-time starters.

➤ They may be more likely to drive horses coming off injury layoffs.

➤ They may drive their difficult horses who need seasoning or careful handling.

➤ They can't pick and choose among several stables' horses.

Their statistics may suggest that they are poor drivers rather than the careful trainers that they actually are. More even than catch drivers, trainer/drivers require examination of past performance and result charts to identify the ones who are effective.

To be sure, you can't always tell the difference between a trainer/driver who wins because he's a good trainer and one who wins because of his driving skills. Some times you can't even separate the two skills. The horse may be trained to perform in a manner that best suits the trainer himself when he drives.

But most bettors aren't going to look a gift win in the mouth. They don't care why a particular combination wins, just that it finishes first. Study the charts, looking for the characteristics of a driver who does the right thing at the right time.

Drivers' Weight

There's been a long-standing belief in harness racing that the weight of the driver doesn't much matter. Unlike in flat racing, where it's universally accepted that weight slows a horse down, weight in harness racing is somehow believed to be more fluid. It's where the driver places his weight, the believers say, not the weight itself.

This is nonsense on its face. If weight didn't matter, sulkies would be safe, secure, untippable, and weigh a couple of hundred pounds, rather than the 50 or so they do weigh. It *is* true that driver position matters a great deal. The reduction in race times when the modified sulky placed the driver behind the wheels rather than over them proves that.

Proponents of the weight-doesn't-matter theory also point out that Standardbreds race from a moving start, unlike Thoroughbreds and Quarter Horses. They already have momentum, and the law of inertia keeps them going. But weight matters most in flat runners in long races and near the end of those. Momentum has nothing to do with it; muscle exhaustion does. Standardbreds rarely go longer than a mile, so weight plays a smaller role.

The fiction that weight doesn't matter got itself established in the era when everybody was a trainer/driver. Some superb trainers who never met a calorie they didn't like still managed to win with their superbly trained horses. Those trainers would rarely get a mount and would never get a win if they tried to be catch drivers today.

Inside Track

The driver's weight matters most on tracks that are muddy, deep, or otherwise less than fast.

Today's most successful drivers almost never weigh more than 150 pounds, and many of them are below 140. Drivers' weight doesn't matter quite so much as riders' weight does, but we do know for sure that horses pulling lighter weights almost always go faster than those pulling heavier weights, all else being equal. The proof of it is in the program. In a sport where driver's weight isn't supposed to matter, most tracks print the driver's weight right below the name of the horse.

Driver's Age

Every now and then, the United States Trotting Association likes to add up the number of octogenarian drivers who have started at least one race during the year. The figure usually stands at about half a dozen. Dozens, possibly even hundreds, of people in their 60s and 70s drive and sometimes win races.

Harness racing may be the only significant sport in the world in which elderly people can compete as seriously and as actively as they do. But should you bet on them?

Conventional harness racing wisdom has it that driver's age, like his weight, doesn't much matter. You're told that you may bet on elderly drivers, or young drivers, or middle-aged drivers according to their records, not their ages. At the same time, harness racing is the only one of the racing sports where the age of the two-legged participant is often included right on the program.

Drivers, like other people, can't deny a couple of basic facts. Age brings experience, information, and wisdom, but it takes away reaction time, aerobic capacity, and muscle strength. In harness racing, the ideal balance seems to be somewhere in the 30s and 40s.

Although some are a little younger, and a few are a little older, most top drivers are in this age range. You don't need to avoid betting on someone not in this age group, but you don't give them any extra points either.

Female Drivers

Until the 1970s, women were formally excluded from obtaining unrestricted licenses to drive in harness races. That's no longer true, but there are still very few women drivers, and none at the top levels of the sport. It's not altogether clear why.

The sulky has been even less hospitable than the racing saddle to women, probably because the weight advantage enjoyed by women doesn't matter in harness racing. On the other hand, Standardbreds are generally less difficult than Thoroughbreds, and upper body strength doesn't matter as much either. The answer to the scarcity of women drivers probably lies in the sport's fascination with tradition. There didn't used to be females in the sulkies, and some people think that's the way it should always be.

When you do come across a female driver, you'll have to consider her experience level, which probably won't be high, as well as her ranking on the lists we've talked about, which will probably be even lower. The charts, not her sex, will probably mean points against her.

Driving Equipment

Harness racing, which by itself keeps hundreds of horse equipment producers profitable, requires the driver, as well as the horse, to wear and carry extraneous items. Like jockeys, drivers must wear safety helmets. Unlike jockeys, they are required to wear safety vests in many racing jurisdictions. Many drivers don't like the vests, claiming that they're bulky and uncomfortable. With weight of less concern, more rather than fewer tracks are requiring the vests.

Neither item of equipment affects the outcome of the race, but they do help assure that you can follow favorite drivers with some confidence that they'll be around next week.

For the Record

Harness racing is safer than flat racing, for both horse and human, with far fewer fatal injuries occurring during either training or racing. Even so, the most celebrated single person ever killed in a horse race was a harness driver, the revered Hall of Famer Billy Haughton, who died in a racing accident at Yonkers Raceway in 1985.

One item of driving equipment does bear watching. There's a growing movement in harness racing to reduce the use of the whip, which is longer and much more visible to the fans in harness racing than it is in flat racing. Several tracks now require drivers to keep both hands on the lines at all times, even when using the whip.

From the Horse's Mouth

The **lines** are the reins that connect drivers' hands to the horse's bit. They are both steering wheel and brakes.

This regulation dramatically limits the kind of whipping that the driver can administer. With both hands on the lines, he can't whale away on the horse's back and rump. The rule helps restore the image of the sport, but some drivers complain that it limits a driver's options too much. In reality, a horse good enough to win or place usually needs only a touch of the whip to urge him to keep moving.

The rule actually helps drivers with good hands because they're the ones who can handle both whip and lines. If the hands-on-the-lines rule is in effect at your track, good drivers will probably do even better.

The Business of Driving

Like jockeys, catch drivers are hired by trainers on a race-by-race basis, but the tradition of trainer/drivers lingers on in the pay arrangement. In most harness racing jurisdictions, drivers receive five percent of the purse money they win. Purses are paid to the first five finishers, with the rest of the field receiving nothing.

Even a math class dropout can figure what that means: Losing drivers risk broken bones and the scorn of bettors while earning absolutely nothing. At a few tracks, drivers are paid a modest fee for losing drives, and most drivers would like to see this policy in effect everywhere.

Supporters of the current system say it encourages an all-out effort on the part of the driver. Opponents believe that it just isn't fair to fail to pay someone for work. It's not fair, of course, but that's the tradition.

Agents are not a significant factor in harness racing. Most drivers negotiate their own drives and make their own decisions about which horse they'll drive when offered more than one. They make up for getting only five percent of the purse by being able to keep it all for themselves.

The Least You Need to Know

➤ Drivers play a bigger part in the outcome of races than jockeys do.

➤ Most drivers try to leave the gate quickly, but leaving quickly with no place to go is worse than a slow start.

➤ Drivers can no longer slow down dramatically on the lead, but those with a good sense of timing can still control the pace to their own benefit.

➤ Catch drivers are usually more effective than driver/trainers, but a trainer who's a particularly good driver can usually handle his own horse better than anyone else.

➤ Provisional and amateur drivers are usually (but not always) poor bets.

➤ Drivers' weight does matter; the lighter the better.

➤ Drivers' age matters too; not too young and not too old is best.

➤ The hands-on-the-lines rule helps good drivers and hurts bad ones.

Chapter 11

The Supporting Actors

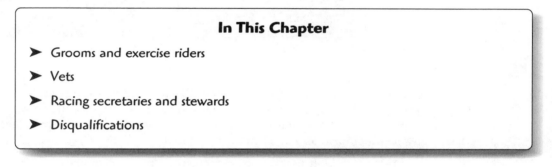

In This Chapter

➤ Grooms and exercise riders

➤ Vets

➤ Racing secretaries and stewards

➤ Disqualifications

Training, riding, and driving make up the tip of the racing iceberg. All the other people, dozens upon dozens of them, form the base. They like to point out that they're what keeps the whole thing afloat. So let's shine a little light on all those people beneath the surface.

The Horse People

Most of the work involved in getting a horse to the racetrack is dirty, smelly, exhausting, and even dangerous. The trainer, king of the backstretch that he is, isn't going to want to do much of that kind of labor.

The groom is every horse's favorite human being.

The Groom

Ask any horse to name the human most important to him, and he's not going to mention the trainer, jockey, or driver. He'll name his groom, although if he's a Standardbred, he may use the word *caretaker*. The groom is his nanny, housekeeper, chef, beautician, physical therapist, and all-around best friend.

Inside Track

If you're at a simulcasting facility, you won't get quite as good a look at the horses, but you should be able to see them being saddled, walking around the ring, or marching in a post parade. Watch this part of the transmission. You'll learn things the best past performance chart can't tell you.

It used to be an exclusively male occupation. Nowadays, many grooms are women. People become grooms because they enjoy the company of horses. After all, you can make more money manning the drive-in window at Burger World, and it doesn't smell so bad.

Grooms don't always retain their affection for horses. A few years of poor pay, no promotions, and odors can do that. A horse with a bad groom will not perform as well as he otherwise might, while a horse with a good one may come up with unexpectedly good races. How do you identify good grooms?

➤ Take a look at them in the saddling enclosure or paddock. Grooms who take clean halters off their horses and who are dressed neatly themselves probably take good care of their charges.

➤ Horses with shiny coats and neatly brushed or braided manes and tails are well groomed.

➤ Horses who don't shy or toss their heads when equipment is being adjusted are used to being handled gently.

➤ Horses from the barns of successful trainers usually have good grooms. Top trainers understand the importance of grooms and permit only good ones around their horses.

Big racing stables have an array of other people who care for the horses. *Stall muckers* take care of the inevitable product of a horse standing 23 hours a day in a his stall. *Hot walkers*, if they haven't been replaced by a machine, cool a horse who's just raced or worked by walking him around the barn area. If the trainer and groom are good, these people will do their jobs and won't affect the horse's races one way or another.

Exercise Rider

The large operations employ their own exercise riders. Smaller ones hire them as needed from the legion of would-be riders who haunt the backstretch.

Some exercise riders are hoping to become jockeys. Others are former jockeys still trying to make a living by riding horses at the gallop. They all hang around trainers looking for a $20 ride in the morning.

Although the pay isn't outstanding, riding workouts is a good job for not-quite-jockeys for a couple of reasons.

➤ It requires most but not all of the skills needed by jockeys. Exercise riders need to be alert and aware of pace, just like jockeys, but they don't have to be as aggressive. They don't need the nerve to charge toward shrinking holes, and they don't have to push their horses beyond exhaustion.

➤ Exercise riders must be light, but they don't have to be as light as jockeys. While no overweight people need apply, exercise riders don't have to make assigned weights or worry about losing a race because of excess poundage.

As we talked about in Chapter 9, jockeys occasionally ride morning workouts to impress trainers, to retain mounts, or to earn new ones, but most workouts are ridden by exercise riders, men and women you've never heard of. You won't know much about the quality of the exercise rider when the horse steps onto the track. You can assume that a good trainer employed an adequate one.

You can make a second important assumption. If a horse you're interested in is coming off a very fast workout with an exercise rider rather than a jockey aboard, he's capable of running even faster. Most exercise riders weigh more than most jockeys, and most exercise saddles are heavier and sturdier than racing saddles. Carrying less weight in a race should result in a faster performance.

For the Record

Many tracks permit fans to watch morning workouts. It's an entertaining, if occasionally confusing, spectacle, and it can be instructive. Even a beginner can tell the difference between the good exercise riders and the rest. The good ones are all business, while the others are bouncing around in the saddle, sawing on the bit, and shouting to their friends.

Veterinarians

There are two kinds of vet at the racetrack, each equally important. One tries desperately to keep the horses sound and healthy. The other tries to identify the ones who aren't and makes sure they aren't made healthy by nefarious means.

All horses need the periodic attention of vets, who vaccinate, worm, examine, and draw blood from the healthiest of them. If the owner and trainer can afford it, the less healthy horses see the vet almost daily for x-rays, injections, and various other treatments. Every racetrack has a number of veterinarians, most of whom operate out of trucks or vans. They go to their patients, not the other way around.

It's emotionally and morally challenging work. Racetrack vets are often asked to patch together a horse who should be retired from racing or to get one ready to race who needs months of rest and recovery. They are sometimes asked to use chemical means to help horses who are otherwise too slow or too unhealthy to win.

Some track vets do the first, helping trainers send out horses who shouldn't be racing. A very few do the second. We've already talked about that, but here let's note that the existence of even one or two of this kind of vet means that every racetrack, state, or racing jurisdiction has vets of their own.

The vets employed by the track or another controlling agency have two separate but not altogether different functions. One is to try to catch illegal drugging of horses, preferably in advance, but after the fact if necessary. They may take blood before the race to test for illegal substances, and they supervise the taking of urine after the race to do the same thing.

They also check all horses before the race, usually in the morning, to certify them as sound enough to race. They watch the horses warm up, and they have the power to scratch any horse deemed unhealthy enough to race.

Although the track vets hope to save both horses and jockeys from injury, the primary purpose of all this prerace observation is to maintain the integrity of the betting process.

The Track People

While some vets work for the track or other agency, most of the other track employees work out front. It's cleaner work, although hardly anybody at the track has a typical nine-to-five job.

Racing Secretary

While the trainers rule their own kingdoms of the backstretch, the racing secretary is the emperor of the entire operation. At the largest tracks, the functions of the racing secretary may be fulfilled by a barnful of different people. There may be a director of racing, plus a racing secretary, plus an assistant racing secretary, plus a stall supervisor. At small tracks, there's just one person to do it all.

However it's divided up, it's important work. The racing secretary's job is to bring together horses and purse money in a way to encourage people to come to the racetrack and bet on those horses. The goal is easy enough to describe, but it can be a challenge to reach.

The first step is to get the horses into the barns. Most tracks provide free stall space to help lure the competitors onto the grounds, and the racing secretary oversees the job of making sure those free stalls are occupied by horses who can actually race, so he has to become a negotiator.

Trainers who start a lot of horses get almost as many stalls as they want, with no questions asked about who's munching hay where. One who rarely starts a horse may not be offered stalls, unless he happens to have next year's Kentucky Derby favorite in his stable. He's welcome whether he enters horses or not.

After he's got the horses on the grounds, the racing secretary designs races to suit the animals filling all those stalls. As he does this, he keeps bettors in mind. They don't like to bet maiden specials? Then he'll schedule races for older horses. The track has given him a potful of money to put into purses but he hasn't got a stakes-quality horse on the grounds? Then he'll be generous with the day-to-day purse distribution, making many trainers very happy.

In the old days, racing secretaries at Thoroughbred tracks designed plenty of handicap races in which they assigned weights to individual horses

From the Horse's Mouth

A **maiden special**, in flat racing, is a race for horses who've never won. You occasionally see a future star in one, but you may see a lot of very poor horses instead. See Chapter 14.

From the Horse's Mouth

A **dead heat** is a tie. They're rare nowadays, thanks to extremely sharp lenses on photo-finish cameras.

according to their talents. In a perfectly handicapped race, all horses would finish in a dead heat.

Racing secretaries still involve themselves with weight, but these days the weight is usually among the conditions of the race. For example, the secretary might set 120 pounds as the base weight for the race, and then allow a three pound reduction for any horse who hasn't won a race in three months.

The possible variations are endless, but they have the same goal: to prompt the closest possible finish. This is what fans and bettors like.

Racing secretaries at harness tracks share the goal and most of the procedures, although weight isn't among their tools. Instead, the harness racing secretary will tinker with claiming prices, allowing less successful horses to be entered at higher prices. This is supposed to encourage an intriguing array of horses in each race by making trainers think twice about entering better horses while enthusiastically starting lesser ones.

Stewards and Judges

At some tracks, terms are virtually interchangeable. At others, the jobs are quite different. In flat racing, you'll find that stewards often do the work that judges do in harness racing. Whichever term is used, the person who holds the title is powerful. He makes decisions that affect who starts, who wins, whose tickets pay off, and who might be suspended. That's power by anybody's standards.

At a flat track, you're likely to find three stewards, two representing the racetrack and another representing the state agency that regulates racing. Depending on the state, that may be a Racing Commission, a Wagering Board, or some other regulatory body.

You'll also find an array of judges reporting to them, including placing judges, paddock judges, horse identifiers, and other people who have something to say about enforcement of the rules of the track and the state.

In harness racing, you'll find the big three called judges, with the biggest of the three designated the presiding judge. In addition, there are people who fill most of the same functions as at the flat track, although the titles may vary. The names of the officials appear somewhere near the front of each day's programs.

Infractions and Disqualifications

Racegoers are most likely to find themselves thinking about stewards and judges if something happens before or during a race that affects the outcome. If a horse runs off in the post parade, exhausting or injuring himself, he may be ordered scratched. If one horse interferes with another, he may be taken down.

Disqualifications occur far less often than interference does. Judges and stewards know how unpopular disqualifications are with fans, and most of them are reluctant to take a horse down unless the foul was blatant and obvious to everybody but the vision-impaired. They may conduct an inquiry on their own initiative or as a result of a claim of foul from a rider or driver.

From the Horse's Mouth

Taken down means disqualified. The term dates from the time winning numbers were hung on results boards. Nowadays, they're electronically zapped, but the old term remains.

Before a decision is made, they look at videotape and listen to comments from everyone involved. Most of them also follow guidelines, whether they're part of the regulations or an unwritten policy. Here are some of the things that lead to disqualification:

➤ If one horse bumps or jostles another in a way that impedes his progress.

➤ If a horse changes course to cause another to pull up suddenly.

➤ If a horse changes course to force another wide.

In each case, the horse causing the interference has to finish in front of the object of the interference. If your horse loses because another horse fouls him, he's out of luck unless the villain profits. If both horses lose, the victim has no recourse.

Sometimes, stewards and judges don't disqualify even if the perpetrator of the foul wins or places. If the bump or change of course is believed not to have affected the outcome of the race, there's often no disqualification, no matter how noticeable the interference. This sometimes happens when the foul occurs at the start, and the rest of the race progresses normally.

Whether claims of foul are upheld or not often depends on the traditions of the particular racetrack. Whether you like it depends on who you bet on.

The Starter

In both flat racing and harness racing, the starter is vital to success for the horses, the bettors, and the track itself. A good starter is worth his weight in winning tickets, making sure that every horse has at least an equal shot at getting out of the gate safely and is ready to race.

Inside Track

If the horses in each race appear to be getting out of the gate in a ragged and awkward manner, avoid betting on short races this day.

Good starts are little noted, but poor ones are long remembered. Legend has it that Man O' War lost the only race of his life because he was turned in the wrong direction when the starter lifted the tape at the start of a six-furlong race in 1919. The invention of the starting gate made sure that can't happen again, but the stalls can open while horses are rearing up, pulling backwards, standing awkwardly, or anything else that a nervous horse can think to do.

Other Track People

Also among the legion of track workers:

➤ The *track announcer* calls the positions of the horses during the race. Good ones are a pleasure and a joy to hear, but even bad ones don't turn a winner into a loser.

➤ The *track superintendent* maintains the racing surface. His ability can affect races. More on him in Chapter 12.

➤ Outriders in flat and harness racing and pony people in flat racing. *Outriders*, mounted on well-behaved horses, lead the post parades and patrol the corners of the racetrack. They catch runaway horses and otherwise maintain equine decorum. *Pony people* (who ride horses, not ponies) lead Thoroughbreds and Quarter Horses to the post, keeping them quiet and under control.

For the Record

Most outriders and pony people prefer not to use former racehorses for their mounts. They find many retired runners get a little too excited at the sights and sounds of racing. On the other hand, they need horses fast enough to keep pace with runaways. You'll see a lot of Appaloosas and stock-type Quarter Horses doing the work.

In North America, most flat runners are led by ponies. In Europe, they go to the post under the exclusive control of their jockeys.

European runners who come to America often keep up the ponyless routine, and you'll occasionally see an American horse without a pony.

Sometimes this works and the horse is beautifully behaved. Other times, he acts like a preschooler and wastes precious energy. You should reach two conclusions when you see a horse step onto the track without a pony:

➤ The trainer may be cheap and reluctant to spend the few dollars he has to pay the pony person.

➤ You should try not to place your bet until you see how the horse behaves.

The Owner

Placing them last in this chapter doesn't mean that they're the least important people in racing. On the contrary, if owners weren't willing to risk huge amounts of money for very little chance of profit, there would be no racing. Or at least there wouldn't be the kind of racing we know today.

Owning a racehorse is the ultimate gamble. Aside from the cost of buying the horse, you'll be paying between $40 and $80 a day just to keep him in training. That doesn't include several thousand dollars a year in vet and shoeing bills, transportation, entry fees, and the percentages of purse money that go to the trainer, jockey, or driver if you're lucky enough to win. But people do it, even people who aren't rich, for a number of reasons.

➤ There's money to be won in races. In two minutes, the winner of Thoroughbred racing's Breeder's Cup Classic takes home $2 million. There are million dollar races in Quarter Horse and harness racing, too.

➤ The residual value of successful horses can be enormous. The owners of the Thoroughbred stallion Northern Dancer once turned down an offer of $20 million for him, even though he was an elderly 19 years old.

➤ Owners get to sit in special sections at the racetrack, join trainers and jockeys in the saddling enclosure, and pose for winner's circle photos if they win.

On the other hand, owning racehorses can be a tough business.

➤ In Thoroughbred racing, you may hear your $50,000 horse referred to as "cheap." A cheap horse doesn't cost quite so much in the other racing sports, but you have to pay serious money to buy a horse you know is going to be good.

➤ Among well-bred, well-trained horses, less than 10 percent ever win stakes races of any kind. Among blue-collar horses, that figure is less than 3 percent.

➤ You'll spend $15,000 to $20,000 per year just to keep a horse in training. That's a lot if all you get out of it is seats in the owners' section.

If you go to the races and find yourself grumbling that the owners seem to get the best seats and most of the excitement, don't resent them. Instead, thank the gods of racing that they exist.

The Least You Need to Know

➤ Horses with good grooms should be comfortable, happy, and ready to race.

➤ Horses with exercise riders heavier than their jockeys may improve their workout times when they race.

➤ The racing secretary's job is to create competitive races. If he's good, there's no runaway winner.

➤ Stewards and judges have the power to disqualify winners, but even if there's a foul, there's rarely a disqualification if there's no harm.

Part 3
The Races

There may not be quite as much variety in races as there is among horses, but it's close. It's not enough for you to know horses and handlers if you hope to win. You've also got to make sense of the races.

In this part, we'll take a look at vital components of the racing equation such as track surface, weather, race classifications, weight assignments, and post position. Each can matter to who wins and who loses, whether it's horse or bettor.

Chapter 12

Courses for Horses

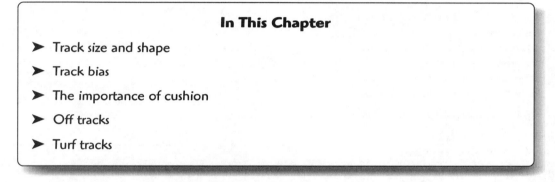

In This Chapter

➤ Track size and shape

➤ Track bias

➤ The importance of cushion

➤ Off tracks

➤ Turf tracks

No horse races exactly alike, which is why people take bets on them. No track is exactly alike either, and this fact should figure into every betting decision you make.

Track Size and Shape

North American Thoroughbred tracks, all of which are more or less oval-shaped, range in circumference from the 1/2 mile of Northampton to the 1 1/2 miles of Belmont Park, with every gradation of distance in between.

Quarter Horse racing usually takes place on a small oval with a chute that creates at least a full 1/4-mile straightaway. Many Thoroughbred tracks also use chutes so that all races, whatever their length, finish at the same place.

Harness tracks come in three incarnations. There are a handful of one-mile tracks, most of which share the year with Thoroughbred racing. Most of the rest are either 1/2-mile or 5/8-mile ovals.

A chute extends from one end of the racetrack, creating a longer straight-away than it might otherwise have.

In both flat and harness racing, the smaller the circumference of the track, the sharper the turns. The more the turn resembles a hairpin, the more likely strategy, accident, and chance will play a part in the result of a race. Here are some of the problems.

Inside Track

A race that begins in a chute often has an unusually long run to the first turn. This takes away much of the advantage of a good start, so habitually poor starters often do well in races that come out of a chute.

➤ Sharp turns exaggerate the ground lost by horses who race wide.

➤ Sharp turns are difficult for horses who come from behind because it's hard to pass other horses on a turn. Small tracks are almost all turn.

➤ Sharp turns are stressful for equine bones and joints since they force the horse to transfer his weight to his left side to maintain his balance.

➤ Some horses are simply too clumsy to race well on sharp turns. They manage to get their feet tangled and their sense of balance confused.

As soon as jockeys figure out bias, they all concentrate on the good part of the track.

Harness racing acknowledges the importance of track size by telling you in the past performance charts the circumference of the track where the race occurred. In Thoroughbred racing, track size in previous races is usually not shown in past performances, but most past performance publications and some track programs have a chart that lists tracks, often including information on track size.

The Biased Racetrack

Every track has a bias. No, that doesn't mean it prefers brown horses to gray ones. It means that it favors certain running styles.

At each track, biases may develop from year to year and even from day to day. They don't usually change from race to race, but this happens, too. A track may favor horses who come from off the pace, horses who take an early lead, or horses who run in a particular part of the racetrack.

It's usually a result of the banking that's designed into the tracks to improve drainage, combined with the structure and the depth of the racing surface. Depending on the temperature, the amount of liquid that falls from the sky, and the kind of track maintenance that takes place, bias occurs. The most important kinds include:

Inside Track

A small, agile-looking Thoroughbred with an average record on a large track may improve dramatically if he moves to a small, sharp-turned track. His odds may be long, based on his previous performances.

From the Horse's Mouth

Bias is a track's tendency to favor one style of running over another.

➤ **Rail bias.** If no bias at all is present, the rail (meaning the part of the track closest to the inside rail) is the place to be since it's the shortest way around the track. But the rail is usually the lowest part of the racing surface, making it vulnerable to either hardening or softening, depending on what material the track is made of. The rail may be good or it may be bad, depending on the individual track bias.

➤ **Position bias.** At some tracks, horses who get to the lead early almost always stay there, unless some far superior horse comes along and catches them. At other tracks, getting an early lead is more like the kiss of death, and even far inferior horses pass them before the finish line. This is probably a result of the depth of the loose material on top of the track (more on that later).

Identifying Bias

You recognize bias by paying attention to the results of previous races. Each day, look at what happened in yesterday's races at the track, trying to pick out patterns. Did every horse who won stay on the rail? Did they come up on the outside? Did early

From the Horse's Mouth

Cushion is the loose material on the surface of the track. It's made of sand, clay, organic materials, or occasionally synthetic fibers, usually in some combination.

speed hold or did it fold? If you have self-control, watch a few races each day before you bet to see if you can identify any bias for that day.

Depth

The racing surface has three elements: sub-base, base, and cushion. The depth of each, particularly the cushion, affects the outcome of many of the races held on it.

When there's a lot of cushion, the surface is considered to be *deep*, and when there's little, it's *hard*. The depth of the track is sometimes reported in racing columns or news reports, but you can usually judge yourself. Get down to the finish line and take a look.

Deep Tracks

A track with more than three inches of cushion is deep, and the horses who race on it have to work as their hooves dig through the surface. The more cushion, the more difficult the work. A deep track is a slow one, producing slower times than others. It also affects race outcomes in the following ways.

➤ A deep track is more tiring to the horses than a harder one, favoring horses with stamina.

➤ Horses can't maintain top speed for long, penalizing front runners.

➤ But horses who like to come from far off the pace suffer too since the slowness of the track makes it difficult for them to make up a lot of ground.

➤ Horses with tendon or soft tissue problems often suffer on deep tracks. Avoid a horse with evidence of a bowed tendon on a track with a lot of cushion.

➤ But horses with sore hooves often suffer less because of the reduced concussion that occurs on deep tracks.

Hard Tracks

Hard tracks suffer from problems of their own, and they produce a special dilemma in the minds of track officials. There's no doubt that hard surfaces produce faster race times, which almost everybody likes.

In the 1970s, fans and racing officials alike were thrilled with the perfection of Ruffian, who set or tied records in every one of her first ten starts on the tracks of New York and New Jersey. They weren't so happy after her 11th start, when she suffered a fatal fracture after a blindingly fast first quarter. That took the shine off rock-hard tracks.

Flat track superintendents walk a fine line between the desire to create a track that's safe and well-cushioned and one that's enticingly fast with little cushion.

In flat racing, few track superintendents nowadays use less than two and a quarter inches of loose material on top of the track surface. Those who lean toward the bottom end of cushioning produce tracks that do this:

➤ They often allow early speed to hold on longer than expected, giving an advantage to quick horses who break well.

➤ They create concussion and can be very hard on horses with any kind of soreness in hoof or joint. Although they don't cause as much tendon stretch as deeper tracks, hard tracks focus and concentrate pain and are in general much harder on unsound horses.

➤ Tracks with little cushion sometimes have less bias of any kind. There's not enough loose material for dramatic variation in depth from one area of the track to another.

Harness Track Surfaces

Harness racing requires a much shallower surface than flat racing since the wheels of the sulky would be bogged down in loose material of any great depth. The relative hardness is no problem for harness horses, whose less stressful gait allows them to remain sound on a track that would cause gallopers to break down. What's more, harness racing thrives on fast times. So, between the sulky's requirements and the desire for speed, harness track superintendents do little experimentation with depth.

Artificial Surfaces

American racing began a lengthy flirtation with artificial track surfaces in the late 1970s. Engineers developed a variety of petrochemical substances to serve as either the firm base or the loose surface material.

Fake dirt seemed like such a good idea. In bad weather, it wouldn't become muddy. After hard use, the surface would remain even because there wouldn't be the compaction that real dirt suffers. Artificial racing surfaces were touted as safer, easier to maintain, and possibly faster.

None of the above proved true, at least to the satisfaction of most flat racing people. The artificial surfaces, they said, weren't any better. They were just different, and the differences weren't something that trainers liked. Most Thoroughbred racetracks that installed them replaced the fake dirt with the real stuff.

Believers in artificial surfaces are still lurking here and there in the racing world, and there are still some in use at various tracks around the world. It's also likely that artificial surfaces will stage a comeback in North America if the composition and maintenance of the material can be worked out to everybody's satisfaction. In fact, Hollywood Park in California recently experimented with a partially artificial surface.

Should you find yourself standing, past performance chart in hand, watching a field of horses march to the post on fake dirt, keep these points in mind.

➤ Artificial surfaces create very opinionated horses. Some horses really love them, and some really hate them. You don't know which it's going to be until the horse races on them.

➤ Betting on a field of horses who've never raced on the track is like betting on a field of first-time starters, except that they probably won't show baby horse antics like trying to run in the wrong direction or biting their lead pony. You pay your money and take your chances.

➤ Artificial surfaces are as prone to bias as any other, in spite of the fact that they're supposed to be consistent. Many are noticeably deeper at the rail, which means that horses who like to go wide aren't as disadvantaged as they are on most dirt tracks.

➤ A horse who shows good form in the mud on a dirt track isn't necessarily going to run well on a wet artificial surface. Some of the good mud form is due to a willingness to be hit in the face by slop, which won't happen in fake dirt.

Artificial Surfaces in Harness Racing

Harness racing has been more hospitable to artificial surfaces, partially because wintertime racing at major tracks has become an important part of the sport. Sleet might cause cancellation at a dirt track, but you can race (if not enjoy it) on icy artificial tracks. They're also better in rain since mud and sulky wheels don't mix.

Harness horses don't seem to have the extremes of attitude toward artificial surfaces as running horses do, and you usually can make wagering decisions based on something other than whether it was God or chemical engineers who made the cushion.

Success in the mud requires specialization on the part of horse, rider, and bettor.

Mud

It's possible to specialize in wet tracks at all levels of Thoroughbred racing. Some stallions produce a high percentage of horses who perform well in the mud. Some trainers are particularly skilled at developing mudders, and some jockeys know how to get the most out of horses racing over off-tracks.

Most important, some horses race consistently well on wet tracks. They probably don't actually enjoy racing on muddy surfaces, but they dislike it less than other horses. Mudders don't mind the sensation of slipping that occurs when their hooves strike the track. If they like to produce their speed from behind, they can tolerate being covered by a layer of mud.

Last on the list of mud specialists are people who bet successfully on rainy days, often to the amazement of their friends. Some bettors are convinced that any wager on any race on a muddy track is just half a step better than dropping your money into a pit and watching it get stuck in the mud on the bottom. While they might acknowledge that some horses are better than others in the mud, they are convinced that identifying those horses requires a Ouija board.

In fact, identifying good wet track horses is not particularly hard. Here's what you look for in a horse who's going to run well on a rainy day.

➤ He has wet track form. Look in his past performances for the symbols *sly, my, hvy*; these symbols describe increasing degrees of wetness in a track. More on the specifics in Chapter 18. If he ran well in a race with a symbol, he should be

143

capable of running on a track that isn't dry. The charts sometimes help you by printing an asterisk next to the name of a good mudder, but they miss some and praise others who don't deserve it.

➤ He is bred for wet track racing.

➤ He has big flat feet (go to the saddling enclosure and take a look).

➤ He has early speed, which tends to last longer in the mud. Come-from-behind horses can't get moving as easily, and when they do they find themselves carrying several extra pounds of mud.

➤ He has run well on the turf. Nobody's quite sure why good turf horses are often good mudders, but it may have something to do with those big flat feet.

➤ He doesn't have to be unsound, but if he is, it might not bother him as much as on dry tracks. Mud is softer and less concussive.

For the Record

Stallions whose descendants run well in the mud include Pleasant Colony, Mr. Prospector and his son Conquistador Cielo, Northern Dancer and his many sons, including Danzig and Nijinsky, and In Reality. Keep your own list by noting the sires and grandsires of horses who win on muddy tracks.

Refer back to Chapter 7 for a discussion of the use of mud caulks on off tracks. A quick summary of these special shoes: they can increase traction, give a horse a sense of security on a slippery surface, and be very dangerous to unsound horses.

You assume that a trainer who often succeeds on wet tracks is capable of assessing both the surface and his horse. If he chooses to use mud caulks, his horse may have a big advantage.

Quarter Horses and Standardbreds

Quarter Horses running on wet tracks have the same sense of slipping that Thoroughbreds do, but rain has far less effect on the outcome of the short races. Since Quarter Horses usually run stretched across the track rather than as a parade, one in front of the other, mud kickback isn't a concern. Neither do you have to consider the effect of early speed lasting longer than usual. It's nice to see previous form on off tracks, but overall past performance is more important.

Harness racing used to be very vulnerable to dramatic form changes in the mud, even though the cushion is shallower and less mud is thrown back to hit the horses in the face and cake on his equipment.

The drag of sulky wheels through any amount of mud would cause misery to horse, driver, and bettor, and serious students of wagering on harness racing would often refuse to place a bet on anything but a dry day. That's changed, thanks to synthetic surfaces, better track design for drainage, better sulky design, and the fact that you would miss a lot of good races if you refuse to bet on an off track.

Harness horses are also opinionated about mud, some racing well and some racing poorly, but you'll find that the extremes are much closer together than in Thoroughbred racing. Racing on off tracks does affect harness racing in one important way. The final time will be slower, anywhere from one to five seconds slower than it would have been on a dry track. Keep this in mind when you're assessing past performances.

Inside Track

Bettors sometimes don't notice the fact that a slow race or two in a horse's recent past took place on an off track. They may dismiss the horse as too slow to bet on. If you're observant, you may get good odds on a horse who's faster than he looks.

Track Grooming

Tracks need grooming even more than horses do. Galloping or pulling a sulky across a dirt track creates craters, furrows, holes, compacted areas, and other nasty spots that may cause a horse to stumble, fall, or just slow down. To smooth all this out, the track needs grooming, and it needs it often.

If Mother Nature doesn't provide water, track maintenance people must.

You'll see the tractor-pulled harrows on the track between races, raking and smoothing the surface pitted by the previous race. You'll also see water trucks depositing thousands of gallons of water during the racing day.

The better the track, the more thorough the harrowing. The noisy, lumbering machine might look like a refugee from a monster truck competition, but it's a welcome sight to all horsemen. It should be just as welcome to bettors because it helps assure that the horse you select will run according to his ability, not according to where he's lucky enough to place his feet.

Turf Racing

Racing on the grass, usually called *turf*, is a special and unique category in North American racing. Although it's the rule rather than the exception in the rest of the world, here it comprises only a small fraction of all racing. But grass races make up a disproportionate number of important stakes races, so most major Thoroughbred tracks now have turf courses in addition to their dirt racing strips.

You won't find cheap claiming races on the turf, and you'll find very few races for sprinters or two-year-olds. American turf racing is mostly for mature, proven horses at middle distances or longer.

As with mud racing, turf racing is better suited for some horses than others. First, look for good past performances in races on the turf. They're identified by a T next to the name of the race. Then, consider these qualifications:

➤ Turf sires and grandsires produce turf runners.

➤ The so-called "turf foot" features a wide hoof with a low heel.

➤ Most good turf runners have long strides but high action, meaning that they raise their knees high as they gallop along.

➤ Turf racing usually favors horses who like to come from behind, even at sprint distances.

➤ Imported horses with good records in their native countries usually perform well. The horse will have a two- or three-letter symbol next to his name in the program (Ire, GB, Fra, and so on).

American turf courses are usually located inside the main track, making them small and sharp-turned. Jockeys who get themselves to the rail usually prosper.

Horses who perform well on them tend to be smallish, agile, and quick out of the gate, but not necessarily front runners. The two most important turf courses on the continent, the ones at Santa Anita and Belmont Park, are 1 3/4 and 1 5/16 miles respectively, and large, less agile horses do well there.

For the Record

Some stallions whose descendants run well on the turf: Northern Dancer, Nijinsky, Roberto, Sadler's Wells, Gone West, Caro, and Silver Hawk.

Wet Turf

Turf courses don't produce mud, but they do change when they get wet. On an extremely rainy day, turf racing will be canceled and the race transferred to the main track. Many of the horses will be scratched, but those who remain may show some good performances on muddy main tracks. Examine the past performance charts to identify them. Foreign horses and those who've never run on a dirt track are usually poor bets when a turf race is transferred to the dirt.

If it's only a little damp and the race remains on the turf, the grass will be listed as good, yielding, or soft, depending on how wet it is. Some excellent turf horses despise wet grass, and you can usually pick them by studying their past performances.

Other Weather Concerns

Most weather-related problems will fit into your analysis of track conditions, but here are a couple of odd points to think about:

➤ Among Thoroughbreds, horses seem to prefer cold weather to warm, and their speed rises when the temperature sinks. Check the dates of previous races to assess good or bad performances.

➤ Mares often race best from the fall through winter, probably because they don't go into heat. A mare who can't beat male horses in the summer may be able to do it in the winter.

➤ Among Standardbreds, the very fastest times of all occur on hot, humid days. A horse who turns in a spectacular time when it's 90 degrees may not be able to duplicate the performance a week later when the thermometer reads 70.

The Least You Need to Know

➤ Most tracks have bias, usually making the rail either good or bad, and it's useful to identify what kind of horse they favor by watching a few races and studying the previous day's results.

➤ The smaller the track, the more it favors agile horses who get to the rail.

➤ Hard, fast tracks favor front runners, while deep slow ones favor horses who come from off the pace, but not from too far behind.

➤ You never know how a Thoroughbred is going to like an artificial surface until he actually races on it, while it doesn't seem to make as much difference to a harness horse.

➤ Muddy tracks favor front runners.

➤ Grass tracks tend to favor come-from-behind horses.

Chapter 13

The Long, the Short, and the In-Between

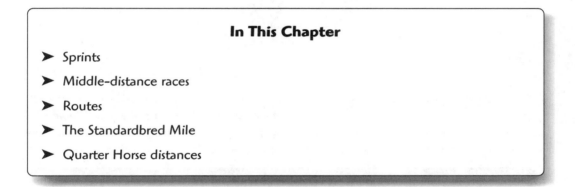

In This Chapter

➤ Sprints

➤ Middle–distance races

➤ Routes

➤ The Standardbred Mile

➤ Quarter Horse distances

In its earliest days, horse racing was intended to prove not only which horse was fastest but also which was longest of wind. There were 20-mile races—not 20 races of one mile each but one race of 20. There were even a few 40-mile races, where the winner was the last horse standing.

In the middle of the 19th century, as American racing was becoming more humane and better organized, the standard Thoroughbred race was still three or more heats of four miles each. People who went to the trouble and expense of racing horses, or even betting on them, wanted their money's worth.

Today, you'll see good horses who don't race that many miles in their entire careers. It's strictly a sport for the fleet of foot rather than the long of wind.

Short and Shorter

The shrinkage of racing probably has something to do with our dwindling collective attention span, but even though modern races are finished before old-time horses would even begin to stretch their legs, our horses do have to run faster than their ancestors.

Since horses vary not only in their speed but in their ability to carry speed over increasing distances, any variation in length matters. That fact can be frustrating to trainers, bettors, and horses alike.

Harness and Quarter Horse racing have dealt with the frustration problem by limiting the variation. Standardbreds race one mile, with a few exceptions that we'll talk about later. Quarter Horses almost always race 440 yards or less, also with a few exceptions.

In Thoroughbred racing, distances do vary. While this can be frustrating, it leads to excitement, opportunity, and even a little mystery.

For the Record

Quarter Horse racing has begun to discover the pleasures of frustration, adding an increasing number of longer distance competitions to their race cards. The fact that so much Thoroughbred blood has been added to the gene pool probably has something to do with it, too. Look for the most Thoroughbred–like horse to excel in any race longer than 600 yards.

What's Short and What's Not

Since racetracks and turf courses vary in shape and size, races of almost any length are possible. You'll see races identified as being "about 6 1/2 furlongs" or "1 mile and 70 yards" and "1 and 5/16 mile." But no matter how odd the number, all races fit into one of three general categories, making everyone's decision-making process a little easier. Here's what fits where:

Race	Distance
Sprint	7 furlongs and under
Middle distance	1 to 1 1/8 miles
Route	1 3/16 miles and up

You may find disagreement with these figures. Some people think that seven furlongs constitutes a middle distance, while 1 1/8 miles is a route. There certainly are some horses who would agree, especially as they're gasping for breath in the last half furlong of these races. But you can begin with these categories as you assess the horse and the race to see if they belong together.

From the Horse's Mouth

A **route** is a distance race, not the path a horse takes to get to the finish line.

The Sprinter

Most Thoroughbreds in North America are sprinters, possessing the physical shape and psychological orientation to run best at a short distance, at least compared to horses of the past. Review Chapter 3 for information on the characteristics of a horse with natural speed. In a nutshell: Look for a short body, wide hindquarters, muscles, and fairly short legs.

Six furlongs is the most common sprint distance, but you'll also see races of five, 5 1/2, and seven furlongs. Early in the year, some tracks schedule 1/2 mile races for two-year-olds.

It's not clear whether the horses were bred to suit the short races or whether the races were shortened to suit the horses, but it doesn't really matter. You'll find yourself paying most of your handicapping attention to the sprint distances.

The rules of sprint racing apply to all races of less than one mile, but you'll find that their importance is greatest the shorter the race is. Here they are:

➤ Inside post positions are best, unless there's an anti-rail bias at the track (see Chapter 12).

➤ A good break from the gate is vital. Otherwise, you lose.

➤ Early speed is equally vital, although a horse doesn't have to get an early lead to win.

➤ Contrary to popular opinion, sprints are often won by a horse who comes from behind, but never from far behind. If there are several horses who are likely to produce early speed, a horse who runs off the pace is likely to be the winner.

Inside Track

If the track's configuration causes a very long run to the first turn (a common occurrence in a seven-furlong race) the outside post position is preferable to an inside one for a horse with early speed.

The Middle Distance Horse

Middle-distance races are usually one or 1 1/8 miles, but you'll also see events of one mile 70 yards and 1 1/16 miles. The difficulty of the middle distance is also its glory. It's too long for a stamina-free sprinter, but it's too short for a speed-free plodder.

Physically, a middle-distance horse can look like a sprinter or a distance horse, but good ones tend to have the best characteristics of each. They'll have strong hindp-quarters, for example, but not so many muscles that they look like four-legged body builders. So they'll have the impulsion for speed but the lighter body weight needed for endurance.

But, as with all races, the proof is in the past performance. Look for your middle-distance winners like this:

➤ If you can't find a true middle-distance specialist (a horse with a good record at the distance), look for a sprinter to stretch out rather than a distance runner to speed up.

➤ Look for a horse with speed to get good early position. A horse can come from behind at the middle distances, but they aren't long enough for a real laggard to get there.

➤ Don't look too much at post position, unless there's an unusually short distance between the starting gate and the first turn. In that case, your horse should be as near as possible to the inside post.

➤ Look at weight, but you rarely have to make it the deciding factor. Figure five extra pounds will lose the horse 1/5 second, which equals a length.

From the Horse's Mouth

Stamina is the kind of endurance a horse needs to win beyond the shortest sprint distances.

Middle-distance races constitute only a small percentage of all races in North America, but they make up the majority of stakes events. So if you want to bet on the big ones, learn to identify the good prospects.

For the Record

Breeders also play close attention to the middle distances, and not just because they're prestigious and lucrative. Good middle-distance horses make the best breeding stock, hands down. Northern Dancer, Mr. Prospector, Seattle Slew—they all won at other distances, too, but they shone at the middle ones.

The most famous route race of all is the 1 1/2-mile Belmont Stakes.

The Router

There are even fewer races longer than 1 1/8 miles, but those few include the most prestigious ones. Routes are challenging to everybody.

Since few are actually bred for them, most modern horses would prefer to be heading back to the barn long before they get to the finish line of a 1 1/2-mile race. Trainers aren't much more enthusiastic, since they are faced with deciding whether to train for the few big ones or the many lesser ones.

Bettors often don't much like them either since past performance information is usually limited. But if you want to pick a winner in the Kentucky Derby, the Santa Anita Handicap, or the Breeders' Cup Classic, here are the rules:

➤ Effective routers are often light of body. They can be tall but not excessively heavy. They usually have modest musculature, but most have deep shoulders and wide chests for lung capacity.

➤ Past position doesn't matter, unless the field is so large that there's a danger of crowding at the first turn.

➤ Early speed isn't vital, but if only one horse in the race has it, he can steal away to a big early lead that nobody else can catch.

➤ Enough speed to stay in contact with the leaders (however fast or slow they are) *is* vital. Routes are almost exclusively for top-class horses, and such a field is rarely going to be caught by a horse who drops much more than a dozen lengths off the pace.

➤ Weight matters a lot. At 1 1/2 miles, figure a loss of two lengths for every five pound difference in weight. At 1 1/2 miles, it's more like 3 lengths.

From the Horse's Mouth

The **Triple Crown** consists of the 1 1/4-mile Kentucky Derby, the 1 3/16-mile Preakness, and the 1 1/2-mile Belmont Stakes, run between the first weekend in May and the second weekend in June.

Dosage

Every spring around Triple Crown time, talk of dosage pops up like tulips. Officially, it's the Dosage Index, a numerical assessment of a horse's distance running potential.

The formula, developed by Dr. Steven Roman, awards points to certain stallions who appear in the first four generations of a horse's pedigree. The mares are ignored, although their sires are included.

The formula has an excellent record, not of predicting who's going to win one of the Triple Crown races, but of separating those who can win from those who can't. Now, some questions and answers about dosage.

➤ Just how accurate is it? Very. Over the past 70 years, only a handful of horses lacking the correct figures have won any of the Triple Crown races. It's less useful in routes later in the year, but in the spring of a horse's three-year-old season, dosage rules.

➤ How hard is dosage to figure? Very. But you don't have to bother since the figures will be printed in racing publications during the five weeks of Triple Crown season.

➤ What's the magic dosage number? This one is easy. A Dosage Index of 1.0 is ideal, indicating a perfect balance of speed and stamina. You might assume that the horse whose dosage is closest to 1.0 is the most likely winner, but the formula isn't that magical.

History has proven that any horse whose dosage is less than 4.0 is equally likely to win one of the big races, whether his figure is 3.9 or 1.0. Since most of the horses entered will probably have the necessary figures, you should use them to eliminate prospects rather than to pick winners.

The Two-Turn Enigma

Some races are longer than others of the same length. Really. It's a result of the two-turn enigma.

Horses who compete in a one-mile race over a track that's a mile in circumference will go around two turns. A mile race on a 1 1/2-mile track will need only one. A horse that can win a one-turn mile may not have enough stamina for a two-turn mile. In fact, a horse who wins a one-turn 1 1/8-mile race may not have enough for a two-turn mile.

Actually, it's probably not such an enigma, since running around a turn requires more energy than running straight. But the problem exists, and if you're looking at a past performance chart that tells you that a horse won at a mile or 1 1/8 miles at Belmont Park, don't assume that he can run that distance at Churchill Downs or any other mile track. Until he's raced around two turns, he's still a sprinter.

Standardbred Racing

Despite its origins in a sport that featured competitions over distances as long as 50 miles, modern harness racing confines itself to short, uniform events. The races are normally one mile, and that fact means that you rarely have to consider distance in your handicapping equation. But rarely doesn't mean never.

Odd Distances

You'll occasionally come across races that aren't exactly one mile in length. They may be a fraction over or under one mile, usually because they have to accommodate a track whose size or circumference doesn't quite allow a mile race to finish at the wire.

If the variation from a mile is minor (it's usually just a few yards), you can analyze the race as if it were the standard distance. Just remember in studying past performance charts that fractional times will be different on these tracks. Use the track variant table published in almost all programs and past performance publications.

The race that's nowhere near a mile is very rare, at least in North America. They're sometimes shorter than normal, perhaps 3/4 mile, or they may be longer, either a 1 1/4 or a 1 1/2. They're generally added to a race card as an experiment to generate interest.

Trainers and drivers don't much like the odd races because they don't know how to condition or strategize for them. Bettors don't like them because there's not much past performance information available. Nobody asks the horses, but they would probably vote for the extra-short ones and opt out of the long ones.

If you're faced with a nonstandard race and want to bet on it, look for the obvious. In the short ones, try to identify horses who always leave well. In the longer races, look for horses who are in the habit of finishing strongly. There's no guarantee they can carry that strength beyond a mile, but there is an absolute guarantee that a horse who struggles at the end of mile won't get a sudden burst of renewed energy from additional yardage.

Inside Track

You'll occasionally find a horse who benefits from extra or fewer yards. Look for one who's usually caught at the wire or who can't get to the front until a couple of strides past the finish.

Heat Racing

There's one other situation where total distance varies: heat racing. This vestige of old-time racing is fast disappearing. When the sport's most famous event, the Hambletonian, shrank from heats to a single dash in 1997, the death knell for heat racing may have been wrung. But the corpse still has a little life in it, and some events, including a few major stakes, are still determined by heats.

In heat racing, a horse usually has to win two separate dashes to win the event. All horses compete in dash one and dash two. If the winner of dash one also wins dash two, he wins the event. If another horse wins dash two, they race off in dash three. Sometimes all horses race in three preliminary dashes, and sometimes the first dash is split.

Obviously, a horse needs endurance to race two or more miles on the same day, even though the miles have a little time between them. If you're trying to pick winners in heat races, do it like this:

➤ Assess the first heat as if it were any other dash, according to past performance, appearance of health and soundness, driver, trainer, and any other statistics you choose.

➤ Assess subsequent heats according to performance in the first heat.

➤ Then pay extra attention to appearance during the post parade in any heats after the first. Try to identify signs of exhaustion: sweating, reluctance to move out. Sometimes a horse will even manage to look a little thinner than he did in the first dash.

➤ Remember that order of finish in the first dash usually determines post position in the second. The winner is on the rail, the second place horse next out, and so on. This gives the first winner an automatic advantage at most tracks, particularly small ones.

➤ Check past performances for horses who always finish well. This might demonstrate stamina for heat racing.

➤ Look at how recently and how often the horse has raced. You want to see that the horse started within two weeks of the current event, but you don't want to see that he's started every week for two months. He's bound to be exhausted.

➤ Or just skip the bet and enjoy the race. Nowadays, only the best horses race in heats, and a good horse is always a joy to watch.

Quarter Horses

The standard length of a Quarter Horse race is 440 yards, although there are events ranging down to 220 yards for very young horses. In recent years, the sport has added races of 660, 770, and 870 yards, but they're still rare.

All but the two longest Quarter Horse races require neither strategy nor pacing since every horse runs as fast as he can for every step. Look for the soundest, most consistent, best-conditioned horse you can find without consideration for distance.

The 770s and 870s usually aren't won by the same horses who excel in the shorter races. Keep these points in mind in the distance events:

➤ Thoroughbred blood is useful. If the sire or dam is Thoroughbred, you'll see the letters TB next to its name. Unless you keep up with breeding, you won't be able to spot Thoroughbred blood any further back in the pedigree.

➤ A horse should show evidence of running very strongly at the end of the shorter races. He shouldn't be in the habit of being caught at the wire at a 1/4 mile.

➤ A horse should have an inside post position since the long races are run around turns.

➤ If you've seen the horses run before, look for one with a longer stride than the average racing Quarter Horse.

➤ Good starts are very important, but they're not quite everything as they are in the short events.

The Least You Need to Know

➤ In Thoroughbred racing, races are much shorter than they used to be.

➤ Races can be divided into sprints, middle distances, and routes, with different qualities needed by horses for each.

➤ Sprints are won by muscular horses with good hindquarters, inside post position, the ability to break well, and early speed.

➤ Most stakes races are at middle distances, although these distances constitute only a fraction of any day's race card.

➤ Middle-distance horses can look like either sprinters or routers.

➤ Middle-distance horses should be able to break well, but they have a little more flexibility than sprinters.

➤ Post position and weight are of moderate importance at the middle distances.

➤ Route races are rare, but they're almost always major events.

➤ Routers should be light of body and wide of chest.

➤ Post position doesn't matter very much at a distance, but extra weight does.

➤ Harness races are almost always one mile, so you don't have to worry about figuring distance.

➤ Don't think about distance in Quarter Horse racing either, except for the few events approaching a 1/2 mile. Then look for the Thoroughbred-type Quarter Horse.

Chapter 14

Keeping It Competitive

In This Chapter

➤ Claiming races

➤ Allowance races

➤ Stakes races

➤ Weight assignments

➤ Standardbred races

There's no such thing as equality among racehorses, any more than there is among NFL teams. Football tries to keep competition strong with a college draft that's supposed to make the bad teams better.

You can't make slow horses faster, but you can help even the slowest of them find races where they can be competitive. That's the job of racing secretaries.

If the Horse Fits

Racing secretaries design races of all kinds: races for good horses and bad ones, inexperienced horses and old campaigners, and male horses and females. Add to the mix the varying quality of racetracks, and you get races for horses of all kinds and talents.

But if every horse entered exactly the race it belonged in, the best of a bad bunch would almost always win, as would the best of a good bunch. No excitement and very little betting revenue.

So racing secretaries add some qualifications to each race to make it harder for everyone—things such as weight breaks for some horses make it harder for others, extra entry fees for stake races make it more expensive to take a shot at big money, and claiming makes it risky for everybody.

Finding the best race that a horse can win is the challenge for the horse's connections, and finding the best horse that can win a race is the challenge for the rest of us.

Claiming Races

The majority of flat races and a substantial percentage of harness races in North America are claiming races, in which every horse is available for purchase at a specified price. On any day's race card, you're likely to see claimers in all but one or two races.

For the Record

Modern claiming is a direct descendant of 19th-century *selling races*, in which the winner was auctioned off to the highest bidder after the race. These disappeared when it became obvious that a lot of trainers and owners preferred that their horses finish second, a fact that became clear to bettors only after seeing too many good horses finish second.

Because of their dominance, you must understand the principles of claiming races if you plan to bet on or even enjoy today's racing.

Who Can Claim?

Even though all the horses are for sale, not everybody can buy them. Rules vary from track to track, but usually only people who train or own at least one other horse at the track can drop a claim into the box.

This matters to all of us because owners and trainers receive at least a minimal background check before they are licensed. The license is no guarantee of honesty, but it does assure that they've never done time at a penitentiary for race fixing and fraud.

How Are Claims Made?

The claims are dropped into the claiming box before the starting gate opens. The successful claimant (more than one claim results in drawing lots) owns the horse as soon as the race starts, win, lose, or dead. This means that casual claims are usually not made.

Are All Claimers Cheap Horses?

No. Claiming prices are determined for each race by the racing secretary to approximate the value of the horses he hopes to attract to the race. Their value is, understandably, based on their racing ability. The price may range from $1,200 for the worst horses at a small track to $50,000 for the best claimers at a big track. Secretaries sometimes experiment with high-price claiming races (upwards of $100,000) but these are rare.

From the Horse's Mouth

A **claimer** is a horse who races in claiming races, not a person who claims him. A **reformed claimer** is one who used to be a claimer but has become too good to be risked, like multimillionaire and Horse of the Year John Henry. To run for a **tag** means to be entered for a claiming price.

Price matters to the bettor because the price the owner is willing to take for the horse is a good indication of his quality. A high price means the horse is sound and probably consistent. A low price, especially at small tracks, means the horse has serious problems. An extremely low-priced claimer who used to race at a higher level is probably very unsound. He's also in possession of an owner who should do the right thing and retire him.

Can They All Be Claimed for the Specified Amount?

Actually, no. Racing secretaries can do a great deal of fiddling with price to lure more horses as well as more interesting ones to any race. A secretary may set a base claiming price of $10,000, then give a three-pound weight break to any whose connections agree to a claiming price of $9,000 for their horse. Or he may give a break in both weight and claiming price to fillies and mares.

In Standardbred racing, where there's no weight assigned, racing secretaries use price almost exclusively to lure intriguing horses, especially better ones, to claiming races. A race for $10,000 horses needs better quality? The secretary will allow a 25 percent increase in claiming price for female horses, maybe 25 percent for three-year-olds, so a four-year-old gelding can be claimed for $10,000 while the three-year-old filly racing next to him will cost $15,000. The fans will probably see a better-quality filly whose trainer wouldn't risk losing her for $10,000 but might for $15,000.

Conditioned Races

In Standardbred racing you'll see conditioned races, in which the horses aren't necessarily subject to claiming. They often feature horses on par in talent with claimers, and you'll notice that their past performance lines may show starts in both other conditioned races and claiming races.

161

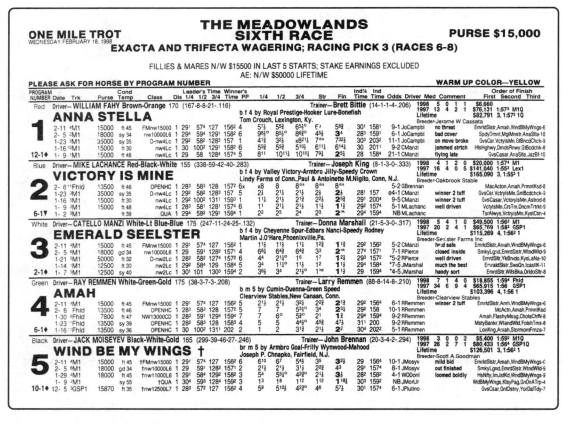

ONE MILE TROT
WEDNESDAY, FEBRUARY 18, 1998

THE MEADOWLANDS
SIXTH RACE

PURSE $15,000

EXACTA AND TRIFECTA WAGERING; RACING PICK 3 (RACES 6-8)

FILLIES & MARES N/W $15500 IN LAST 5 STARTS; STAKE EARNINGS EXCLUDED
AE: N/W $50000 LIFETIME

PLEASE ASK FOR HORSE BY PROGRAM NUMBER — WARM UP COLOR—YELLOW

(Standardbred past-performance chart for horses: 1 ANNA STELLA, 2 VICTORY IS MINE, 3 EMERALD SEELSTER, 4 AMAH, 5 WIND BE MY WINGS — with full race lines, drivers, trainers, times, and orders of finish.)

Here's a typical set of conditions in a Standardbred race.

Bad Bet

Never skip reading the conditions and qualifications at the top of the program page before every race. You may find a phrase that allows in a top horse against weak competition.

Conditioned races have qualifications for entry. The race may be open only to horses who haven't won $1,000 in their last five starts, horses who've never won anything, horses who haven't won as a three-year-old, or horses who *have* won in the past few months.

The conditions allow the racing secretary to fit the races to the available horses, just as claiming prices do. You'll even find claiming races with conditions, optional claiming races, and a few others.

Quinella,Exacta & Trifecta Wagering
1st Leg Pick 3
Freedom Village

6th

Allowance **Purse $9,700**

(INCLUDES $2,000 FOA). FOUR YEAR OLDS AND UPWARD WHICH HAVE NOT WON TWO RACES OTHER THAN MAIDEN, CLAIMING, OR STARTER SINCE OCTOBER 17, 1997 Weight 122 lbs. Non-winners of two races since November 17 allowed, 3 lbs. A race since November 17, 6 lbs. (Races where entered for $12,500 or less not considered in weight allowances).

Start · 5 Furlongs · Finish

Track Record: Arion Fair (4), 116 lbs; :57.1 (03-20-82)

Red
1 **GO KAZ (L)** — 8-1
Ch.g.'93 Sensational Luck-Phillip's Nannie by Sir Woodley
Breeder: S & K Stables (OH) (March 31, 1993)
Red, Blue "LL" on White Star
Owner: Miguel Feliciano & Leonard Longo
Trainer: Miguel Feliciano
Benny Feliciano 119

Turf:	1	0	0	0	$700	
Off Track:	2	0	0	1	$1,294	
1998:	1	1	0	0	$5,040	
1997:	11	2	2	1	$30,980	
Life:	28	6	5	4	$67,344	

01Jan98	6Tam	6f		ft	:2280	:4580	1:1140	4↑ Alw10400nw1/x	5	4	2hd	1hd	1½	1¾	Feliciano,B	bfL	116	10.10	81	GKz ¾,OrMthew ½,ThndringStorm hd	long drive, prevailed	8
08Nov97	4Tdn	1		wf	:4740	1:1260	1:3836	3↑ Alw12000nw2/r/x	5	21	21½	1hd	2½	33	Feliciano,B	bfBL	116	2.40	84	Jy'sMne 3,AlgbrHndrson ns,GKz 1	drew even, outfinished	6
26Oct97	12Tdn	1		ft	:4886	1:1340	1:3946	3↑ [S]Alw19800cnd	7	11	11	1½	2hd	21½	Feliciano,B	bfBL	116	28.00	81	PlsantAfair 1½,GKz 2¼,J.J.Hny 1½	set pace, second best	8
13Oct97	9Tdn	6f		ft	:2200	:4518	1:1104	3↑ [S]OhioSprint-50k	12	3	64½	54	77½	88¼	Felix,J	bfBL	122	24.90e	78	BuckCreek 3,GrapeJuice 1½,InandOver ¾	faded	14
21Sep97	12Beu	6f		ft	:2238	:4576	1:1045	3↑ [S]HoneyJayH-30k	5	7	64	1212	1216½	1226¼	Murphy,C	bfBL	114	64.10	55	Dnzcode 5,InndOver ½,AncentSecret nk	failed to menace	13
23Aug97	11Tdn	6f		ft	:2270	:4584	1:1100	3↑ Alw14000nw1$/x	6	1	42½	63¾	55	56¼	Feliciano,B	bfBL	116	8.00	77	RylOplnce 1¾,DncLgcy 2,OptmmMde 1	lacked late response	7
03Aug97	11Tdn	1		ft	:4806	1:1284	1:3950	3↑ Alw14000nw2/r/x	3	11	1hd	1hd	11	2nk	Feliciano,B	bfBL	116	7.20	82	ClMMarfa nk,GKz ½,Nsrlah'sFlet nk	outfinished, gamely	6
20Jul97	11RD	1 1/16	Ⓣ	fm	:4800	1:1240	1:4340	3↑ [S]Buckeye Na-35k	6	21½	2hd	2hd	76½	66¾	Troilo,W	bfBL	113	20.70	71	Dnzcode hd,TsAndy'sTm 4,Rchrd'sRb 1½	pressed pace, gave way	12
22Jun97	4Tdn	1		ft	:4774	1:1216	1:3776	3↑ Alw14000nw2/r/x	3	11	1½	2hd	42½	47½	Feliciano,B	bfBL	122	14.50	79	BckCrek 3,ImprialPas 3¼,RyalOpulence 1¼	dueled, tired	8
28May97	6Tdn	1		ft	:4854	1:1292	1:4010	3↑ Alw13000nw1/r/x	5	1½	1hd	1hd	1hd	1nk	Feliciano,B	bfBL	116	4.20	79	GoKaz nk,DJNorth ns,OutforGold 1¾	long drive, all out	7

Workouts: **15Jan Tam 3f ft :36.00 b** **23Dec Tam 4f ft :50.20 b** **15Dec Tam 4f ft :50.40 b** **05Dec Tam 3f ft :37.80 b**

White
2 **DEFENSE WITNESS (L)** — 9-2
Ch.h.'91 Skip Trial-Phi Theta Kappa by Arts and Letters
Breeder: Arthur I. Appleton & James R.Chapman (OH) (March 25, 1991)
White
Owner: Y. J. Games
Trainer: Gary Johnson
Heriberto Rivera Jr. 116

Turf:	4	0	0	0	$1,980	
Off Track:	4	1	0	1	$12,022	
1998:	0	0	0	0	$0	
1997:	1	1	0	0	$10,590	
Life:	32	11	3	4	$374,882	

15Nov97	11Tdn	6f		sy	:2284	:4626	1:1210	3↑ Alw13000nw1/9mx	3	4	1hd	11½	13	12½	Lumpkins,J	fBL	116	2.70	87	DfnsWtns 2½,OptmmMde 1¾,StrkWvngMd hd	led throughout,driving	6
14Oct95	12Tdn	1¼		sy	:4787	1:3860	2:0381	3↑ [S]OhioEndurc-150k	3	46	33	22	21	DNF	Madrigal, Jr.,R	fBL	122	1.70	---	RckyHi 11¾,MjrAdversary 2¼,DltHuse 2¼	pulled up lame late	11
30Sep95	10Tdn	1 1/16		ft	:5071	1:1501	1:4524	3↑ Alw11000nw2$/6mx	4	2½	2hd	2hd	12	15	Castillo,F	fBL	122	*1.10	91	DfnsWtns 5,KngTryOn nk,StrfthNght 1¾	drew off,much the best	6
02Sep95	11RD	1¼		ft	:4720	1:3860	2:0540	3↑ [S]GovBkyeCp-100k	6	39	32	24	24	1hd	Madrigal, Jr.,R	fBL	122	9.90	101	DfenseWitnes hd,MjorAdversary 3,KngTryOn 1½	long drive	13
06Aug95	12Tdn	1⅛		ft	:4806	1:1194	1:5023	3↑ [S]GLewisMemH-30k	6	43½	44	43	34½	56½	Madrigal, Jr.,R	fBL	122	*1.70	89	RockyHi nk,ReggiesTimeEx 5,KingTryOn nk	no excuse	7
23Jul95	9Tdn	1		ft	:4685	1:1225	1:3880	3↑ Alw12000nw1$/x	7	67	54	1hd	11½	11	Vidal,F	fBL	122	*.80	89	DfnsWtns 1,KngTryOn nk,Mr.Prmo 1	quick move, held well	7
25Jun95	7Tdn	1		ft	:4948	1:1465	1:4044	3↑ Alw9000nw2/x	3	42½	42½	41¾	11	12¾	Castillo,F	fBL	116	*.30	82	DfnsWtns 2¾,Mr.Prmo ½,J.J.Hny 4	closed wilingly,handly	5
16Jun95	10Tdn	6f		ft	:2208	:4438	1:1030	3↑ Alw9500nw2/x	3	6	56½	510½	46	22	Madrigal, Jr.,R	fBL	116	2.00	84	PlsPsePaul 2,DfnsWtns ¾,Dn'tstmpthflg ns	up for place	6
03Dec94	9Med	1 1/16		ft	:4588	1:0997	1:4213	3 WinterQtrs-40k	6	69½	510½	56	614	69¾	Molina,V	L	118	4.60	90	GlfRckng nk,NxtWve 5¼,Algdlmprson 1½	failed to respond	8
22Oct94	14Beu	1¼		ft	:4594	1:3638	2:0085	3↑ [S]OhioEndur-150k	9	1315½	106¾	54¼	41¾	31½	Madrid, Jr.,A	fBL	117	3.00	97	It'sJstMe 1½,Nlwn hd,DfnsWitnes 1½	outfinished for place	14

Workouts: **10Jan Tam 3f ft :39.00 b** **02Jan Tam 3f ft :37.20 b** **09Nov Tdn 5f ft 1:02.60 b 2/7** **31Oct Tdn 5f ft 1:03.80 b 6/6**

Blue
3 **HE'S DYNAMITE (L)** — 2-1
Ch.g.'92 Pancho Villa-Diggyliggylo by Olden Times
Breeder: Tom Gentry Farm (KY) (April 21, 1992)
White , Red "W "
Owner: Majestic Stables & Winning Stables
Trainer: Gerald Bennett
Ronnie Allen Jr. 119

Turf:	5	1	2	1	$39,160	
Off Track:	2	0	0	1	$2,790	
1998:	0	0	0	0	$0	
1997:	17	7	3	1	$78,959	
Life:	33	10	4	5	$119,605	

20Dec97	8Tam	5f		ft	:2180	:4500	:5800	3↑ Alw11500	2	4	2½	4¾	1½	1nk	Allen,R	bL	116	*1.50	84	H'sDynmte nk,BrscJck ½,FlshyLnk 2	dueled, just lasted	10
13Dec97	5Crc	5f	Ⓣ	fm	:2154	:4483	:5692	3↑ Alw28000	2	6	42¼	53	53½	52½	Allen,R	bL	117	7.00	87	Prklo ½,Mgabuck ¾,Hckofaralph ¾	good position inside	11
12Nov97	7Haw	5f	Ⓣ	fm	:2232	:4553	:5746	3↑ Alw30000	9	7	54	55	41¾	2¾	Lasala,J	bL	122	2.70	92	Mrks'Pwrply ¾,H'sDynmte ¾,LmnGrs 3	closed with a rush6w	9
11Oct97	7Kee	5½f	Ⓣ	fm	:2118	:4417	1:0296	3↑ Nureyev-65k	1	3	33	21½	21½	34¾	Albarado,R	bL	123	3.70	82	Ssaro ¾,Frd'sHofer 4,H'sDynamite ½	bid,hung stretch	10
04Oct97	8AP	5f	Ⓣ	fm	:2220	:4472	:5646	3↑ TaylorSpec-35k	2	7	92½	51¾	41¾	11¼	Lasala,J	bL	113	9.70e	94	H'sDynamite 1¼,GH'sPlasure ¾,LmonGras 2¼	rallied rail	10
11Sep97	5AP	a5f	Ⓣ	fm	:2249	:4600	:5757	3↑ Clm30000	3	6	62¾	52¼	21	2¾	Lasala,J	bL	113	20.30	81	Ziploose ¾,He'sDynamite 3,MovinOnBy 2	angled in hung	9
31Aug97	9Tdn	5f		ft	:2216	:4554	:5760	3↑ Clm25000	1	4	21½	22½	22	24	Cox,R	bBL	118	3.10	81	CmbrlndGap 4,H'sDynmte ¾,BprOn 2	no match for winner	5
23Aug97	7Det	6f		ft	:2200	:4520	1:1080	3↑ Clm23000	3	4	1hd	11	1½	*21¾	Allen,R	bL	115	5.00	79	JmJmJm(**dq6**) 1¾,H'sDynmt(p1) 2,AdrblRcr(p2) 1	weakened ,p1	6
16Aug97	9Det	6f		ft	:2220	:4480	1:1080	3↑ Alw18000nw2$/6mx	1	6	42¼	65¼	65	69¼	Skinner,C	bL	116	20.50	69	PongoBoy ½,Beamn'Reason 1¼,SilentEra hd	gave way turn	6
02Aug97	7Det	6f		ft	:2240	:4520	1:1120	3↑ Clm25000	6	2	31	2hd	1hd	43½	Skinner,C	bL	116	4.10	75	Kt'sDpty 1½,CmnchTril 2,RrRg ns	duel turn to lte strch	6

Workouts: **07Dec Tam 4f ft :52.00 b** **24Oct Det 5f ft 1:01.20 b 1/3**

Here's a typical set of conditions for an allowance race.

Allowance Races

These Thoroughbred and Quarter Horse events usually attract better horses than claiming races because the horse is not for sale. But they feature varying levels of competition, just like claiming races, and trainers still have to try to find the best race while bettors try to find the best horse.

Allowance races are similar to harness racing's conditioned events since they usually limit entry to horses who haven't won a certain number of races in a certain length of time. But racing secretaries can design allowance races for almost any horse they want to see entered. A race for horses who haven't won a race in 1999 might seem like one for pretty feeble animals, but it could allow in the millionaire Kentucky Derby winner of 1998. Always read those conditions.

The word *allowance* in allowance races means a break in the weights. A nonwinner since July might get a reduction of three pounds, while a nonwinner all year may get five. We'll have more on what weight breaks mean later, but note now that the reductions, as well as conditions, give trainers and bettors a chance to shop for the most lucrative potential race for a particular horse.

Maiden Specials

In flat racing, maiden specials are scheduled for horses, usually two-year-olds, who've never won a race but are too valuable to be entered for claiming prices. Unlike maiden claiming races, which usually feature the worst horses around, maiden specials may include potential champions.

Almost every horse makes its debut in a maiden special. Secretariat did, Cigar did, Silver Charm did. The joy of the maiden special is the possibility that you may see one of the great ones. The agony is that they are remarkably difficult to figure out.

Many serious bettors avoid maiden specials, without exception. Others look for signs of life in breeding, workouts, appearances, and connections and bet accordingly. Some of us prefer to watch and hope.

Stakes Races

Stakes represent the pinnacle of the sport, whether it's flat, harness, or steeplechase racing. Stakes races are always the most lucrative that the track offers, and the purses are increased by the addition of entry fees paid by the owners.

The presence of a horse in a stakes race isn't a guarantee that he belongs there. Some owners are willing to pay the fees for the pleasure of being in the saddling enclosure along with the owners of the really good horses.

It's more complicated, as well as more expensive, to enter a horse in a stakes than in other kinds of races, so you'll often find horses that belong in big races simply not there. Some races require modest eligibility payments by owners months or even years in advance. Most will allow horses not originally made eligible to be entered late by paying a stiff fee, but some still do not.

For the Record

Invitational stakes races feature the best horses available at the track. They're not all great (sometimes the track has to stretch its standards to fill up a field) but each theoretically has a fair shot at winning.

The Breeders' Cup in Thoroughbred racing and the Breeders Crown in harness racing require owners of stallions to pay fees to make their offspring eligible. The young horses' owners then pay continuing eligibility fees. Most owners of good horses are willing to make the investment since there're millions of dollars available every year in each series.

Handicap Races

In Thoroughbred racing, many stakes and some allowance races are handicaps, although there are fewer of them than there used to be. In handicap races, the racing secretary or an assistant assigns weight to each horse to try to even them up. The goal is to have every horse finish in a dead heat for first.

In reality, that's the last thing any track would really want since the outside horse would probably be racing so wide he'd be knocking the hot dogs out of the hands of the crowd at the finish line. But a blanket finish that includes several horses within a length of each other is among the most exciting events in racing.

A handicap is a challenge to assign, particularly nowadays with quick and easy transportation to other racetracks. Racing secretaries walk a fine line. If handicapping is done right, the best horse will receive so much weight that his trainer will probably take him elsewhere, and the worst horse will carry so little that his trainer will have trouble finding a jockey who can make the weight.

Most handicaps aren't really done well, and the race isn't going to come out anywhere near even. But there will be some variation in weight between the entries, and you will have to try to figure out what difference it might make in the outcome.

Weight Watching at the Racetrack

Weight has no official role in Standardbred racing, and it doesn't make a lot of difference in Quarter Horse racing, but it's important—sometimes the deciding factor—in Thoroughbred racing.

165

It's the subject of several of racing's favorite aphorisms:

➤ If a good horse is assigned a huge weight, you'll hear that "weight will stop a freight train."

➤ If he's had a big reduction in weight since his previous start, you'll hear that "weight off will move an elephant up."

➤ If he receives a very light weight, he's "in with a feather."

In nonhandicap events, weights are usually assigned according to the standard scale used in North America. The Jockey Club's Scale of Weights, also known as the weight-for-age scale, is the bible of weight assignments. It's a massive chart, with recommended weights for horses of varying age and sex, racing at each possible distance.

Both feathers and freight train-stoppers are included, with weights ranging from the 96 pounds to be assigned a three-year-old racing two miles in January to the 130 to be carried by an older horse going a 1/2 mile in December.

In the real world of racing, no three-year-old is ever going to race two miles in January, and conditions would assure that few horses will carry 130 pounds in any race at any time of the year, but the scale has some basic principles.

➤ Weight assignments go up as distance goes down, for horses of both sexes and all ages.

➤ Weights go up as the season wears down since the horses are supposed to be in better condition later in the year. Actually, many are never again as sound and fast as they are in the early spring.

➤ Female horses carry less than male horses. Two-year-old fillies carry three pounds less. Three-year-olds and up carry five pounds less until September, and then three pounds less (mares rarely come into heat in the fall and tend to be more competitive then).

The top weight in the average race at the average racetrack will probably be about 122 pounds, with conditions and allowances bringing the weight down for most of the horses entered. The weight each horse is to carry is always printed prominently in the program or past performance publication.

Why It Matters

Horses can carry a lot of weight, even at the gallop. Cow ponies, most of whom are considerably smaller than Thoroughbreds, can dash around under riders who weigh at least 50 pounds more than the heaviest jockey.

What horses can't do under a lot of weight is run as fast as they might otherwise. How much slower they run under how much more weight is the question. Unfortunately, there's no easy answer.

Here are some guidelines, subject to disagreement and variation from track to track. Remember that 1/5 second equals a length. Here's what extra weight means at the finish line:

➤ At a sprint distance, a horse will lose 1/5 second for every five pounds extra he carries.

➤ At a middle distance, he loses that 1/5 second for three to four pounds.

➤ At a route, he loses the 1/5 second for every two to three extra pounds.

➤ The heavier the weight, the more speed he loses, whatever the distance. If he's carrying 110 pounds, he probably isn't going to be much slower than the horse carrying 105, all else being equal. But at 125, he may be several lengths slower than the horse carrying 120 who is in all other ways his equal.

The Alluring Weight Loss

We're not talking newly discovered good looks here. Remember that one about a reduction in assigned weight making an elephant run faster? Don't rush to the betting windows to put your money on pachyderms. Some bettors are thrilled to see a horse assigned a lighter weight than he carried in his last start. They figure he'll be equally thrilled, running much faster with the joy of a reduced burden.

In fact, horses usually receive lighter weight assignments because they haven't been accomplishing anything. A horse who's been performing well recently should pick up a few pounds, not shed them.

There's one exception. A horse who's been racing under high imposts in handicaps will greatly appreciate the lighter weight of a scale weight event. He may move up dramatically.

Racing for Sport: Non-Betting Races

Racing has always tried to find a point of balance between its dual reasons for being: sport and betting. Every now and then, you'll come across a race that's just for sport. You can't bet on it, but you can learn from and enjoy it. Here's what you might see.

Walkovers

Only one horse shows up, having scared the other horses away. This only happens in stakes races where the racing secretary can't play around with conditions to lure opposition, and is even rare there since second money is normally 20 to 25 percent of the total purse. Horses don't walk when they walkover; they usually do a slow gallop around the track. You don't learn much from a walkover, but you do usually see a very good horse stretch his muscles.

Match Races

In these, two horses compete in special races designed for the matchup. The horses are almost always similar in ability and accomplishment. You are usually allowed to place win bets, but the odds on both horses are likely to be so low that it won't make sense to risk $2 for a $2.20 payoff, especially since match races often develop in inexplicable ways, with speed horses foolishly laying back and come-from-behind horses trying to make the pace. If you want to place that risky win bet, remember these points:

➤ Post position generally doesn't matter at all in a match race.

➤ Choose the horse who usually breaks fastest and hope that his rider or driver doesn't change policy. Match races are almost always won by the first horse out of the gate.

➤ If both horses like to break fast and race best on the lead, pick the horse whose record shows the most endurance, even if the two are sprinters. Fast, head-to-head racing early in a race is exhausting.

Steeplechases

Racing over fences is sometimes a betting sport, but it's often not. Major tracks such as Belmont, Saratoga, Monmouth, and Keeneland schedule occasional steeplechases as part of the regular racing calendar. These are betting races, with wagering accepted just like any other.

Major tracks rarely run claiming steeplechases since most owners believe that asking their horses to jump a dozen fences during the course of a two-mile race is plenty risky enough. Steeplechases of any kind aren't particularly popular with bettors, probably because they too believe they risk enough by watching their bets fly through the air before coming down on four fragile legs.

Other jump races are held at steeplechase meets, sometimes in states where there's no legal betting on horses. These meets are wonderful sport, with mostly amateur riders and well-cared for horses competing for sport more than money.

If you're hoping to pick steeplechase winners, whether there's money or pride on the line, follow these rules:

➤ A steeplechase is always a route race, so follow the route rules in Chapter 13.

➤ A good record on the flat is admirable, but success at sprints is no more useful than no experience at all. Look for flat race appearances in middle distances and routes to judge potential.

➤ Past performances in steeplechases are significant, but you're looking for consistency first. Avoid horses who fall. Unless they finish the race, they can't win, no matter how much speed and stamina they have.

➤ Post position and early speed don't matter, unless the first jump is close to the starting gate and the horse has only a short space to get into a good spot to take off.

➤ Behavior does matter since steeplechasers have a great deal of opportunity to bolt, stop, dump their riders, and otherwise destroy their chances. Horses are essentially out of control as they take off and descend from a jump, and any horse who wants to misbehave can opt out of the race at every obstacle.

Qualifiers and Training Races

All Standardbreds take part in non-betting races at some point in their careers. They are required to compete in qualifiers, proving that they are sensible and at least modestly fast, before they're eligible to race with fans' money on them.

Some qualifiers are held at training tracks and some at the regular racetrack. You can't bet on them, but you can usually watch. Qualifiers are hands-down the worst races to try to figure since you're dealing with a field of horses not ready to race for real.

Don't try to pick winners, but do pay close attention. Whether you attend or just review the qualifier in past performance charts, you'll find a horse's performance to be instructive. Just remember that a qualifier is not quite the same thing as a race. The differences to keep in mind:

➤ Qualifiers are usually slower than a betting race with the same horses would be. There's no money on the line, and the last thing the trainers want is pressure on the horse. He might break stride and fail to qualify.

➤ The trainer probably drove his own horse, and he might not be as talented at driving as the catch driver he'll hire for the actual race.

➤ Unless you were there or recognize the names of the other horses, you won't know the level of the competition. You may see that a horse won a qualifier by 10 lengths, but you won't know if he beat Mr. Ed or a future Niatross.

➤ Some trainers don't want more than an adequate performance by their horses in qualifiers. They want to be able to surprise the competition (and maybe cash a good bet) when real money is on the line.

But here's one final point to remember: Fast is fast. If a horse trots or paces a fast mile in a qualifier, he's a fast horse and is worth your attention in any race he enters.

Training races (you'll sometimes hear them called *trials*) for both Thoroughbreds and Standardbreds usually take place at training centers, and the public may be invited.

169

They are usually for very young horses, and they're often shorter than normal racing distance.

You may be able to pick out a future star, and you'll certainly enjoy watching the young animals, but training races may not be particularly instructive. Very young horses shouldn't be racing fast, so if you spot one who does, you're probably watching a future breakdown rather than a future champion. If you spot one who's slow or foolish, you can as easily chalk it up to immaturity as lack of talent.

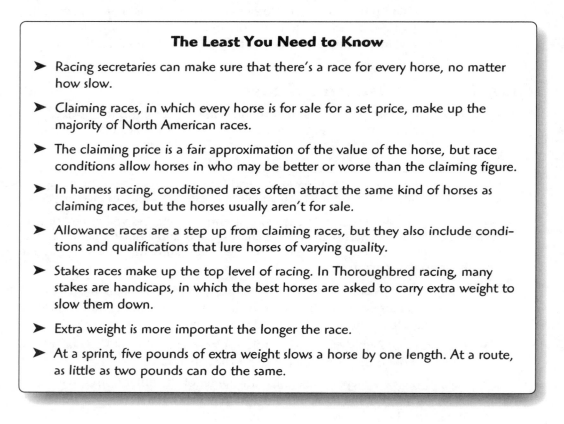

The Least You Need to Know

➤ Racing secretaries can make sure that there's a race for every horse, no matter how slow.

➤ Claiming races, in which every horse is for sale for a set price, make up the majority of North American races.

➤ The claiming price is a fair approximation of the value of the horse, but race conditions allow horses in who may be better or worse than the claiming figure.

➤ In harness racing, conditioned races often attract the same kind of horses as claiming races, but the horses usually aren't for sale.

➤ Allowance races are a step up from claiming races, but they also include conditions and qualifications that lure horses of varying quality.

➤ Stakes races make up the top level of racing. In Thoroughbred racing, many stakes are handicaps, in which the best horses are asked to carry extra weight to slow them down.

➤ Extra weight is more important the longer the race.

➤ At a sprint, five pounds of extra weight slows a horse by one length. At a route, as little as two pounds can do the same.

Chapter 15

Are Races Fixed?

In This Chapter

➤ Fixing and track size

➤ Ringers

➤ Jockeys and drivers

➤ Mechanical devices

➤ Drugging

There's no more dreaded pair of words to be uttered at any racetrack than "fixed race." At the same time, most track people would probably try to find out which race, what horses, and how it was to be done before turning in the malefactor.

How Prevalent Is It?

Race fixing frightens, angers, and intrigues everybody involved in racing. If you judge by the money, personnel, and worry that go into the prevention of race fixing, you'd think that skullduggery is rampant at the racetrack. It's not, for several very good reasons:

➤ There's no sport more closely watched for integrity than horse racing, probably because fraud at the track is both lucrative and alluring, and everybody knows it.

➤ Technology is fully involved in prevention of race fixing, what with DNA testing, ELISA tests, instant computer analysis of betting, and so on.

➤ It's not easy to fix a race. Horses are notorious for not doing what's expected of them.

Does this mean that there's no race fixing these days? No, because the allure is too great. There's not much, but it exists. Here's where it's most likely to occur:

➤ **At small racetracks.** It's not common, but the smaller the track, the more likely fixing is to happen. Smaller tracks usually have less security and more underpaid people close to the horses.

➤ **In low-purse races.** When a big purse is on the line, the people connected to the horses would rather take an honest shot at the honest money. Of course, some of them want more than an honest shot and try to improve the chances of their horses illegally, but even they tend to stick to lower-level races. Big events attract too much attention.

➤ **In races that offer exotic wagering.** The high payoff potential of the trifecta has lured the occasional group of jockeys into a few minutes of crime as they maneuver certain horses in or out of the top three.

From the Horse's Mouth

Exotic wagering is any bet other than the traditional win, place, or show (first, second, or third) individual bets. The **trifecta**, also called the *triple*, requires the first three horses to be chosen in order. More in Chapter 16.

The possibility of race fixing is not something to spend much time worrying about. If you hear somebody talking about it, you can probably assume it's not true. Even if it is, rest assured that it hasn't been undertaken to help you. Still, the concept is intriguing even to devoted nonparticipants. Here's what's possible.

Ringers

A *ringer* is a horse who races under a name and identity other than his own. The first ringer probably raced in ancient times when a sharp-eyed charioteer noticed that two brown horses, one fast and one slow, looked an awful lot alike. What might happen, he asked himself, if he hitched the fast horse to his chariot and told everybody it was the slow one? He would have two things: a horse that would run faster than anyone expected and the first ringer.

Why Ringers Work

Horses may not look alike to other horses, but many of them do to even observant humans. The three primary racing breeds are not known for their gaudy and unusual coat colors. Standardbreds are mostly bay, and many have no white at all on their faces or legs.

Thoroughbreds and Quarter Horses are a little less uniform, but even they come in only a handful of colors. Theoretically, it would be possible to get easy purse money and big payoffs at the betting window with little chance of being caught, just by entering one horse in the name of another.

But it's also no secret that many horses look alike, and the racing industry puts a great deal of time and money into making sure that the 20-1 shot Gray Mouse that runs in a race you're betting on really is Gray Mouse, and not a Silver Charm looking for a big win at long odds.

The lip tatoo is the simplest and most widely used method of race horse identification.

How They're Stopped

The antiringer techniques range from basic to high-tech. The methods are slightly different for each racing sport, but a horse can be identified in the following ways:

➤ He's photographed and described on his registration papers when he's a young foal, long before anyone knows whether he's going to be fast or slow.

➤ His unique hair growth patterns on the head and neck, known as *cowlicks*, are carefully described. Horses also have chestnuts, or night eyes. These vestigial horny growths on the leg are like fingerprints, unique to each horse. They're difficult to photograph, but they can serve as an identification tool.

➤ He's tattooed on the inside of his upper lip before he races. The tattoo is the primary on-track identification tool, and each horse's lip is checked before each race.

➤ He's probably had a DNA test, or at least his parents have. All three racing breeds are in the process of establishing a DNA registry, primarily for parentage verification. The science doesn't yet exist for DNA to be used for prerace identification, but it may someday.

For the Record

The horse identifier stands at the entrance to the paddock or saddling enclosure. He folds up each horse's lip to check the number against a list of the horses entered for each race. It's possible to alter a tattoo, but the identifiers are highly skilled at noticing changes.

All the antiringer techniques except DNA testing have been in use for decades. Even so, a ringer case pops up every now and then. A few altered tattoos have been discovered, as have a couple cases of young horses being misidentified and tattooed with the wrong number, probably by accident.

The most celebrated recent ringer case occurred during the 1970s in New York. It involved a veterinarian who imported two South American horses who looked a great deal alike. They didn't run alike; one was an outstanding stakes horse while the other was a cheap nobody.

The cheap horse, starting at extremely long odds, surprised everyone in America with a big win and high payoff. Except it wasn't the cheap nobody, who was actually dead and buried under the good horse's name. The vet was caught, proving that it isn't that easy to fix races, at least not with ringers.

Mechanical Means

The good thing about the use of mechanical means to affect the outcome of races is that they're usually obvious and reasonably easy to detect. The bad thing about them is that they're almost always cruel to horses.

Some are designed to slow a good horse down, while others encourage him to run faster. Here are some of the possibilities.

Pain-Causing Devices

Although, in general, horses don't perform well when they're hurting, momentary pain can prompt a burst of speed. It's the nature of horses to run away from things that frighten them, particularly painful things, and everybody who works around horses knows it.

One pain-causing device is legal. It's the whip, used in all the racing sports.

For the Record

Spurs are illegal in flat racing and pointless in harness racing. They'd be difficult to apply, anyway, given the length of jockeys' stirrups.

The kind of whip and the style of whipping is regulated and closely watched by the stewards. Jockeys and drivers are regularly given fines and even suspensions for excessive use of the whip. But some still try to sneak in illegal, unusually painful whips, perhaps shorter and stiffer ones that cut, or whips with a spiked end. The cheaters are usually caught because illegal whips often draw blood.

Batteries

A little harder to detect than an illegal whip is the portable shocking device known as a battery or a buzzer. The jockey applies it to the horse's neck or flank, surprising him into sudden speed.

Paddock judges, outriders, and stewards pay close attention to the actions of riders before and during races, particularly at smaller tracks. Batteries have been known to fall out of the pockets of cheating riders as they mount or dismount.

Sponges

The mechanical device of choice these days seems to be the sponge. This seemingly benign object, present in every tack room and kitchen, can stop a horse cold when stuffed into his nostrils.

That's exactly what race fixers have been doing at some Midwestern tracks for the past couple of years. Someone, probably a person with legitimate access to the backstretch, inserted sponges into the nostrils of certain horses before selected races, causing them to run much slower than expected.

They weren't detected immediately because equine nasal passages are long and the sponges were pushed deep inside. Their use was eventually discovered after enough good horses ran poorly, appearing to be unreasonably short of wind. In one case, the use of a sponge contributed to the death of a horse.

So nostrils are more likely to be examined before races these days, or at least some nostrils are looked into at some racetracks. It's difficult and time-consuming to examine horses for the presence of sponges.

Human Hands

Without mechanical assistance, there's no way that a jockey or driver can fraudulently make his horse win. Yes, he can commit fouls against other horses, but these will be spotted and the win will be taken away. But there are several things he can do, ranging from the terrible to the not-quite-right to the occasionally okay, to help his horse not win.

From the Horse's Mouth

Two or more horses trained and/or owned by the same person constitute an **entry**. If you bet on one, you bet on them all, getting two or more horses for the price of one.

Bad Bet

Most trainers want each of their horses to run as well as they can, but some prefer one to another. Watch out for nonentry horses trained by one person. You don't know his preferences.

The Terrible

Jockeys and drivers have been known to ask their horses to slow down so that another horse can win or finish in the top three. It's known as *pulling, stiffing,* or *stopping* a horse.

Some do it because they were paid to do it with an up-front fee or a cut of the winnings on the other horses. Some do it at the request of trainers they want to please.

Most racing jurisdictions have rules regarding multiple horses entered by the same trainer or owner, requiring both (or all) horses with the same connections to be considered one horse for betting purposes.

The entry rule is intended to reduce the possibility that a bettor might be victimized by a trainer or owner who would prefer that one of his horses wins rather than another. Some tracks join horses either owned or trained by one person, while others require only horses owned by the same person to be considered an entry.

Entries aside, trainers and owners occasionally want their horses to lose for reasons that have nothing to do with the current race. They may believe that if the horse loses today, he'll run next week at longer odds, with better conditions, with lesser weight, and won't attract claims.

Whatever the possible motives, the jockey or driver who wants to pull a horse has to be subtle about it because the stewards are watching closely for evidence that horse and human aren't making the effort they should.

The Not-Quite-Right

Sometimes jockeys and drivers, once they know they're not going to win, allow their horses to give up. Their fee for a second or third place finish isn't that high, after all.

But that second or third place can be vital to a bettor who has money on a horse in an exotic wager or for place or show. So every rider and driver is expected to persevere to the finish line, and stewards will punish them if they don't, even though their motive may be laziness rather than larceny.

The Occasionally Okay

Trainers sometimes ask riders and drivers to take it easy with a horse. Strictly speaking, they're not asking that the horse lose. They would be perfectly happy with a win, as long as it's easy and non-stressful for the horse. But the horse is really in the race for conditioning, sharpening, or testing and not for winning. Stewards tend to look the other way on this practice, as long as nobody makes an obvious effort to lose. Of course, money put unwittingly on the horse is just as lost.

Bad Bet

Most horses should be avoided in their first race after a long layoff. They're probably out of racing condition anyway, but they're the ones most likely to have a trainer who neither expects nor wants much of an effort.

This intentionally modest effort, done for the sake of the horse rather than betting fraud, is the most likely kind of less-than-straightforward race that you're likely to see at a major racetrack. This is especially true for top-quality horses whose health and condition are more important than any single race.

Drugs

Drugs are used on race horses for legitimate reasons, to cure disease and ease pain. They're also used for not-so-legitimate purposes, to make horses run faster or slower than God and circumstance intended them to do.

Refer to Chapter 5 for information on the kinds of drugs used on horses, what they do, and how testing takes place. Note a couple of points here on how illegal drug use effects the bettor, other than the obvious one of making the race turn out differently than it might have if all the horses ran clean:

➤ There is little prerace testing in any of the racing sports. An official vet gives each horse a quick look and sometimes a simple blood test in the hours before the start, but only obviously drugged animals are detected. This may change as drug testing becomes more sophisticated and offers quicker results.

➤ Postrace test results are slow in coming. The race is made official, the bettors are paid according to the order of finish, and the urine samples go off to the lab. If, weeks later, the samples turn up positive and the results are overturned, the purse is redistributed, but the betting payoffs are not.

➤ Sometimes you won't even know from past performance charts if a horse won or lost because of an illegal drug. A disqualification notation is eventually printed, but a horse may start again one or more times before a drug disqualification for a previous race is finalized.

Track Security

Several private and governmental agencies are involved in protecting the integrity of American racing.

➤ The track provides the first level of protection against race fixing. It employs guards to protect the barn area against intruders and the front side against thieves, pickpockets, and other scoundrels.

➤ The state provides the next level, through its racing commission, gambling board, or similar agency. This agency is the most powerful in racing within each state, since it maintains the right to license, suspend, disqualify, and otherwise control who participates and who doesn't. Drug testing is under the supervision of the state.

➤ The breed registries—the Jockey Club, the American Quarter Horse Association, and the United States Trotting Association—each control registration and identification of young horses. The Jockey Club and the USTA also maintain the rules of racing for their sports. The states may override these rules, but they seldom do except in the minor cases.

➤ Racetracks themselves finance two related investigative agencies. The Thoroughbred Racing Protective Bureau and the Standardbred Investigative Services look into people and incidents that threaten racing's integrity, mostly involving race fixing.

Race fixing is a crime, and suspected cases are investigated and charges are brought by the appropriate police agency. In many cases, it's a federal crime since simulcasting, off-track betting, and shipments of horses and drugs involves racing in interstate commerce.

The Least You Need to Know

➤ Race fixing exists, but it's less common than interest in it might suggest.

➤ Fixed races are more likely at small tracks with lax security and poorly paid employees, in low-purse races, and in races that offer exotic wagering.

➤ Ringers are unlikely in modern racing, thanks to several levels of identification.

➤ Mechanical devices like batteries and sponges can be used to make horses run faster or slower than they might otherwise, but the detection level is high.

➤ Jockeys or drivers may pull a horse to allow other horses to win for betting purposes, but that's watched closely by the stewards.

➤ They may follow a trainer's orders not to make the horse work too hard, and stewards may not mind as long as it's not obvious.

➤ Illegal drugs are tested for after every race, but a drug positive that overturns the results won't effect the bettor. He's paid or not paid according to the finish on the track.

Part 4
The Game

Finally, we've reached the nitty gritty, the dollars and cents, the crux of the matter. If you've gotten this far, you have sufficient background to understand what's going on at the racetrack. Now, you've got to understand what happens at the betting window.

In the first couple of chapters, we'll take a look at what really happens when you put money on a horse. You'll get a little background on the way people used to bet and learn about how old-fashioned betting has evolved into the modern pari-mutuel game. Then you'll hear about the betting pools and how they create the odds, the kinds of bets you can make, and what you can expect to collect if you win.

You've just spent considerable time reading about all the complications involved in picking winners, so we'll tell you about how to simplify it all with systems and money-management methods. Finally, we'll see how the computerization of the world has impacted—and in a big way—the racing world.

Chapter 16

Pari-Mutuels, Bookmaking, and Other Risky Business

> ### In This Chapter
>
> ➤ Private bets, bookmaking, and auction pools
>
> ➤ How pari-mutuel betting works
>
> ➤ Odds and payoffs

Gambling, for better or worse, has been around about as long as human beings have. In fact, a couple of *Homo erectus* probably made a bet on whose children were going to evolve into *Homo sapiens* first.

Horse racing proved to be a natural for gambling, providing both excitement and mystery whenever one horse tested its speed against another. For most of its history, betting on horses was a private transaction between individuals. It was enjoyable, but not necessarily lucrative.

Unless your companion in wagering was wealthy, there was a limit to how much money you could win. What's more, it was hard to get paid when you did win. Many bets were made with promises rather than cash, and it could be impossible to collect money that the losing bettor didn't have. Add to that the difficulty of finding a fellow bettor with the precise opposite opinion to yours, and you had a problem.

The First Betting Business

Professional bookmaking found an audience waiting for it when it emerged in England around 1800. The bookmaker took bets from a number of people, paying off the winners with the money of the losers.

In effect, he was making private bets with each person, and he stood to win everything if they all bet on losers, but he also stood to go bankrupt if they all chose winners. Bookmakers helped their own chances by offering odds so that people who wagered on highly regarded horses wouldn't get much in the way of payoffs, while those who bet on outsiders had the chance of winning a jackpot.

Bookmakers varied in their ability to set odds for the best chance of profit for themselves. Some individuals failed, but the institution of bookmaking flourished.

In spite of its success in England, the institution initially found limited welcome in America. Private betting lasted longer here, possibly because bettors were willing to wager and accept in payment items other than cash. Andrew Jackson, a few years before his presidency, wagered and won $1,500 worth of clothing, as well as several ladies' saddles when his great horse Truxton won a match against another horse.

For the Record

Early presidents were great racing fans. George Washington's diary reports wins and losses in bets on Narragansett Pacers, a now extinct breed. Andrew Jackson was the biggest fan, though. Truxton's winnings, and Old Hickory's winning bets on him, helped finance his presidential campaigns.

When the American sport was ready for more, it was auction pools rather than bookmaking that swept the racing world.

A Dip in the Auction Pool

The auction pool form of betting was lucrative to its operators, popular with the well-to-do, and unfair to the small bettor. It worked a little like the Calcutta bet in golf: The pool organizer would auction the chances of each horse to the highest bidder, with all money going to the person who bought the winner (after a healthy deduction to the operator).

The problems with the pools were obvious. People with the most money going in could buy up all the good horses, leaving only the bad horses to everybody else.

From the Horse's Mouth

The word **pool** refers, of course, to the concept of pooling the money before dividing it. In New York, the rooms where auction pools were conducted were called poolrooms, and fans played billiards to pass the time between auctions. Poolrooms live on, but not in racing.

Bets in auction pools were very public, and a good handicapper's lead could be followed by anyone.

Enter the bookmaker, who would take bets on any horse from anybody. You didn't need a lot of money to place a bet on a good horse, and the bets you did make could be make in private.

Bookmaking, American-Style

By the end of the 19th century, bookmaking had come to dominate racetrack betting in North America. Bookmakers set up at tracks, paying a daily or yearly fee to the management, and they also set up off track. Almost everybody who wanted to bet did it through bookmakers, even though many bettors weren't entirely satisfied.

Unlike in pools, people could bet on any horse they chose, and they could pick and choose the odds they were willing to accept. Once their ticket was paid for, however, the odds were set in stone, no matter what the horse looked like when he actually stepped onto the racetrack.

The fact that odds were inflexible and that different bettors could get different odds on the same horse, and the even more significant fact that the bookmakers themselves got to keep anything they didn't pay back to winners, led to rampant abuses. Bookmakers paid for information and paid for horse tampering. They suckered people to bet on horses they knew wouldn't start. They bribed jockeys with a cut of their winnings.

Enter Monsieur Pierre Oller and his machine for conducting a new kind of auction pool.

Pari-Mutuels

In France, 19th century bettors referred to pools as *mutuels*. Most of the big races were in Paris, so when M. Oller's machine arrived in America, it became known as the Pari-mutuel. It's appearance in North America in 1875 horrified both bookmakers and the remaining pool operators. They managed to suppress the new device for a few years, but its eventual takeover was inevitable. Today, pari-mutuel wagering is the only legal form of betting on horses available in almost all of North America.

M. Oller's system answered the complaints about both of its rivals. It was less subject to cheating by dishonest operators, it was private, and it allowed anyone to bet on any horse.

Bettors were slow to take to it because some people didn't trust the calculations and didn't believe that the operator couldn't care less which horse won and which lost. But that's the entire point. You don't beat the racetrack or beat the pari-mutuel machine when you win big. You beat everybody else who bet on the race.

How Pari-Mutuels Work

At its most basic, the pari-mutuel system is simple. Every bettor who wants to participate in a race picks the horse he thinks will win. The money paid by all of the bettors is pooled.

When the race is over, the pooled money is divided up evenly among everyone who bought a ticket on the winning horse. It makes no difference to the track, which operates the pool, which horse wins. It isn't their money that's paid out; it's the money of the people who hold the losing tickets.

Although the winners each get a share, they don't get exactly the same amount. First, all winners are repaid for their initial investment. The person who bet $2, gets $2 back. A $50 bettor gets back $50. This is the *return* on the bet. The remainder of the pool is then divided among the winners according to units of $2. The $2 bettor has one unit, while the $50 bettor has 25 units.

The *profit* on the bet is figured by dividing the number of units possessed by all the bettors into the pool that remains after the return, and then distributing it to the bettors according to the number of units each owns.

Let's pause now for a little arithmetic (proving that the required four years of math in high school really was worthwhile). Here's an example. Follow the steps, or just leap to the conclusion.

➤ Total pool of an imagined race: $450

➤ Two people bet $50 each on the winner (each has 25 $2 units)

➤ Twenty-seven people bet $2 each on the winner (each has one $2 unit)

➤ Return to winning bettors on their initial investments: $154

➤ Profit due to winning bettors: $296

➤ Units outstanding = 77

➤ Each unit is worth $296 ÷ 77 or $3.84

➤ The winning $50 bettors each receive $146 ($96 profit plus their $50)

➤ The winning $2 bettors each receive $5.84 ($3.84 profit plus their $2)

➤ Totals: $146 × 2 = $292; $5.84 × 27 = $157.68

➤ Returned to winning bettors: $292 + $157.68 = $449.68

Now, having used all that remembered math, here's some bad news. That's not really what you get back.

Takeouts and Breakage

There's *takeout* and *breakage* in each race, and this doesn't mean that a losing bettor had a temper tantrum in a nearby Chinese restaurant. What it means is that less than 100 percent of the entire pool is divided up among the holders of the winning tickets.

The track withholds between 14 and 18 percent of the pool before distribution as the combined profit of the state and the racetrack. The figure varies, depending on how much the state thinks it deserves. That's takeout.

The track's percentage goes to its operating expenses, including salaries, plant maintenance, and purse money. Admission, parking, and food prices at racetracks are usually much lower than at other sporting events, and they make up only a small percentage of the money needed to put on the racing show. The tracks rely on takeout from betting to keep going.

Both bettors and tracks wish state legislatures would be a little less greedy in demanding their cut, but they've had little luck in convincing politicians to reduce what is in effect a tax on gambling so racing's takeout remains higher than in most forms of gambling.

The track and the state have another sneaky little way of separating money from winning bettors. It's breakage, which is the policy of rounding off payoffs to the next lowest dime.

Say the computation of the total pool and the amounts due each winning bettor works out to a payoff of $4.74 for each dollar bet. The track pays out $4.70, keeping the 4 cents for itself. The money is often placed in a special fund to make up the difference in a minus pool, but it's sometimes just added to the overall profit figure.

There's a separate pool maintained for each kind of bet in each race. For example, if you're betting to win, your money is combined with that of everybody else who's betting to win and not those who are betting to place or show.

In these days of high-speed, high-capacity computers, a remarkable number of pools can be maintained for bets on the same race. In the next chapter, we'll talk about the different kinds of bets you can make, and how you go about it. But whatever the bet and whichever the pool, the principle of odds applies. Since we're in a mathematical mood, let's cover that area now.

Inside Track

The fact that racing's takeout is high doesn't mean you should spend your money on lottery tickets or video slots. Racing always gives you more opportunity to use skill and less reliance on chance than any other betting sport.

From the Horse's Mouth

A **minus pool** is one in which there's not enough money to pay back everybody who bet on a horse, plus the track's minimum profit of 10 cents on the dollar. It can occur when an outstanding horse is heavily bet and wins as expected.

Odds Are, You'll Be Confused

Using the common definition, odds are nothing more than somebody's estimate of the relative chances of two or more competitors. Three-to-one means that something or someone has three chances in four of winning.

In racing, odds have a more specific meaning. A horse's odds represent the percentage of the pool wagered on him. They're the figures used to determine the payoffs.

The odds you hear are always based on the win pool. It's possible to determine odds for place and show, but it requires more mathematical skills and patience than most of us have. In those pools, the winner has to be taken out of the equation, so you potentially have dozens of possibilities.

Consider any odds you hear to be for the win. Here's an example of how odds are determined.

First Race at Heavenly Downs

Win Pool: $100,000		
#1 Angel Toes	$50,000	1-1
#2 Winged Glory	$25,000	3-1
#3 Gabriel's Triumph	$20,000	4-1
#4 Saint Peter	$5,000	23-1

Inside Track

Notice that lists of odds don't include any shorter than 1-9 or longer than 99-1. Modern pari-mutuel systems can figure odds shorter and longer, but most boards can't display them. You'll get the real payoff, not the payoff for 99-1 if the odds are more or less than displayed.

At odds shorter than 1-9, you're in the minus pool anyway and will get the minimum amount.

Only at Heavenly Downs will these odds actually be in effect. Down here on earth, takeout and breakage come out of the pool before you determine odds, so the real ones (as well as the resulting payoffs) are lower. Fortunately, you usually don't have to know the pool and its breakdown or do the math yourself to figure a horse's odds.

Every track calculates odds for each horse based on the amount of money currently in the pool. Once the race has started and betting is closed, it will figure the final odds on which the payoffs to the winners will be based. By tradition, payoff figures are based on a $2 bet, even though odds are worked out based on one dollar. There's a reason for this. Two dollars used to be the minimum bet.

Tradition survives, even though most tracks now permit bets of any amount from a dollar up. Once you know the payoff for $2, you can figure what you'll get for any other amount.

➤ For $2, divide the amount in two.

➤ For $5, multiply by two and a half.

➤ For $10, multiply by five.

➤ Et cetera.

As for the payoffs you'll get for a win at various odds, here's the simplest way to figure them. First, make sure the odds are based on one. Change 5-2, for example, to 2 1/2 to 1. Then multiply the first number by two. Add your initial $2 investment to the total, and you have your payoff for a $2 bet.

The formula isn't entirely accurate at very short odds because, among other things, there's a minimum profit that you'll get even if everybody holds a winning ticket, and there's no losers' money to spread around. But you'll find it works just fine for most horses in most races. If you don't want to do the math, the following table shows a selection of payoffs on a $2 bet for various odds.

Odds	Payoff
1-9	2.20
1-5	2.20
2-5	2.80
1-2	3.00
Even (1-1)	4.00
7-5	4.80
2-1	6.00
5-2	7.00
3-1	8.00
7-2	9.00
4-1	10.00
5-1	12.00
6-1	14.00
7-1	16.00
8-1	18.00
9-1	20.00
10-1	22.00
15-1	32.00
20-1	42.00
50-1	102.00
99-1	200.00

The tote board is both map and lifeline to people hoping to win at the races.

The Tote

Racing was an early and enthusiastic user of computers, and racetracks feature the largest video display terminal around. It's the tote board, which sits in massive splendor in the middle of the infield directly across from the grandstand. Smaller, less informative versions are scattered around the track. One or another is visible from most of the public areas. People who go to the racetrack and sit in front of a television screen to watch the races will see an electronic version of the tote on the screen, as will people who go to simulcast facilities.

For most racegoers, the tote board is the map that directs you in and out of the labyrinth of the racing game. The name comes from the Totalisator Company, which used to operate most of the computerized betting systems in North America. Today, other companies operate systems and boards, but the behemoth of the infield is still known as the tote board.

Depending on how much money the track is willing to spend on the board and the computer system, the tote can display a lot of information or hardly any.

The bare minimum shows:

➤ Time of day

➤ Post time to the next race

➤ Approximate odds of each horse in the next race (you'll see program numbers rather than names)

➤ Results and payoffs of the last race. These are removed as betting progresses on the next race, so nobody is confused. The win, place, show, and fourth-place positions are then used to show the changing order during the next race.

A mid-range board will add:

➤ Dollar amounts of pools for win, place, and show

➤ Fractional and final times of the last race (this disappears as betting progresses)

➤ Fractional and final times of the current race

➤ Track condition

➤ Scratches

➤ Inquiry sign

Top of the line will add:

➤ Weather

➤ Equipment or jockey changes

➤ Mud caulks

➤ Potential payoff for win bet

➤ Pools or potential payoff for exotic bets

➤ Any other information the track deems important

When a track has limited tote space, information other than betting figures will be given over the public address system. You have to both listen and remember to take advantage of it. The tote is much more convenient, and serious racegoers believe that there's no such thing as too much on the tote.

There is, however, such a thing as too big a tote. At some tracks, you can miss much of the race because the horses disappear behind the board for a good chunk of the race. This is one case in which viewers of simulcasts have an advantage.

The information on the tote board is tied directly to the computers that keep track of the money bet. The figures are constantly changing, but they do lag behind reality. You won't know the true size of the pools and the actual starting odds until the race is over. Betting is closed at post time, which is supposed to precede the actual start by only a couple of seconds. That isn't time to show you the money that got into the system just before the windows close. You'll have to wait until the race is over to get the final odds and the payoff.

Bad Bet

While it's useful to pay attention to the pool, the odds, and any money that comes in late (late money is supposed to be smart money—from knowledgeable people), cutting it too late can get you cut out of betting. Because of similcasting, most betting facilities close the windows precisely at scheduled post time.

The Least You Need to Know

➤ The modern pari-mutuel betting system has become the legal system of choice in America, beating out bookmakers and betting pools.

➤ In pari-mutuels, winners' winnings come from losers' losses. If you win, you don't beat the track, you beat other bettors.

➤ The bets are pooled for each category of wager, and payoffs come out of that pool alone.

➤ Odds and payoffs are determined by what percentage of the pool was bet on the winning horse.

➤ Figure what you'll get for a $2 bet by multiplying the first number of the odds by two and adding $2.

Chapter 17

Picking Your Spots

In This Chapter

➤ How to place a bet

➤ Straight bets

➤ Exotics

➤ Wheeling and boxing

There may be no group of people, other than maybe Bill Gates and his heirs, who have benefited more from the computerization of the world than people who bet on horses. To bet legally, you used to have to travel to the racetrack and line up at the window that sold tickets in the amount you wanted. Then, if you were lucky enough to win, you'd line up at a pay window to collect your money. After pocketing your winnings, you'd return to the betting window to put it on the next race. No wonder illegal bookmakers were appealing.

Today, racing offers bettors convenience beyond what even the most customer-friendly bookie could dream of. Tickets no longer have to be pre-printed in set amounts, so you can go to any window and put down any amount of money you choose, within reason. No odd change.

*The lines aren't as long at
the $50 windows.*

Winning tickets require neither skill nor particularly good eyesight to verify, so the
same clerk who sold you the ticket can give you your winnings. But all this simplifica-
tion created a vacuum. What with quick and efficient ticket selling, what would the
bettors do with all the extra time on their hands? It didn't take long for the tracks to
figure it out. The bettors would spend this newly available leisure time calculating
new and complicated bets, bets that were harder to win but created the opportunity
for huge payoffs.

So the gods of racing created *exotics*, which racing purists insisted on calling gimmicks.
The complexity of the new bets served to make the betting window transactions longer
and more difficult. The vacuum was neatly filled.

For the Record

Most tracks ease the way for big bettors by offering separate windows for people wagering higher than average amounts. There may be a $50 window, a $100 window, or higher. The lines are always shorter at these windows.

How to Place a Bet

Whether you're a purist or an aficionado of exotics, the process of betting is the same. Racetracks, simulcast facilities, and off-track betting outlets will have a sign near the betting windows telling you how to announce your bet to the pari-mutuel clerk. If you get the required items a little mixed up, the clerk isn't going to refuse your bet. He or she will help you work out the wager you want. The closer you get to the correct order, the quicker you'll have your ticket in hand, and the happier you'll make the people standing in line behind you.

Have your money in hand as you ask for the ticket. You will be expected to give the following information in the following order:

➤ The name of the racetrack, provided that the windows take bets from more than one racetrack. Otherwise, the present track will be assumed.

➤ The number of the race.

➤ The amount of money you want to bet.

➤ The kind of bet.

➤ The number (not the name) of the horse.

Inside Track

Speed matters. If you (and the other people in line) don't get your bets in before post time, you'll find yourself shut out. Just don't ask for your ticket so fast that you get the numbers wrong.

There's no need to get nervous if you can't remember the numbers. Clerks have copies of the program, and most of them will work out what race and what horse you mean.

Some bets, particularly multirace wagers like Pick-Sixes (more on them later), are best submitted on slips located on counters near the betting windows. Fill them out according to the directions and take them with you to the window.

You may also write down details of any other bet that you find too intricate to remember. In fact, it's a good idea if you're combining several complicated bets in one visit to the window.

After you've successfully announced your requests and paid your money, the clerk will give you either one ticket that includes all your bets or several different tickets. You may request different tickets for each bet, which is invariably a good idea if you've taken somebody else's money to the window to place a bet or two for him or her. This may matter if one of you wins.

Once you get your tickets from the clerk, check them immediately to make sure they're exactly what you asked for. You can get a correction as you stand there, but you can't come back later. There are no return privileges in betting on horse races. Once you accept the ticket and walk away, put it in a safe place and enjoy the race.

Betting Machines

Some racetracks offer a couple of additional ways to place a bet. You may find a betting machine, or ticket terminal, or whatever the track wants to call it. The machine is like a reverse ATM. You put your money in, punch some buttons according to directions, and get a ticket back.

The machines haven't proven very popular at racetracks or even at OTB outlets, and they haven't taken many jobs away from pari-mutuel clerks. That may change someday. The machines really do give you a quick and efficient way to place a bet.

The machines known as television, telephones, and home computers also allow you to place bets in some areas. We'll have more on that in Chapter 22.

Kinds of Bets

Some big money bettors will tell you that the simplest bets aren't worth your time. They don't pay enough, so the argument goes, to be worth the risk that exists every time you put money on a fragile and unstable animal. Not so quick.

Betting a horse to win, place, or show is called *straight wagering*. There's something to be said for being straight. It's the easiest to do and the most likely to succeed, but it's also usually the least lucrative and—let's face it—the least exciting.

But even the most devoted fans of exotics have to pick winners first, and sometimes second and third, too. Straight betting forms the wide and sturdy base of the game.

Betting to Win

If you bet a horse to win and only to win, you get a payoff only if the horse actually wins. But, like almost everything else that touches on horse racing, it's not as simple as that appears.

The winner doesn't always have to finish first for you to win your bet. A race is unofficial for a few minutes after the horses cross the finish line. Before it's made official and payoffs become available, the stewards may launch an inquiry into the results, either because of something they've noticed themselves or because of foul claims made by jockeys or drivers. The stewards, after viewing videotapes and talking to participants, have the option of taking down the winner or any other horse that finishes in the money. See Chapter 11 for more on disqualifications.

So don't tear up your tickets in a fit of annoyance when your horse staggers across the finish line. If he's last in a field of twelve, there's probably no readjustment the stewards can possibly make that will change your ticket into a winner. Occasionally, however, the second- and even third-place horses will find themselves awarded a win because of interference caused by the horse who finished first.

As for picking the horse you're going to bet on to win, take a look at Chapter 20 for systems, methods, and ideas.

Betting to Place and Show

The advantage of making a straight bet, but not to win, is that you get extra chances for a payoff. If you bet a horse to place (finish second), you get a payoff whether he finishes first or second. If you bet a horse to show (finish third), you collect if he finishes first, second, or third.

From the Horse's Mouth

Finishing **in the money** normally means finishing in the first three positions. But purse money is paid for the first four (and sometimes five) spots, and disqualifications from fourth and fifth are also made regularly.

From the Horse's Mouth

Stoopers go around the track after a few races, studying the ground for foolishly discarded tickets. They stoop down to pick them up when they find them.

The disadvantage of betting to place or show is that the pools, which are separate, must be divided in more ways since there are more people holding tickets eligible for payoffs. That means that the dollar amount of each payoff is going to be smaller—most of the time anyway. The following table shows a typical set of payoffs in a race where the favorite wins and well-regarded horses finish second and third.

Horse	Win	Place	Show
#2	$6.00	$3.40	$2.40
#6		$4.40	$3.60
#3			$2.40

If you bet $2 on horse #2 to win, you receive $6.00. If you bet him to place, you receive $3.40. If you bet him to show, you get back $2.40.

If you bet horse #6 to win, you get nothing, since he didn't win. If you bet him to place, you receive $4.40. If you bet him to show, you collect $3.60.

As for all of you who bet on horse #3, you get nothing if you bet him to win or place, but you will receive $2.40 if you bet him to show and he does indeed come in third.

As you can see, the payoffs aren't exactly spectacular for place and show, particularly for show. But remember this: Favorites win about 30 percent of their races, a little less in Thoroughbred and Quarter Horse racing, a little more in harness racing. In most of the races they don't win, they finish second or third. So show bets are *very* likely to pay off for good horses, even though the amount of the payoff won't give you much profit.

Occasionally, place and show betting can be more lucrative than normal. If a horse of exceptional quality, one heavily favored in the win pool, is inexplicably underbet in the place or show pools, you can anticipate a bigger payoff than the horse deserves.

Any horse that's underbet, given his ability and form, is called an *overlay* (an overbet horse is an *underlay*), and it's up to you to find overlays in the win pool. But the tote board can do it for you in the place and show pools.

Normally, racegoers bet horses to place and show in pretty much the same proportion they bet the same horse to win. A horse who is responsible for 50 percent of the win pool is probably going to get about 50 percent of the place and 50 percent of the show wagering too, but sometimes that doesn't happen. There's no reason for it, other than perhaps people are so convinced the horse is going to win that they don't bother with other bets.

If the tote board at your track displays regularly updated show and place pools, you may see a horse who has a much smaller percentage of the place and show pools than he deserves. In this case, a place or show bet gives you not only two or three chances to collect, but also the chance of collecting a good chunk of money when you do because you're not going to have to divide it up among so many other ticket holders.

The underbet good horse can show up in either the place or show pool, but a win is likely to be much more

From the Horse's Mouth

A **bridge jumper** is a person who puts a huge wager on a supposedly sure thing to show, even though the guaranteed profit is only 5 percent. He figures that that profit is just fine for a couple of minutes work. He only has to jump if the horse finishes fourth or worse.

Bad Bet

Other bettors will probably notice the show and place pool overlays, particularly at big racetracks. Don't rely too much on it being a secret. You may see that the percentage of the pool that's bet on the big horse grows as race time approaches. You can hope, though.

lucrative if it's in the place pool. Don't reject a dramatically underbet horse in the show pool, but if you're choosing between the two for one bet, choose the bet to place.

Exotics

The name is appealing, conjuring up images of icy pink drinks with lots of coconut and an umbrella stuck in the top. But exotics at the racetrack are usually more exasperating than they are refreshing. Some of them aren't much more intriguing than a little lemon in your diet cola. Others can plunder both your pocketbook and your peace of mind as effectively as the most ruthless pirate. Maybe that's where they got the name.

All exotic wagers have two things in common. They're difficult to figure out, and they can pay extremely well when you do manage to figure them correctly.

Daily Doubles

The oldest and simplest of the exotics is the daily double, in which you're asked to pick the winners of two consecutive races, usually the first two of the day. Racetracks happily embraced the concept of the daily double decades ago, as soon as they realized it got people to the racetrack well in advance of the first race.

Many tracks then went on to the *late double*, in which you're asked to pick the winners of the last two races. This kept the fans at the track to the bitter end. Tracks can also offer doubles on any other two races on the card.

Doubles are popular with bettors for a number of reasons:

➤ They can pay very well, particularly if both races are won by longshots.

➤ They can be exciting, but only to people who've picked the winner in the first race.

➤ They're simple bets to place since you only have to pick winners for two races.

➤ A successful double wager usually pays more than you'd win if you put the equivalent amount into two win bets on the two races, probably because people are more willing to throw money away on impossible longshots in daily doubles, hoping to win a stupendous payoff.

So much for the good news. The bad news about doubles is that most tracks make sure that at least one of the races involved in each double features large fields of horses that are extremely hard to figure. Maiden claiming races designed for the worst horses in the barns are a particular favorite for the second race in a double.

Because of the unlikelihood that both races in a double will be easy to figure, most serious bettors in doubles work some kind of a *wheel* into their wager.

A daily double wheel might consist of the horse you're confident of in the second race, combined with separate bets on every horse in the first race. That's a lot of bets, possibly costing more than you can recoup even if your horse in the second race does win. You can bet something less than the entire field in the first race, eliminating those you think have no chance at all, but this is risky.

Some large tote boards will show you potential daily double payoffs with various combinations of first race entries with potential second race winners. If your sure horse is in the first race, look at the payoff you'll get with the most favored horse in the second. If the figure is higher than it will cost you to wheel the entire second race, do it. It probably will happen only if your first race selection has fairly long odds.

Exactas

These bets, called *perfectas* at some tracks, are second in popularity only to daily doubles. Most racetracks take exacta wagering on almost every race.

To win an exacta, you have to pick the first and second finishers in one race in exact order. The bet isn't especially lucrative if the top two choices finish first and second, usually only about double what you'd collect if you had a win ticket on the winner and a place ticket on the second-place horse. Of course, your single exacta bet would cost you half as much as your two separate tickets.

But exactas can be lucrative in certain situations:

➤ When a heavy favorite fails to finish in the first two. A race that features a strongly bet horse that you think isn't going to be anywhere near at the finish is ripe for big payoffs, regardless of who wins.

➤ A race where the favorite has only lukewarm support. If even the two most heavily supported horses in the race finish 1-2, the payoff can be substantial.

Exactas pay poorly when:

➤ A heavily favored horse wins, particularly if the horse is odds-on or shorter.

➤ Two horses seem heads above everybody else in the field, and they run 1-2, in whatever order.

Boxing is a favored betting tactic in exactas when you're sure of horses but not sure of precisely where they'll finish.

Quinellas

A *quinella* (sometimes spelled "quiniella") wager will take care of boxing for you, and it will only cost you the price of a single bet. This wager requires you to pick two horses to finish first and second in any order. It's about twice as easy to win as an exacta and tends to pay about half as much.

The quinella isn't as widely offered as the exacta. It's not as popular with bettors, probably because it doesn't have the same potential for big money payoffs. Tracks, too, would probably prefer that people box exactas rather than bet quinellas since the track makes more money that way.

There's one situation in which you might enjoy profits from a quinella bet. Here are the circumstances:

➤ You've narrowed your choices down to three horses.

➤ No more than one of those horses is among the top several choices.

➤ You're willing to make three separate bets.

You box the three horses in a quinella. In other words, you bet 1 and 2, 1 and 3, and 2 and 3. In a $2 quinella, that's $6 in bets. If any of the three finish first and second, you'll win your quinella bet, and it will certainly pay more than $6.

Trifectas

In this bet, also called a triple, you're required to pick the first three finishers in exact order. The payoffs can be extremely high if a longshot finishes anywhere in the top three. Unfortunately, the trifecta is also extremely difficult to win.

It's not particularly difficult to pick the best three horses in any race. Even in races where there's no one standout, there are usually three that seem noticeably better than the rest. What's difficult is figuring in the effect of the random events that plague every horse race.

No matter how confident you are that you've identified the best three, there's no way you can predict which jockeys or drivers (of your horses or others) are going to make mistakes, or are going to be quick enough to take advantage of somebody else's mistakes.

You can't predict which horse is going to injure himself. You may be sure your picks are sound, but what about the horse that breaks down in front of one of yours?

Bettors solve the problem by boxing. There's probably more of it in this kind of wager than any other. Using a $2 trifecta bet as an example, here's what boxing does and costs.

201

Trifecta box using horses 1, 2, and 3, covering every order in which they can finish.

1-2-3	$2.00
1-3-2	$2.00
2-1-3	$2.00
2-3-1	$2.00
3-1-2	$2.00
3-2-1	$2.00
	$12.00 for 6 separate bets

If you're a little less sure and want to add a fourth horse to the mix, that will work out to 24 separate bets totaling $48.00.

The problem with boxing exactas is clear: It's expensive. It can be worth the investment in these situations:

➤ When your confidence lies in three rather than four horses. When you're looking at four good, well-supported horses, the box may cost more than the payoff.

➤ When at least one of them hasn't been noticed by other bettors. An extacta box of three short-priced horses isn't going to pay much more than your bet. It's risky business for a small profit.

➤ When you love the chances of a true longshot, even if you're not sure he's good enough to win. A longshot finishing anywhere in the first three means a big trifecta payoff.

➤ When you like to dream about taking a couple of thousand dollars home with you in exchange for a $2 investment. At many tracks, the trifecta offers the biggest chance of lottery-sized payoffs for a minimum bet.

If you like the part about dreaming, but you don't want to make six separate bets, here's a compromise method of playing a trifecta.

➤ Pick your winner and put him on top of your trifecta ticket.

➤ Pick two more horses and box them in second and third place, so you'll have a 1-2-3 trifecta and a 1-3-2 trifecta. That's $4 worth of tickets. If you have no idea who's going to win, do a more traditional box or put the $4 into a hot dog and fries while the race is being run.

Some tracks offer what they call *superfectas*, in which you're supposed to pick the first four horses in order. Everything that's true of trifectas is super-true of superfectas, including the amount of money necessary to box horses. Most people will find that their time is better spent picking winners than working out possible superfecta bets.

Pick-Six (or -Three, or -Four)

These bets call for picking winners in six (or three or four) straight races. Not every track offers them. Needless to say, they're difficult to win, but serious bettors often put a couple of dollars on them whenever they're offered. They're appealing for several reasons.

➤ The payoff tends to be the biggest available at the racetrack, especially if a longshot or two figures into the list of winners.

➤ Even when nobody wins, a decent consolation prize goes to the near-winners, at least for the Pick-Sixes.

➤ When nobody wins the big prize, the money in the pool carries over to the next day, creating huge pools that sometimes last for weeks.

➤ Since most people pick potential winners before they figure any other kind of betting, they feel they might as well place a single bet on all their choices. It's a cheap thrill.

On the other side of the argument, some bettors believe that Pick-whatevers are poor bets because:

➤ Even if random and unexpected happenings don't occur in one or even two races, you can be sure they will in the next one.

➤ Whether they mean to or not, racing secretaries seem to place at least one race right into the middle of the schedule, in which, on paper, not a single horse is good enough to win. (They probably mean to.)

➤ Some races, whether they feature good horses or bad, should never be bet on because the patterns aren't clear.

For the Record

The Breeders' Cup, the once-a-year event that features seven different million–dollar races for Thoroughbreds, includes a special Pick-7 bet that's offered at more than 500 simulcast facilities around North America. You can bet $1, and if you choose all seven winners, you own or share a payoff pool that can exceed a million dollars.

The Least You Need to Know

➤ The pari-mutuel clerks will help, but you need to know the track, the race, the amount you want to bet, the kind of bet you want to make, and your choice of horse before you go to the betting window.

➤ Straight bets are wagers to win, place, or show. They're the simplest and often the least lucrative.

➤ Other kinds of bets are known as exotics, and they range from the relatively easy to win, such as the quinella, to the very difficult, such as the Pick-Six.

➤ Success in exotics usually requires wheeling and boxing.

➤ Wheeling consists of picking one certain horse and then betting him in combination with every other horse.

➤ Boxing consists of separate bets on two, three, four, or more horses in every possible combination of order of finish.

Chapter 18

Get with the Program (and the Past Performances)

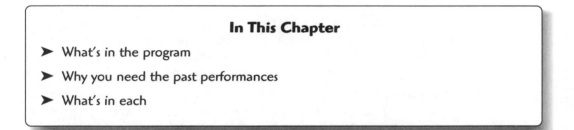

In This Chapter

➤ What's in the program

➤ Why you need the past performances

➤ What's in each

Think of them as the map to Captain Kidd's treasure, plus the key to help you interpret that map. They're better known as the *program* and the *past performances*. You used to need both to succeed at the racetrack or even to understand what's going on. Today, the two documents tend to overlap, and it's sometimes possible to get by with one or the other. Let's start with the most important and fundamental one.

The Program

Every racetrack publishes its own program, a different one for each day of racing. In every program, no matter how cheap the track and small its publication, you'll find basic data, some of which you can happily overlook. Other information is vital if you expect to bet successfully.

Even a bare-bones program gives you information you need before you make your betting decisions.

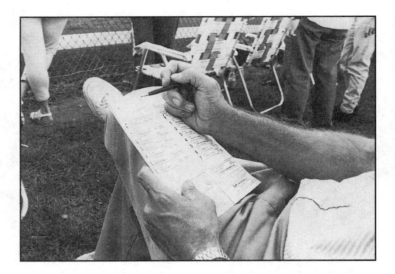

Most racetrack programs only cost a dollar or two, and it's well worth the investment even though most of the same data will also be in any past performance publication that you purchase. Included in every program will be:

➤ The names of track officers, stewards, and other people whose identities are more important to those who work at the track than those who bet on the horses. Pay attention only if you're looking for someone to whom to address a complaint about the quality of the food.

➤ Conditions for each race on the card. These are listed at the top of the page devoted to the race and include purse, distance, and claiming price, as well as the age, sex, and any race record limitations of the horses permitted to be entered. In Thoroughbred and Quarter Horse racing, the information also includes the base weight to be carried, plus provisions for weight allowances. If the race is on the turf, that too is included here.

➤ The list of entered horses, plus the numbers they're going to wear on their saddlecloths. In most cases, the horses' numbers coincide with their places in the starting gate, with the lowest numbers nearest the rail. If there's a multiple interest entry (see Chapter 15), you may find an additional number with the letters PP next to the horse's name. The plain number is the horse's saddlecloth number, while the PP number is his post position.

From the Horse's Mouth

The **morning line** is the predicted odds breakdown of the race. The oddsmaker isn't predicting the finish; he's guessing what the real bettors are going to do (more in Chapter 19).

➤ A description of the horse, including his age, sex, and color.

➤ The horse's sire and dam.

➤ A description of the jacket colors worn by the jockey or driver.

For the Record

In Thoroughbred and Quarter Horse racing, the colors belong to the owner, while they belong to the driver in harness racing. Drivers don't have to spend much time changing during the course of a racing day.

➤ The weight to be carried by the individual horse (in Thoroughbred and Quarter Horse racing).

➤ The name of the jockey or driver.

➤ The name of the trainer.

➤ The name of the owner.

➤ Morning line odds.

➤ The kind of wagering permitted on the race.

Slightly more complete basic programs give you the following (either on or apart from the pages devoted to the race entries):

➤ A selection of track records so you can judge as the race day progresses just how fast the horses are going.

➤ A description of the wagering process.

➤ A diagram of the racetrack, showing you the location of the starting gate for each race distance.

➤ Current jockey and trainer standings, including starts and placements.

➤ Statistics on winning percentages of each post position.

➤ Early entries for the following day.

Extremely complete programs give you:

➤ Past performance charts for each horse entered in each race.

➤ Choices of one or more handicappers (other than the morning line oddsmaker).

➤ Tips on how to win at the races.

➤ Interesting statistics, such as the most successful jockeys on the turf, the best trainers in claiming races, and so forth.

Past Performances

For decades, harness racing's policy has been for the racetracks to provide programs with almost all the information a bettor needs, while flat tracks have expected bettors to buy past performance publications. Almost all harness programs include a reasonable selection of past performances, as well as each horse's lifetime statistics for victories, earnings, and speed records. Most programs also include tables for track variants, so you can adequately compare times earned at different tracks.

The tradition probably developed because there's no harness equivalent of the *Daily Racing Form*, at least in terms of its hundred-year history and database. There is *Sports Eye*, a past performance publication whose information is every bit as good as the *Form*'s, but its presence has never been quite as pervasive in the harness sport as the *Form* has been in Thoroughbred racing, and tracks have always felt it necessary to provide at least modest past performance data themselves.

A few years ago, some Thoroughbred tracks decided to get into the past performance business. Some wanted to break the stranglehold of the *Daily Racing Form* on racing data, while others simply realized that fans like a program that tells them more than the basics. Many flat tracks are now providing past performances in their programs.

Most Thoroughbred racetracks and simulcast betting outlets get their past performance data from Equibase, a company that was formed by the Jockey Club and the Thoroughbred Racing Association, an organization of racetracks. The Equibase data and past performance charts have much in common with those of the *Daily Racing Form*, although there are slight differences.

Deciphering the PPs

If you hope to win at the races, not just enjoy them, you've got to learn to read and understand past performance charts, also known as the PPs. It doesn't matter whether you get them from the track program or from one of the specialty publications.

All of the basic program information, except possibly for the colors of horses and jackets, can play some part in your betting decisions. We've talked in previous chapters about the importance of the various characteristics of horses, humans, and racetracks. Some attributes matter a great deal, some very little, but none matter as much as the information you'll find in the past performance charts.

Exacta / Trifecta / Pick Three (Races 6-7-8)

6

START
7 Furlongs
FINISH

The Spendthrift

Julep Cup - Mr. Ted Taylor

Allowance. Purse $41,000($31,640 Plus $9,360 from KTDF).For Two Year Olds which have not won two races. Weight, 121 lbs. Non-winners of $21,000 allowed 3 lbs. $15,000 5 lbs. $10,000 8 lbs.
Seven Furlongs

Win	Place	Show	No.

Track Record: **Binalong (4), 112 lbs; 1:20.39 (10-13-93)**

Pgm# | Owner | Weight | Jockey (Record) | Class | Trainer (Record) | Claiming

Foxhill Farm (Rick Porter) — **115.9** — **Nicholas P. Zito** (15-3-3-3)
Red and white quarters; red bars on white sleeves, white cap.

1 — **Swig (L)** — **118** — **Pat Day** (39-8-6-9)
7-2
Dk.B./Br.c.2 Fly So Free-Cassa Gay by Cassaleria
Breeder: Sa Long Farm & Dennis Swartz, KY (February 25, 1995)

Life :	3 1 0 0	$21,510	Turf :	0 0 0 0	$0
1997:	3 1 0 0	$21,510	Off Dirt :	1 0 0 0	$1,110
1996:	0 0 0 0	$0	Keeneland:	0 0 0 0	$0

21Sep97	Bel9	ft	2	FuturityG1	1	:45[62]	1:10[44]	1:35[69]	86/89	**65**	9/10	8[4]¼	9[4]¼	10[8]½	10[16]½	10[30]¼	Smith,M	122		55.00	GrndSlm 6½,K.O.Pnch 2¼,Dvl'sPrde 4½	bumped strt,no bid
28Aug97	Sar8	my	2	Alw37000N2L	6f	:21[80]	:45[22]	1:11[95]	80/87	**72**	6/6	6	6[9]	6[7]	6[9]	5[4]¾	Smith,M	118	c	2.40	AlymorB. 1,Overlord 2,SpicyAward ¾	mild rally
01Aug97	Sar2	ft	2	Msw	6f	:22[22]	:46[38]	1:12[57]	84/89	**81**	2/8	5	6[6]¼	4[2]½	2[hd]	1[1]¼	Smith,M	119		28.25	Swg 1¼,Sctmnd(dq6) 1,Mnt(p2) 5	got through inside

Workouts: **12Oct KEE 5f ft 1:02.40 b** **05Oct KEE 5f ft :59.60 h** **28Sep BEL 5f ft 1:03.71 b** **13Sep BEL 6f ft 1:15.46 b**

Earl Levine — **110.6** — **Owner** (0-0-0-0)
Yellow; red hoops, red bars on sleeves, yellow cap.

2 — **Fleet Crossing (L)** — **121** — **Willie Martinez** (50-5-8-3)
20-1
Ch.c.2 Afleet-Rivers to Cross by Riverman
Breeder: Earl Levine, KY (April 24, 1995)

Life :	6 1 0 0	$27,961	Turf :	0 0 0 0	$0
1997:	6 1 0 0	$27,961	Off Dirt :	2 0 0 0	$5,555
1996:	0 0 0 0	$0	Keeneland:	0 0 0 0	$0

02Oct97	TP8	ft	2	Alw28700N1$X	6f	:22[01]	:45[81]	1:11[69]	93/95	**70**	7/8	2	2[1]	2[hd]	3[3]	5[8]	Torres,F	121	L	27.00	Homeward 5½,Cattin 1,Wilcrest [hd]	drew even, gave way
10Sep97	TP9	gd	2	Alw28700N1$X	6f	:22[41]	:46[52]	1:12[81]	93/93	**53**	5/6	3	2[hd]	1[1]	3[3]	6[17]	Albarado,R	121	L	6.10	ClmthGold 3½,Wlcrst 6,O.K.Crby 5	drew clear, stopped
27Aug97	ElP2	ft	2	Alw25900N2L	1	:47[40]	1:11[80]	1:38[60]	85/77	**67**	2/6	1½	2[hd]	2[hd]	5[8]	5[8]¾	Castillo,O	107[5]	f	5.80	NiceRide ½,DeputyCommand [nk],Fiamma 1½	dueled, tired
20Jul97	ElP10	ft	2	Sequoia	6f	:22[20]	:45[40]	1:11[00]	73/47	**--**	4/8	2	8[10]½	8[24]	8[35]	DNF	Hebert,T	112	f	10.80	Tomaso ½,Ontou 2½,RegaintheFame 2	outrun, distanced
26May97	CD9	gd	2	KyBC	5½f	:22[60]	:46[45]	1:04[80]	93/95	**75**	6/8	3	3[2]	2[2]½	3[6]	4[13]¾	Hebert,T	115	f	26.80	FvriteTrick 8½,JsM [nk],CteLutie 5	drew even, gave way
01May97	CD1	ft	2	Msw	4½f	:23[35]	:46[79]	:53[22]	86/--	**76**	3/6	1	1[1]½	---	1[2]	1[hd]	Hebert,T	119	f	13.90	FltCrsng [hd],CpTwn 2,OldTrste 4	drew off, just lasted

Workouts: **12Oct KEE 6f ft 1:15.20 b** **29Sep TP 5f ft 1:02.60 h** **21Sep TP 5f ft 1:03.40 b** **21Aug ELP 5f m 1:01.20 h**

Kyle Nagel and Terry Raymond — **114.1** — **Dale L. Romans** (2-0-0-0)
Orange; black sunrise, orange cap.

3 — **Felon (L)** — **118** — **Sebastian Madrid** (24-1-3-3)
3-1
Dk.B./Br.c.2 Fortunate Prospect-Super Fantastic by Super Concorde
Breeder: Gerald Robins, FL (April 12, 1995)

Life :	5 1 1 1	$33,880	Turf :	0 0 0 0	$0
1997:	5 1 1 1	$33,880	Off Dirt :	1 0 0 1	$3,140
1996:	0 0 0 0	$0	Keeneland:	0 0 0 0	$0

21Sep97	TP1	ft	2	Alw28700N1$X	6½f	:22[58]	:45[82]	1:19[23]	90/94	**79**	4/6	3	2½	2[1]	2[hd]	2[1]½	Torres,F	121	bL	*.40	MrBert 1½,Felon 6,DesertAir 7	pressed pace, gave way
16Aug97	Mth11	ft	2	Sapling	6f	:21[50]	:44[42]	1:09[75]	94/88	**53**	5/8	3	4[1]½	6[7]	8[16]¾	8[23]¼	Martinez,W	122	b	13.70	DoubleHonor 2,Jigadee ¾,EZLine 3	stopped turn
24Jul97	Sar9	ft	2	SanfordG3	6f	:22[34]	:45[95]	1:10[23]	67/80	**83**	4/7	7	7[12]½	5[6]¼	4[4]½	4[6]	Sellers,S	116		9.60	PlshdBras ½,DblHonor 1,Jgde 4½	crowded strt,good fin
22Jun97	CD1	ft	2	Msw	5½f	:22[50]	:46[47]	1:04[88]	85/95	**91**	6/11	3	4[5]½	3[3]½	2½	1[ns]	Sellers,S	120		*.70	Felon [ns],Ontou 6½,Tomaso ½	dueled, prevailed
01Jun97	CD1	my	2	Msw	5f	:22[36]	:45[87]	:58[84]	97/--	**86**	1/6	1	1[hd]	2½	3[2]½	3[3]¼	Sellers,S	120		*.90	Emigre 1¼,DiceDancer 2,Felon 8	dueled, weakened

Workouts: **30Sep CD 4f ft :52.60 b** **15Sep CD 4f ft :51.60 b**

J. M. Jones, Jr. — **114.9** — **Albert M. Stall, Jr.** (5-0-0-0)
Yellow; blue hoops, yellow bars on blue sleeves, blue cap.

4 — **Summer Salute (L)** — **118** — **Fabio Arguello, Jr.** (25-1-2-3)
6-1
B.g.2 Sheikh Albadou (GB)-Seattle Summer by Seattle Slew
Breeder: G. W. Humphrey Jr., J. Pierce, A. Gilman & K. Koontz, KY (April 14, 1995)

Life :	1 1 0 0	$17,185	Turf :	0 0 0 0	$0
1997:	1 1 0 0	$17,185	Off Dirt :	0 0 0 0	$0
1996:	0 0 0 0	$0	Keeneland:	0 0 0 0	$0

21Sep97	TP2	ft	2	Msw	6½f	:22[72]	:46[28]	1:20[07]	81/82	**75**	11/12	6	6[4]	4[4]	2[1]½	1½	Arguello,F	121		6.30	SmrSlte ½,SqMy 7,CptnsChr 2½	saved ground, driving

Workouts: **13Oct CD 4f ft :50.00 b** **06Oct CD 4f ft :52.00 b** **12Sep CD 6f ft 1:16.20 b** **06Sep CD 5f ft 1:03.00 b**

Here's a typical past performance page as compiled by Equibase.

For the Record

Yes, both post position and past performance are known as PP. They're equally important.

Remember about Captain Kidd and how the PPs are the map to the buried treasure? That's not entirely accurate. The PPs are more like the buried treasure itself. Hidden in the tiny lines of type (bring your reading glasses) are the secrets of a horse's soundness, speed, and stamina. They tell you if he's in the kind of race he can reasonably expect to win or if he's in over his head. They give you hints (although not firm proof) about whether he's in condition to live up to his potential.

Almost anything you might want to know about a racehorse is right there, but you have to do a little digging to find some of it. No matter which source of past performances you use, you'll find most of the same information, although the publishers offer exclusive items that they hope will convince you that you must buy their product if you want to win.

The charts are divided by race, with one set of past performances for each race. The set includes information about every horse entered in the race. In past performance publications such as the *Daily Racing Form* and *Sports Eye*, note that the top of the set of charts for each race includes the same basic information that you'll see in the program. You'll see the conditions of the race, the qualifications for entry, the purse, the type of wagers to be accepted, the length, and—if it's for Thoroughbreds—the racing surface. For harness horses, you'll see if it's a trot or a pace.

In these details, it's like the program. But past performance charts, whether they're part of an elaborate track-produced program or a specialized publication, go further.

By the way, the *Daily Racing Form* has recently undergone a change in ownership. There may be changes in its past performance formatting and statistics, but most of the traditional information should remain.

Jockey, Driver, and Trainer Statistics

What you see depends on the sport and the publication. In Thoroughbred and Quarter Horse racing, you find the name of the jockey plus a number indicating any apprentice allowance that he claims. The *Daily Racing Form* prints a summary of his starts and finishes, plus a figure that indicates winning percentage. For most races, you'll see two sets of figures. The first is for the current race meet, and the second is a less complete summary for the year to date. The jockey statistics look like this:

SHAKESPEARE, W (49 8 6 6 .16) 1998: (1149 164 .14)

This means that Willie Shakespeare has ridden in 49 races in the current meet at Avon Downs, of which he's won 8, finished second in 6, and third in another 6. He's won 16 percent of his races. In 1998, Willie has started 1,149 races, of which he's won 164 for 14 percent. It's been a pretty average year for Willie.

The *Form* also prints extensive jockey charts elsewhere in the publication, telling you things such as a jockey's performance in sprints, in routes, with favorites, on the turf, and more.

Racetracks that use Equibase past performances vary in how much jockey information they print in the program, whether on the PP page or elsewhere. The stats they do offer will probably appear in a format similar to the *Form*'s.

In harness racing, driver statistics are always a vital part of past performance charts. A complete one looks like this:

Driver GEOFF CHAUCER 150 (red/blk) (771-135-111-92-.295)

Geoff, who's having an excellent year, weighs 150 pounds and will be wearing his red and black. He's started 771 races, with 135 wins, 111 seconds, and 92 thirds. The last figure is not winning percentage as in flat racing, but the Universal Driver Rating. See Chapter 10 for an explanation of UDR. Some tracks and publications also include Geoff's birth date, making it impossible for him to lie about much.

In both flat and harness racing, some past performance charts also include the statistics enjoyed by the horse's trainer, although not his weight and age.

The Horse

All past performance charts also include summaries of the horses' racing careers, printing breakdowns of entries, placements, and earnings for some combination of the current year, the past year, and the horse's entire racing career. In flat racing, it will look something like this:

1998 9 2 2 1 $101,502

This horse has started nine times, won two, finished second twice, third once, and earned $101,502 in 1998. His next line shows you that he's not improving:

1997 6 4 3 1 $295,713

Then comes his lifetime record:

Life: 18 8 7 3 $492,105

Most past performance charts add similar breakdowns for the horse's performances on turf courses and on wet tracks. The *Daily Racing Form* adds the horse's record over the current track and at the distance of today's race.

In harness racing, charts include the starts and placing percentages, and they add a statistic that's vital in determining a horse's quality: his best mile time for the year.

Bad Bet

Take good wet track stats with a grain of salt. There are sloppy wet tracks, hard and fast wet tracks, and everything in between. Look down the charts to try to see what kind of wet track the horse has excelled on before concluding that he'll be good in today's mud.

Some programs include his best from the previous year, his best lifetime, or both. These appear on the same line as the win-loss statistics, either to the right or left. A harness horse's record might appear like this:

1998: 14 3 2 4 $37,502 1:54 M 1

This horse, who's won 3 of 14 starts in 1998, went a mile in 1 minute 54 seconds at the Meadowlands Racetrack, a one mile oval. You'll find a chart identifying the racetrack symbols elsewhere in the program or the past performance publication. The size of the track matters because harness horses race faster over the larger tracks. You'd be more impressed if you saw a 5/8 for a 5/8-mile track, or no symbol at all, which means the track was 1/2 mile around.

Next, and most important, are the lines describing each horse's previous races. The various publications each use slightly different formats, but learning to read one ensures that you can read the others. Here's the first third of a typical line, reading left to right:

19Sep98 SA 8 6F ft :22 :44 :56 1:09 3U Clm12000

Translation: The horse last raced on September 19, 1998, in the 8th race of that day at Santa Anita. The race, six furlongs in length, took place on a fast track.

Track Condition Symbols

Symbol	Meaning
Main Track	
ft (fast)	Hard and dry
gd (good)	A little soft and maybe damp
sly (sloppy)	Wet, but probably still hard underneath
my (muddy)	Wet and soft
Turf Course	
fm (firm)	Not too dry and not too wet
gd (good)	A little soft and damp
yl (yielding)	A little softer and damper

In past performance lines for European races, you're likely to see hd (hard) and sf (soft).

Next come the running times of the horse leading the race (not necessarily the horse you're examining) at the points of call. In this race, you're looking at the leader's running time at the 1/4 mile, the 1/2 mile, the stretch (about five furlongs), and the finish. Next, you discover that the race was for three-year-olds and up (you may see an arrow pointing upward rather than a U), and that the race was a claiming event with a price tag of $25,000 for entries.

The *Daily Racing Form* and the Equibase programs differ in the next notation. In the *Form*, you'll see a double-digit number in boldface; it's the *Beyer Speed Index*, a figure worked out according to a formula developed by *Washington Post* columnist and horseplayer extraordinaire Andrew Beyer. The figure is designed to quantify the quality of speed shown by the horse in the race, taking into account not only the time of the race, the distance he finished behind, but track biases and conditions for the day.

Following the Speed Index comes the horse's positions at the calls of the race. The middle third of the line will look like this:

$5\ 2\ 3^{hd}\ 4^{1/2}\ 5^1\ 5^2$ Shakespeare.W L118 3.60

The horse, who broke out of post position 5, jumped out of the starting gate in second place, dropped back to third after the first quarter, moved up to fourth at the 1/2 mile, was fifth in mid stretch, where he remained at the finish. The smaller superscript shows his distance in lengths behind the horse in front of him.

Willie Shakespeare rode our horse in the race. The animal was given Lasix (see Chapter 5) prior to the race, and he was assigned 118 pounds. Some past performance charts place the medication symbol after rather than before the weight assignment. Our horse started the race at odds of 3.60 to 1.

From the Horse's Mouth

A **length** is a horse's body length, minus his neck and head.

The final third of the line might look like this:

(82-14) or (93) Hamlet[1] 1/2, Macbeth[2], King Lear[1] bid, hung stretch 12

First comes one of two speed figures. The *Form*, in addition to the Beyer figure, offers a less precise assessment of the speed of the race. The first half of the double figure (84 in this case) represents the horse's time in relation to the track record (that would be 100), and the second half represents the track variant for the day. The total of the two is the figure you'll use. In this case, the horse gets a 96.

The Equibase program past performances include the second figure, a Speed Index similar in intent to the Beyer Index. Again, highest is best. This horse ran a pretty quick race last time out in spite of his fifth-place finish and gets a 93 by the Beyer method.

The three names that follow are the first three horses in order of finish, followed by the lengths they finished in front of the next horse. Then, we learn by the word "bid" that our horse made a run at the leaders but was unable to make up ground in the stretch and "hung." Finally, we discover that there were 12 horses in the race, making our horse's fifth-place finish a little more impressive.

At the bottom of each horse's array of previous races you'll find his most recent public workouts. See Chapter 3 for a discussion of workouts and what they mean in terms of speed and readiness.

From the Horse's Mouth

Past performance comments are usually self-evident. Among the comments that might mean the performance was better than it looked: **checked** (had to slow down to avoid traffic), **impeded** (his progress was affected by another horse), **taken up** (his jockey came close to stopping him to avoid a collision), and **wide** (he lost ground and ran farther than the rest of the field).

From the Horse's Mouth

Among the harness comments you may see: **cvr** (the horse raced behind another horse providing him cover and less wind resistance), **ruff** (rough gaited). The comments that indicate a better effort than the finish would suggest: **Equip** (equipment problem), **unc** (uncovered), **wd** (wide).

In Quarter Horse racing, the past performance line is similar, except there are fewer interim times and positions since most of the races are much shorter. In the average sub-quarter mile race, the first number indicates how the horse broke out of the gate. It's the one (other than finishing position) that means the most. Some Quarter Horse past performances also include information on any head or tail wind that might have affected the final time.

In steeplechasing, you also see fewer calls and may see little indication of interim time and distances. In jump racing, horses tend to string themselves out, making the assessment of leads difficult.

In harness racing, the data is supplied to tracks by the United States Trotting Association. You'll find past performance lines similar to what you find in Thoroughbred charts, with a few exceptions:

➤ Harness PPs include the final time for the horse in question, no matter where he finished. You don't have to extrapolate from the winning time and the lengths behind. It's printed right there for you to use.

➤ Both purse and claiming price of previous races are included, giving you a better assessment of the quality of the race.

➤ There's no equivalent of the jockey's weight.

➤ Since each track produces its own program, you'll find that some charts include comments on the race, while some don't.

The harness line also includes symbols to tell you any trouble the horse may have had during the course of the race. These are important to note because you can assume a horse who had a troubled race would have raced faster with a cleaner race. What you're looking for is x's and o's.

RACE 1 | **PACE** | **ONE MILE** | **PURSE $50,000**

4 YEAR OLDS - OPEN
LATE CLOSER - 2nd LEG

1ST HALF OF DAILY DOUBLE AND $2 PERFECTA WAGERING THIS RACE

$1 PERFECTA BOX

1 — 3-5 — RED

RED BOW TIE
JOHN CAMPBELL wh-maroon-blue
b g 4 Raging Glory-Cheers Lauxmont-Royce
C.D.Siegel,Brooklyn Ny.,Tlp Stable,Kearny Nj.,etc.
Tr.-Monte Gelrod
1998 4 3 1 0 $93,750 1:51^2 M1
1997 23 12 4 1 $438,800 1:50 M1
Lifetime 3, 1:50 1 $662,026
LAST 6 STS. - $162,000
BREEDER - DANA L.IRVING,.

2-7^{98} M1	ft 38	25000	4yr Opn Lc	1 27^2	55^1	125	152	2	3	1$^{1\frac{3}{4}}$	1$^{1\frac{1}{2}}$	1^2	1^{nk}	27	152	*.30	JoCampbell	RdBowTi,RdStarLongshot,Manfcnt -6
1-24^{98} M1	ft 40	110000	D-FFA Lc	1 26^4	55^1	124^3	151^2	8	4°	1$^{1\frac{1}{4}}$	1$^{1\frac{1}{4}}$	1$^{1\frac{3}{4}}$	1^1	26^4	151^2	*.50	JoCampbell	RdBowT,MastrBarny,ThWrathofPan-10
1-17^{98} M1	ft 40	35000	FFA Lc	1 27	55^3	124	151^2	5	7	6^{o5}	4^{oo4}	2^4	2$^{1\frac{1}{4}}$	26^4	151^3	*.50	JoCampbell	MastrBarny,RdBowTi,LDsJonathan-11
1-3^{98} M1	ft 50	35000	FFA Stk	1 27	55^3	124	151^2	3	6	6$^{o5\frac{1}{2}}$	4$^{o2\frac{1}{4}}$	2^{hd}	1$^{1\frac{1}{2}}$	27	151^2	*.30	JoCampbell	RdBowTi,MastrBarny,RalghFngrs-11
12-26^{97}M1	ft 45	100000	D-3yr Inv	1 27^1	55^4	123^2	150^3	6	1	1$^{1\frac{3}{4}}$	1$^{1\frac{1}{2}}$	1$^{1\frac{1}{2}}$	1$^{2\frac{1}{2}}$	27^1	150^3	*.60	JoCampbell	RedBowTie,DMDilingr,MastrBarny-10
12-13^{97}GSP1	ft 36	36500	w25000 Lt	1 27^2	55^4	124^3	151^1	4	2	1$^{1\frac{1}{4}}$	1$^{\frac{1}{2}}$	1$^{1\frac{1}{2}}$	1$^{4\frac{1}{4}}$	26^3	151^1	*.70	JoCampbell	RedBowTie,CaConction,MastrMils -9
12-7^{97} Wdb⅞	ft 37	100000	GOLD-CUP	1 27	55^3	123^2	153^2	1	2	3	3ix°	9$^{13\frac{1}{2}}$	10^{16} pl9		156^3	*.95	LOuellette	NorthernLuck,DMDilinger,Arturo-10
11-30^{97}DD⅝	ft 54	137400	MATRON	1 26^4	55^4	123^3	151	5	1°	1	1^2	1^2	1^4	27^2	151	*.30	LOuellette	RedBowTie,ParkPlace,ParsonsDen -8

2 — 3-1 — BLUE

RED STAR LONGSHOT
JACK MOISEYEV black-wh-gold
ch h 4 Vereen-Tiffisue Hanover-Big Towner
Robert M.Murphy,White Rock Bc.
Tr.-Archie Mc Neil
1998 4 2 1 1 $40,080 1:52^4 M1
1997 20 9 5 3 $217,341 1:54^4 Clgy ⅝
Lifetime 4, 1:52^4 1 $299,009
LAST 6 STS. - $90,080
BREEDER - ROBERT M.MURPHY,.

2-7^{98} M1	ft 38	25000	4yr Opn Lc	1 27^2	55^1	125	152	3	1	2$^{1\frac{3}{4}}$	2$^{1\frac{1}{2}}$	2^2	2^{nk}	26^4	152	3.10	JMoiseyev	RdBowTi,RdStarLongshot,Manfcnt -6
1-31^{98} M1	ft 38	25000	4yr OpnLc	1 28	56^3	125^3	152^4	1	2	2$^{1\frac{3}{4}}$	2$^{1\frac{1}{4}}$	1$^{1\frac{3}{4}}$	1^3	27	152^4	e2.60	JMoiseyev	RdStarLongshot,Rockrby,BrnThatBrdg -8
1-10^{98} FRD	ft 32	40500	PROVINCIAL	1 27	59	127^3	156^3	3	1	1	1	1$^{1\frac{1}{2}}$	1$^{\frac{3}{4}}$		156^3	e*.30	BBeelby	RdStarLongshot,RdStarTrx,ScrfyBn -8
1-4^{98} FRD	sy 32	9000	INVITATION	1 29	100^4	131^2	159^4	2	2	2	2	2$^{1\frac{1}{2}}$	3$^{2\frac{1}{2}}$		200^1	e*1.25	BBeelby	JstDodln,Nordlgato,RdStarLongshot -7
12-14^{97}FRD	gd 48	10000	INVITATION	1 29	100^2	129^3	159^1	6	5°	5°	3°°	3^1	7^4		200	e*1.10	BBeelby	Nordlgato,JustDodln,BlMadowKng -8
11-30^{97}Edm⅝	ft 39	100000	COLIN-FORB	1 28^1	58	127^1	156^2	3	4	4°	1°°	1^2	1^3		156^2	e*.25	TBeelby	RdStarLongshot,BgBarsRoln,Oscaroad -8
11-23^{97}Edm⅝	ft 28	7500	COLIN-FORB	1 29^2	59^3	129^1	157^3	3	1	1	1	1$^{2\frac{1}{2}}$	1^3		157^3	*.35	TBeelby	RdStarLongshot,ScarltandGold,Rains -6
11-9^{97} FRD	ft 59	105800	BCSS-3YR-C	1 28^2	58	126	155^3	4	5	4°	4°	3$^{1\frac{1}{2}}$	1$^{1\frac{3}{4}}$		155^3	e*.45	TBeelby	RdStarLongshot,RdStarTrx,ScrfyBn -8

3 — 15-1 — WHITE

MANIFICENT
RON PIERCE red-white-blue
b h 4 Falcon Seelster-Troubled Heart-Troublemaker
M and L of Delaware Inc, DE & Potkin Stables, NY
Tr.-Bruce Saunders
1998 3 0 0 1 $4,250 1:55^4 M1 Q
1997 27 6 2 3 $233,208 1:51^4 GSP1
Lifetime 3, 1:51^4 1 $255,438
LAST 6 STS. - $29,116
BREEDER - CASTLETON FARM,KY.

2-7^{98} M1	ft 38	25000	4yr Opn Lc	1 27^2	55^1	125	152	1	2	3$^{3\frac{1}{4}}$	4$^{3\frac{1}{4}}$	3$^{3\frac{1}{4}}$	3$^{1\frac{1}{2}}$	26^3	152^1	16.60	RPierce	RdBowTi,RdStarLongshot,Manfcnt -6
1-31^{98} M1	ft 38	25000	4yr OpnLc	1 28	56^3	125^3	152^4	5	6	7$^{o6\frac{3}{4}}$	7^{o5}	7$^{5\frac{1}{2}}$	5^5	27^1	153^4	e*1.20	RPierce	RdStarLongshot,Rockrby,BrnThatBrdg -8
1-24^{98} M1	ft 40	35000	w 25000 Lt	1 27^2	56^3	125^2	152^3	4	4	4^4	4$^{2\frac{1}{2}}$	4$^{3\frac{1}{4}}$	6$^{2\frac{1}{2}}$	27^1	153	18.70	HParker	Hauckuls,SolarGalaxy,MastrMils -8
1-16^{98} M1	gd 32		QUA	1 29	59	127^4	155^4	2	3	1$^{1\frac{1}{2}}$	1^2	1^6	1$^{11\frac{1}{2}}$	28	155^4	NB	HParker	Manfcnt,ChathamHoch,SprngToLf -7
11-30^{97}DD⅝	ft 54	137400	MATRON	1 26^4	55^4	123^3	151	6	6	8	8^{o6}	6^7	5$^{8\frac{1}{2}}$	27^4	152^3	6.30	HParker	RedBowTie,ParkPlace,ParsonsDen -8
11-23^{97}DD⅝	ft 49	45800	MATRON	1 26^4	55^4	124^2	151^3	7	3	4	4$^{3\frac{1}{4}}$	4$^{3\frac{3}{4}}$	3^5	27^3	152^3	3.40	HParker	RedBowTie,ParkPlace,Manificent-10
11-16^{97}DD⅝	ft 45	25000	PROGRESS	1 27^2	55	124^2	153	1	3°	1	1$^{1\frac{1}{2}}$	1$^{2\frac{1}{2}}$	1^6	28^3	153	*.50	HParker	Manfcnt,AtPontBlank,ParsonsDn -6
11-9^{97}DD⅝	gd 53	25000	PROGRESS	1 27^3	56^4	125^3	155^1	7	7	7	7$^{o3\frac{1}{4}}$	6$^{9\frac{1}{2}}$	6$^{7\frac{3}{4}}$	30^3	156^4	8.30	HParker	DreamAway,Megamind,DauntlsBuny -7

4 — 20-1 — GREEN

PARTY STOP (L)
LUC OUELLETTE red-white-black
b g 4 Circle of Light-House Party-Keystone Ore
Brittany Farms,Versailles,Ky.
Tr.-Chris Ryder
1998 6 0 0 0 $4,400
1997 17 4 2 4 $44,226 1:52^2 M1
Lifetime 2, 1:52^2 1 $102,174
LAST 6 STS. - $4,400
BREEDER - BRITTANY FARMS,KY.

2-7^{98} M1	ft 38	25000	4yr Opn Lc	1 27^2	55^1	125	152	6	6	6$^{8\frac{1}{4}}$	5$^{o3\frac{3}{4}}$	5$^{6\frac{1}{4}}$	4^4	27	152^4	45.20	L LOuellette	RdBowTi,RdStarLongshot,Manfcnt -6
1-31^{98} M1	ft 38	25000	4yr OpnLc	1 28	56^3	125^3	152^4	6	7	8^8	8$^{oo6\frac{1}{2}}$	8x$^{11\frac{1}{2}}$	8^{34}	32^4	159^3	12.10	L LOuellette	RdStarLongshot,Rockrby,BrnThatBrdg -8
1-22^{98} M1	ft 32	17500	nw4 Lc	1 28	57	125^3	153^2	7	9	8$^{8\frac{1}{4}}$	8$^{o7\frac{1}{4}}$	7^8	7$^{5\frac{1}{4}}$	27^2	154^2	3.20	L LOuellette	MagntcKlan,GoyaBlChp,PalmtoDar -9
1-15^{98} M1	sy 35	17500	nw4 Lc	1 28^3	57^1	126^3	155	12	7	8$^{8\frac{1}{4}}$	7$^{5\frac{1}{4}}$	5$^{2\frac{1}{2}}$	4$^{3\frac{1}{2}}$	28	155^3	14.00	L LOuellette	BrnThtBrdg,LkNoRn,TkHomThGld-12
1-8^{98} M1	gd 55	17500	nw4 Lc	1 28^2	55^4	123^4	153	12	7°	3$^{o1\frac{1}{4}}$	2^{ons}	8$^{7\frac{3}{4}}$	10^{13}	31^4	155^3	5.50	L LOuellette	SothwwMat,UltmatFalcon,SlgofJn-13
1-3^{98} M1	ft 50	20000	nw18775L6	1 28^2	56^1	123^1	152	3	7	4^{o2}	2^{o2}	4$^{4\frac{1}{2}}$	5$^{4\frac{3}{4}}$	29^2	153	*2.10	L LOuellette	SakraMania,BadBert,Rockapella-10
12-27^{97}M1	sy 34	20000	nw17500L6	1 26^4	54^3	124	152^2	2	4	3$^{3\frac{1}{2}}$	2$^{1\frac{3}{4}}$	1$^{2\frac{1}{2}}$	1$^{2\frac{1}{2}}$	28	152^2	14.50	L LOuellette	PartyStop,UltmatFalcon,HokdOnaFlng -9
12-12^{97}GSP1	sy 36		QUA	1 28^1	57	127	154^2	3	3	3$^{3\frac{3}{4}}$	3$^{o2\frac{1}{2}}$	3$^{3\frac{3}{4}}$	3^5	28	155^2	NB	L RSiegelman	KpYourPansOf,RodsDal,PartyStop-10

Here's a typical past performance page as compiled by the United States Trotting Association.

Here's the section of the line showing the horse's position at various points of the race:

6 6° 7^{oo5} 6^x 12 12$^{9\ 1/2}$

This unfortunate horse should have stayed in the barn. He was forced wide shortly after the start, then was pushed two horses wide at the 1/4-mile mark. At a 1/2 mile, while running 6th, he broke stride. His driver was forced to drop him back to 12th, where he stayed to the finish. He crossed the finish line 9 1/2 lengths behind the winner.

But before you assume too much about his potential, take a look further back in his past performances. Some horses are better at finding bad racing luck than they are at finding the winners circle. Make sure he's not a horse who's always in trouble.

The Least You Need to Know

➤ You must buy a program or a past performance publication. Some tracks provide past performances in their programs, while at others you have to buy both.

➤ The program gives you details about the races, the horses, the jockeys, and the betting permitted for each one.

➤ The past performances provide the secrets about the horses' speed, form, and current condition.

Chapter 19

Psst...Here's a Horse for You

In This Chapter

➤ Inside tips

➤ Tout sheets

➤ The morning line

➤ Public handicappers

➤ The favorite

Let's face it. It's what we're all looking for: the inside scoop on who's going to win. The idea of being in on a secret is almost as alluring as the chance for a financial windfall.

What's purported to be inside information is available from several sources. Some are truly inside, while others consist of nothing more than people who think that they're more skilled at reading the PPs than the rest of us. So who's a bettor to believe?

Inside the Stable Door

Much of the supposed inside information comes from the connections of the horse. Horse caretakers do talk, but what they say might not be useful. It depends both on the kind of information and its source.

The Trainer

If anyone knows whether a horse is ready for the race of his life, it's the trainer. He's also the one who knows if the horse should be locked in his stall and the key hidden from anyone tempted to enter him in a race. The horse's groom knows, too, but he may be a little less aware of the implications of workout times, the reasons for entry in a particular race, and future plans. Here's the inside information on tips from the inside.

When the tip is that the horse is ready for a big race:

➤ Trainers (and grooms) often indulge in wishful thinking about their horses. They're like proud parents, seeing the best and overlooking the worst.

➤ Some trainers are inclined to aim too high when their horses are in top condition, so it's not just a question of a horse being ready—it's also how ambitiously he's been placed.

➤ Trainers like to bet, too, and if they really do know that their horses are going to run better than expected, they don't like to share the information and drive down the odds.

➤ But this is also true: trainers are better able than anyone else to hide signs of impending success by working horses in the dark before the clockers are out, and by working them at farms and training centers where clockers aren't welcome.

When the tip is that the horse has no chance:

➤ Trainers know perfectly well when their horses are too unsound or unfit to compete, and most of them aren't going to bother entering such an animal. In most cases, if a horse is entered in a race, the trainer thinks he has at least a slight chance to earn part of the purse.

➤ But this is also true: Trainers have been known to enter horses for the exercise or experience, expecting a poor performance. This is most likely with young horses with quality breeding and with good horses who've been out of action for a month or more. If either situation exists, you might well believe the tip about the trainer's pessimism.

➤ Also true: Certain high-prestige races attract hopeless horses whose owners want to sit in the owners' box and hobnob with the rich and famous. Every Kentucky Derby features a few horses who have a chance only if everybody else in the race falls down. A negative tip from one of their trainers can be believed.

The Jockey or Driver

Jockeys and drivers can know much about a horse's condition and readiness, or they can know about the same as the people on the other side of the rail. Less, even, since few have the time to study the past performance charts in depth. Believe that the driver or jockey knows something in the following situations:

➤ When the jockey rides morning workouts. As we mentioned in Chapter 9, that's not always easy to find out. You'll sometimes see it noted in the workout tabulations.

➤ When the driver is the horse's regular handler. Catch drivers rarely drive workouts, but many drive the same horse week after week. A regular driver knows much more than one who hasn't driven the horse for a while.

➤ When he's a top jockey or driver. The leaders of the pack know more than any other kind because they are in a position to pick and choose their horses. They're not going to waste a race on a horse with no chance. This rule doesn't apply with top horses coming off layoffs or injury. In this case, they want to keep the mount and will give up a chance at a win in order to do it.

When the Tip Whispers Fix

The inside information you hear may include the word "fix," but before trying to cash in, remember this: Anybody who's trying to fix a race wants as few people to know about it as possible, both so he won't get caught and so that the odds don't shrink on the horses he's planning to bet on. He isn't doing it for the benefit of the average racegoer, and the story is unlikely to get around, at least before the race. Rumors may even be designed to discourage betting on good horses to lengthen the odds. When they win fair and square, the payoffs will be higher than they might have been otherwise. Here are the rules when your tipster says "fix":

➤ Ignore the tip.

➤ If you're convinced that the tip is legitimate, stay away from the race.

I've Got the Horse Right Here...

People who offer supposedly inside information to all comers for a price are known as *touts*. They used to stand outside the entrances to racetracks with handfuls of quickly printed tip sheets, most of which bore names that included the words *edge*, *advantage*, *secret*, and—most often—*inside*.

The best thing about most of the touts was that their publications were relatively cheap, usually only a dollar or two. You still see a few of the old-time touts outside the gates, but you're more likely these days to see them advertising in the newspapers or past performance publications, using 900 numbers or internet addresses.

These technoworld touts charge considerably more than a dollar or two. Tout services sound very impressive in their ads. Some claim 80 percent winners, others claim 100 percent profit, and still others claim an unbeatable daily double formula. How straight their faces are when they make these claims you'll never know because you almost never see them in person.

Their ads can be very convincing, and in fact, they're often true. So it's a great investment, then, sending a little money to a tout? Rarely, and here's why.

➤ The 80 percent winners may be a result of touting several horses in each race. Yes, there were winners, but there were even more losers.

➤ The 100 percent profit may be for one week, one day, or even one race. Unless the clients' betting was limited by some kind of divine intervention to that one unit of time, you can be sure that the real total profit was considerably less—or even nonexistent.

➤ The unbeatable daily double formula may involve wheeling almost every horse in both races. It's a guaranteed winner in terms of horses, but a guaranteed loser in terms of investment.

➤ And here's the biggest reason of all to avoid most touts. If they really know who's going to win at profitable odds, they can make all the money they need by placing bets themselves, not by advising others to place bets, thereby driving the odds down. The concept of touting usually fails on this account alone.

Some touts are undoubtedly better than others, and you may find situations in which you find it useful to buy their tips.

➤ Many offer a free sample. Take it and judge if their selections appear to be based on a sensible system or method. If they are, you may find it worthwhile to allow them to do the figuring for you.

➤ You may enjoy the whole process of receiving special information: the anticipation, the arrival, the follow-through.

➤ Some modern touts offer past performance analysis rather than names, or in addition to names. These sheets often include elaborate demonstrations of a horse's lifetime racing patterns. They help you discover which horse is due for a performance bounce up or down, and they can be both useful and accurate. Unfortunately, they're usually extremely expensive.

Touting for Free

General-interest newspapers that cover horse racing, specialty racing publications, and even the track programs themselves offer advice from experts on who's going to win which race. You get their advice for the price of the publication, and most of them are as good at picking winners as anybody else around the racetrack.

These are the public handicappers. The worst of them is pretty good or else he wouldn't keep his job for long. The best are excellent. Many public handicappers (or rather their editors) publish a running tabulation of their successes for the race meet. Sometimes they also report their theoretical profits. You'll be able to spot which ones you should believe. In the meantime, keep in mind the following points about public handicappers:

➤ They are required to pick winners for every race, every day, no matter how difficult some races are to figure. Their percentages are lower than they would be if they were permitted to skip a few races.

➤ Some publications allow each of their handicappers to make a top pick of the day, for which (presumably) the winning percentage is higher. It is called the Best Bet, the Super Pick, or the Top Choice. You'll be able to find it.

➤ Past performance publications summarize the selections of their handicappers into what's called a *consensus pick* for the race. Consensus horses tend to have the best winning percentages of all. You can have a superb winning record, but not necessarily a running profit, if you bet only on consensus picks.

➤ The fact that public handicappers are so public almost guarantees that their selections will have short odds. The more people who follow their advice, the more they will bet on the selections, and the lower the odds will be.

The Morning Line Handicapper

Every racetrack employs its own handicapper, but his role is a little different from the others. He's the morning line oddsmaker (he actually does the work one or more days in advance). Here's the inside information on the morning line man.

➤ He is estimating what the closing odds will be, not who's going to win. In reality, it usually works out to the same thing, but it can be difficult for him to leave his opinion out of the equation. He often makes the favorite his own choice to win. Most oddsmakers do their most accurate predictions on an average race day in which the hardcore fans are in attendance. On promotional days, or big race days, inexperienced bettors come to the track and sometimes place bets in an inexplicable manner.

➤ He works for the racetrack, so it's not in his interest to set odds that discourage betting. That means that horses who should be 1-9 will probably show up as 1-2 at most, and horses that should be 99-1 will probably be 20-1 at best. Otherwise, hardly anybody would bet on either one.

➤ His work constitutes a kind of self-fulfilling prophecy. It's the one prediction that everybody at the racetrack sees. Even if they don't buy a program, they're the odds that first go up on the tote board when betting opens, so the morning line has an inordinate influence on the decisions that people make about betting. They often become an accurate reflection of how people are going to bet because they tell people how to bet.

Democracy in Handicapping

Fans handicap races with their dollars, and they usually do a pretty good job of it. The starting favorite wins about 30 percent of the races, give or take a point or two in either direction. Harness favorites win more often than Thoroughbreds, with Quarter Horses between the two. The inside information on favorites follows:

➤ The favorite is, hands down, the most likely horse to win a race.

➤ The shorter the odds of the favorite, the more likely he is to win.

➤ The fans sometimes give unreasonably short odds to horses ridden or driven by crowd-pleasers. Famous jockeys and drivers get that way because they're good, but the horse is still most of the race. Sometimes their horses aren't the best, but the crowds make them favorites anyway.

The Least You Need to Know

➤ Trainers are often unrealistically optimistic about their horses, but they are also in the best position to hide signs of an impending good performance.

➤ Unless they work or race the horse regularly, jockeys and drivers don't know much more than anyone else about his readiness.

➤ Tout services tend to be selective about the successes they advertise, and most of them are not worth the cost.

➤ Public handicappers are skilled at picking winners, but their winning percentages would be higher if they didn't have to make selections for every race.

➤ The morning line oddsmaker is predicting how the public is going to bet on the horses, not ranking them as to who he thinks is going to win.

➤ The favorite of the betting public is usually most likely to win, and the shorter the odds, the greater the probability of victory.

Chapter 20

Super Systems and Marvelous Methods

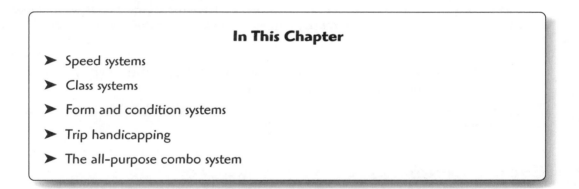

In This Chapter

➤ Speed systems

➤ Class systems

➤ Form and condition systems

➤ Trip handicapping

➤ The all-purpose combo system

Here's a likely scenario. You've studied the horses' appearance, their behavior, their breeding, and their past performances. You've looked at the skills of their trainers and their riders or drivers. You've analyzed the conditions of the race and the racetrack, and you've discovered one of two things:

➤ Every horse in the race appears to have a chance to win.

➤ No horse in the race appears to have a chance to win.

Two additional things then happen:

➤ The racing secretary does private handstands, having written a highly competitive race.

➤ Bettors do public handwringing, being unable to separate the contenders and place their bets with confidence.

The dilemma is solved by a system, sometimes printed or spoken with a capital S (feel free to call it a Method, with a capital M). A System isn't magic and it provides no guarantees, but it does help you separate horses without devoting every waking hour to your decision-making process.

Mostly Mindless Methods

You have two ready-made systems to call upon for your betting choices. In each of them, you can take the choice and make no further decisions yourself. You will get a respectable number of winners this way, but you'll probably lose money in the long run (and even in the not-so-long run). Or you can modify them, using some of the techniques mentioned later in this chapter.

Bet the Favorite

As we discussed in the last chapter, the betting public is pretty good at predicting winners. Unfortunately, the betting favorites also have the shortest odds, so the ones who win for you probably won't pay enough to make up for the ones who lose for you.

Your Favorites System might be this:

➤ Bet favorites, but only when they're tops in one of the other categories upon which more specialized systems are based.

➤ Bet favorites, but only when their odds are higher than 3-2, 2-1, or whichever you choose.

Bet the Consensus

You heard about him in the last chapter, too. He's the best bet in the race, figured by averaging the choices of a group of handicappers working for a newspaper or past performance publication. The consensus is usually the favorite, and his payoffs probably won't be high enough to make up for his losses. But he differs from the favorite in that he's the pick of at least three racing specialists, people who aren't likely to be overly influenced by the name of the jockey, trainer, or anything other than potential performance.

Your Consensus System might be this:

➤ Bet the consensus, but only when he's second or third choice.

➤ Bet the consensus, but sit out the race when he's not the top choice in at least one of the other systems.

The Sensible Systems

Serious bettors use hundreds of systems, some more successfully than others, but almost all systems fit into just a few general categories. You will also find systems that take the Chinese dinner approach, selecting a point from one, a couple of points from another, and a tiebreaker from a third. Will decisions never end?

Speed

Since the race goes to the horse who gets to the finish line first, systems that use speed as the primary factor lead our list of categories. The recognition of speed's importance exists in each of the racing sports. In Quarter Horse racing, it's almost everything. A horse *is* his speed. If he's fast, he wins. If he's slow, he loses.

In Standardbred racing, it's almost everything. Throughout his life, he'll be identified by his best-ever time for a mile. Tar Heel wasn't just Tar Heel. He was Tar Heel (1:57 2/5).

In Thoroughbred racing, speed is a little more ambiguous. There are so many variables in distance, track design, weight carried, and so on, that a lot of very intelligent people spend considerable time developing figures that are supposed to quantify race times. These figures have become so well respected that past performance publications offer dueling numbers in order to sell copies.

A well-designed method of determining figures manages to factor out weather, track bias, and things that make both the final and fractional times of races misleading. The figures make sure that you don't look at a race in a past performance line, see a plod-dingly slow final time, and assume that the horse can't outrun a Budweiser Clydesdale.

Refer back to Chapter 18 for information on where you find the most useful (and free for the price of a past performance publication) figures. Use them in a system like this one, the simplest of all for figures users.

From the Horse's Mouth

Speed figures are often called **figs**, and people who use them to bet are called **fig players**.

➤ Bet the horse with the highest printed speed figures, either total or average, over his past three races (use three races to eliminate the chance of an aberration that can occur with even the most careful figures).

But speed figures, no matter how carefully computed, lose their effectiveness in certain situations, making them a little less simple than they appear. Here's when the problems occur:

➤ When the current race is substantially different in length from previous ones. Although they're worked out so that distance isn't supposed to matter, you simply can't assume that a horse will run well or poorly when he tries a new distance.

➤ When either the current race or the previous ones takes place on an unusually wet or dry track. Yes, the figures take into account how slow or fast the track is on the day of the race, but there's no way you can quantify a horse's individual reaction to the feel of the track surface under his hoofs. He may hate to slip; he may enjoy splashing; he may hurt on a hard dry track.

➤ When either the current race or the ones that provided the figures are 1 1/8 mile or longer. Speed figures lose their importance as distances increase because pure speed becomes less significant.

If you choose not to put your faith in figures, you can still use speed to develop betting systems. Here's a system for the most common sprint distances. It's based on the fact that a horse with enough natural speed to get to or near the lead early has a good chance of holding on for a win, while a slower horse who has to come from behind more often fails.

➤ Examine each horse's last three races on fast or good tracks.

➤ Write down the horse's position at the first two calls in each of the races. Add the numbers (if he was second and third in one race, first and fourth in another, and sixth and fourth in the third, his total is 20).

➤ If two or more horses have the same numbers, adjust by subtracting 3 points for each race actually won by the horse, 2 points for second, and 1 for third.

➤ The lowest point total gets your money.

Here's another method of using speed, in this case the kind of speed that enables a horse to gain ground in the stretch. But don't neglect the value of early speed. Look for a horse who, in his last race:

➤ Was leading or was within 3 lengths of the lead at the first and second calls, and...

➤ Who gained at least 1 length between the final call at the middle of the stretch and the finish line, and...

➤ Who finished either in the money or within 6 lengths of the winner.

If there's more than one horse who qualifies:

➤ Look at the next-to-last races to try to find a horse who's gained ground more than once.

➤ If there's still a tie, prefer the higher placed finish if the class of the race is similar.

In each of these non-figure speed systems, it is worth your while to check your choice with the figure choice. If you and the numbers agree, the horse is a particularly appealing bet.

In harness racing, almost everybody who employs a sensible system of picking winners uses speed as the primary differentiator. Almost all races are one mile, making time comparisons far easier than they are in Thoroughbred racing. Even the differences in track speed are quantified in almost every program and all past performance publications. You'll find the chart displayed prominently, along with a key to figure a par speed for a race you're studying. You may find, for example, that if your horse raced a 2:01 mile at Freehold Raceway and his main competition raced 2:02 at Yonkers, you need to subtract 2/5 second from your horse's time to get a fair comparison. Here's the simplest harness speed system of all:

➤ Write down each horse's final times in his last three races.

➤ Adjust them according to the track variants published in your past performance charts.

➤ Average the times, and the horse with the fastest mile gets your money.

This super simple system works best in the following situations:

➤ When the previous races were on one-mile racetracks (less chance of interference on the big tracks means the final times represent race speed more accurately).

➤ When the horse who comes out first in the figures won his previous race or races going most of the way in front, suggesting that his time wasn't a result of being sucked along by a faster horse in front of him. It also suggests that he might have gone even faster if he had been pressed.

➤ When there isn't evidence of rough races or other trouble, such as the parked symbol (⁰), or other signs of interference.

You'll find that times in most previous races need to be adjusted, at least a little. Two examples:

➤ If the horse was parked, he covered extra ground, and you must take a fraction off his time to get an accurate picture of how fast he went. Here's a rough formula: A horse who has one ⁰ was forced to travel a whole extra horse and sulky wider than the others. If you see that at the 1/2-mile mark, take 2/5 off his final time. Take another 2/5 off for additional ⁰ symbols.

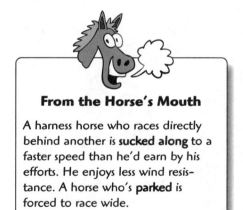

From the Horse's Mouth

A harness horse who races directly behind another is **sucked along** to a faster speed than he'd earn by his efforts. He enjoys less wind resistance. A horse who's **parked** is forced to race wide.

➤ Give the horse a little extra credit for a poor post position when the race took place on a 1/2-mile or 5/8-mile track. Give no additional time off for PPs 1 through 4, 3/5 second for 5 through 7, and a full second for any PP above 7.

Form and Condition Systems

A horse has to be in physical and mental condition to use his speed effectively. It doesn't matter how much talent he has or how good he used to be. He has to be good enough *now*.

Current condition matters so much that some Thoroughbred bettors use a system that says:

> Bet the horse with the fastest recent workout, particularly if it's a bullet (the fastest of the day).

This system assures you that you put your money on a horse who's both fast and ready. Of course, this system presumes that the workout was accurately timed and that it was at a racing distance, not the more common short workout distance.

Other bettors believe that form is different from condition, and they ask more of their systems. They want not just physical readiness, but also real-life proof that their bet is on a horse who's ready to race.

Some systems pay so much attention to the real world that the first step is this one unbreakable rule:

> Bet on NO horse who hasn't started in the last 30 days. You miss a few very good, pampered horses, but you probably save a lot of money that you might put on ones not at their peak.

Some bettors believe in recent racing so much that their system for picking winners goes on to say simply:

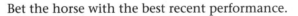

Bet the horse with the best recent performance.

Here's a slightly more elaborate, step-by-step procedure for a system based on current form and condition:

➤ Count the days since the last start for each horse.

➤ Add that to the number of the horse's finish in the race.

➤ The lowest total gets your bet. Example: A third-place finish seven days ago equals 10 points. A second-place finish 14 days ago equals 16 points. The 10 pointer wins.

Inside Track

While you usually shouldn't bet a horse in his first race after a long layoff, he's often ready for the performance of his life in his second start after a break.

This system, like all very simple systems, works best when there's little difference between the current race and previous ones in terms of class, track, weather, and so forth.

Here's another one whose simplicity is both virtue and vice. It's designed to pick a horse whose form is improving:

➤ Write down each horse's finish in his last three races.

➤ Pick out the horse who's last finish was an improvement on his next-to-last.

➤ If there's a tie, pick the horse who's finish in his third race back was an improvement over his next-to-last.

Some very expensive tip sheets offer an examination of each horse's racing career in terms of the circumstances surrounding his best performances. Their goal is to spotlight those horses that reach for a big *bounce* in performance. The race analysts who produce the sheets look at every race in a horse's career, not just the six to ten included in past performance charts.

They identify career-long patterns: Does a horse tail off in performance after five races? Does he bounce after a 60-day layoff and then two mediocre prep races? People who can afford a thousand dollars or more a year to subscribe swear by them, but you have to wonder why their publishers aren't just keeping the information for themselves.

From the Horse's Mouth

If you hear somebody claim that the **sheets** say a horse is ready, they're referring to the high-priced analysis publications, not the cheap tip sheets that give you four selections in a six-horse field.

Class

Some systems rely most heavily on looking at the class of the horses' previous races, the class of the current race, and figuring out what the differences between the two might mean to the outcome of the race. The simplest class betting system is this:

Pick the horses dropping down in class from their last races.

The rationale here is that a horse who's used to running against better horses will be overjoyed at the softer competition and will dominate them. The great weakness in this system is that horses usually drop in class (since purses and claiming price drop along with class) only when they can't win at the next higher level. If you bet on a drop-down, you're betting on a horse in the habit of losing.

To be fair, most horses do have an easier time the first time they face lower-class horses, but it's difficult to figure out if the horse is dropping because he can't quite handle the next level up or because he has such a physical or behavioral problem that he's not going to win at any level. Some people who glorify class choose another approach. Their system says that money talks:

Pick the horse who has the highest average earnings per start over his lifetime. Divide the total lifetime earnings (printed in all past performance charts) by the number of starts. Money is a pretty good indicator of class since the highest purses go to the highest class races.

If several of the horses earned the bulk of their money more than one year ago, modify the system like this:

Pick the horse who has the highest average earnings per start over his last six starts. This is a little harder because it probably requires that you do some adding yourself, but it gives you a better idea of current class than the lifetime figure.

Finally, here's a method that helps you pick a horse who's ready. It's based on the class of the horse's recent company, but it's the opposite of the first class-based betting system.

Pick a horse who's moving up in class.

What? You pick a horse who's about to face more difficult competition? Yes, and here's why. A horse who's moving into tougher competition is doing it because his connections believe he's in good form, good condition, and he's too good to risk at a lower claiming price. That's certainly a vote of confidence from the people who know him best.

To make sure he's not moving up because of trainer and owner delusions, look for this in the horse moving into better company:

➤ A win or close finish in his last start.

➤ No big increase in assigned weight, especially if the race is one mile or more. It's too much to ask a horse to beat faster horses carrying a heavier weight at the same time.

➤ As a tiebreaker: a previous race, even a while ago, at the new class level.

Trip

Trip handicappers are bettors looking for trouble. Their systems are based on finding horses whose past performances were better than they look because of problems they encountered during the races.

This approach can certainly help you find horses whose odds are longer than they should be, given the horse's form and talent. It can also help you find unexpected winners since the horse may have been dropped down to softer competition in an effort to change his luck.

Trip handicapping doesn't really offer a system, but it does give you guidelines to consider when looking for a likely bet. Here's the procedure:

➤ Examine each horse's past two or three races to see what kind of racing experiences he had.

➤ Look first for trouble. It's easier in harness than in Thoroughbred racing since the symbols are included at each point on the race line. Refer to Chapter 18 for details on this.

➤ Look for indications that the horse raced well in spite of the trouble. You may see evidence that a horse ran well early, dropped back while losing ground, then moved up again. He probably had racing trouble from which he recovered.

➤ After examining the charts, give a horse coming off a troubled race credit for being at least a little better than his finish or speed figures indicated.

➤ If he finished well, give him a lot of credit.

➤ If he appeared to have an untroubled race, racing on or near the lead the whole way, and still couldn't hold on, take away credit.

The Combo System

If you're serious about winning at the races, systems based exclusively on one category are a little too simple. A fast horse has the best chance, but a determined one, a sound one, or even a lucky one, can often beat him.

Class is nice, but many a fine stakes horse ends his career struggling against cheap claimers because of injury or age.

You have to pay attention to trips, but a bad trip in a previous race doesn't turn a slow horse fast. All it will help you do is get longer odds in a bet on him.

If you had the time, you might figure each race with simple systems from each category and then pick the horse that came out on top in the most systems. Or you might try this quick system to pick winners, taking factors from most of the categories. Analyze each horse like this:

➤ Quantify form by writing down the horse's finish in his last three races, then add those three numbers. If he's finished second, fourth, and first, his number is seven.

➤ Quantify condition by writing down the number of days the horse has been away from the races. A horse who last started a week ago gets a seven. This rule is a little unfair to high-quality horses who are asked for fewer races, but it's a useful standard in the vast majority of races.

➤ Quantify speed by writing down the number of lengths the horse finished behind the winner. (A winner gets a zero.)

➤ Quantify class by adding the odds to one the horse enjoyed in his last three races (you may have to break down some of the odds to a factor of one). 4-1, 3-2, and 2-1 equals 7 1/2.

231

➤ Add all the figures for each horse. The horse with the lowest total gets your money.

You notice that there are no speed figures, no attempt to assign numbers to different classes of races, and no race times. This system's attraction is its ease and quickness. It also shows that you can develop any system you like, using any combination of points from the categories. Try it. You may discover the best and most effective one of all.

The Least You Need to Know

➤ Systems and methods are designed to make picking winners quicker, easier, and less subjective.

➤ Betting only favorites and consensus picks is the simplest system of all.

➤ Other systems are based on speed, form, class, and trip handicapping.

➤ A particularly effective system takes points from each of the categories and combines them in a way to identify those horses ready to win.

Chapter 21

Money Matters

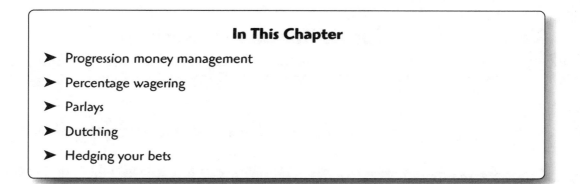

In This Chapter

➤ Progression money management

➤ Percentage wagering

➤ Parlays

➤ Dutching

➤ Hedging your bets

Let's pause for a minute to admire the people who can go to the racetrack, enjoy the races, bet on a few of them (because it really is more fun that way), and go home, writing off their net losses as the price of enjoyment. Let's admire them, but let's not spend too much time trying to emulate them. Unless you're happy to lose money, you can't be quite so lackadaisical about it. It's hard to pick winners, and it's even harder to make money when you bet on them.

How to Lose Even When You Win

The shadow known as takeout darkens every betting transaction you make, and to keep the gloomy metaphor going, you have to get out from under its murky depths if you hope to break even, much less win. Remember Chapter 16 and the story about takeout and its little brother, breakage? The evil twins see to it that 15 to 20 percent of the betting pool is spirited away before the money is distributed to the winning bettors.

The result is that you have to make sure that your winning bets give you at least 15 to 20 percent profit on those bets, plus enough additional profit to make up for all the bets that you lose altogether. You *will* lose races, since even the world's best handicapper isn't going to pick more than about 35 percent winners and 80 percent in-the-money finishers.

Making enough profit on your wins is a tall order since most of those 35 percent winners (more like 30 for normal people) are going to be favorites with modest payoffs. To make a profit of any kind, you need to pick more than a good share of winners. You need to manage the money you bring to the racetrack with caution, common sense, and a little bit of courage.

Your goal is this: You must win more when you win, and you must lose less when you lose. And you must make sure that you have enough money left to enjoy all the races you hope to.

There are methods and systems to help you do this. First, though, some basic and essential rules.

The Golden Rules of Racetrack Betting

These rules aren't much fun since they're designed to minimize your losses rather than maximize your wins. Follow them anyway, or else you won't have the money to try to win with.

From the Horse's Mouth

A *spot play* is a bet on a race that fits certain characteristics. A sensible bettor puts his money into spot plays, not an entire race card.

Rule #1 Don't bet every race.

Some races are so difficult to handicap that it's not worth your time to handicap them and not worth your money to bet on them. If you simply can't enjoy your day at the races if you don't have a little something on each race, do it this way.

Rank the races according to the confidence you have in your selections: those you think you've figured, those you hope you've figured, and those you have no idea about. Bet the most you can afford, be it $10, $20, or whatever, on the races in the first group. Halve that for the races in the second group, and put the minimum the track allows on races in the third group.

Rule #2 Don't go into debt to bet.

If you take your cash advance credit card to the track, you're almost guaranteed to lose, even if you win some bets. Not only does the interest on the credit card, added to the takeout, make it almost impossible to make a profit, but you'll keep doing it until you lose big. If you don't have it, don't bet it.

Rule #3 Quit while you're ahead.

This is what you're supposed to do whenever you bet, whatever you bet on. It's also the hardest rule to follow since it's human nature to want to repeat successes. It's also the nature of racing to make you believe (because it's true) that your skill and not just luck contributed to your win. So it's even harder to walk away from the window.

Do it anyway, and here's a method to help you. Decide before the first race exactly how much money you can realistically hope to win, given your bankroll and the looks of the races. Count your money after each race, and the moment you reach your goal, stop betting. Tell yourself that the satisfaction of reaching the goal is yet another win. (This works, if you're loud enough with yourself.)

Now, on to the systems for money management.

Being Progressive

Most of the systems you'll hear about involve what's known as *progressions*. Being progressive sounds very sensible, but the system sounds a lot less reasonable when you realize that it requires you to bet more after you've lost a race and less after you've won.

Actually, there is reason behind the concept. Progressive betting is supposed to allow you to recoup your losses after a series of losing bets, which—by all statistics—are likely to be more frequent than winning ones. The following table shows how progressive betting is supposed to work, using a flat $2 win bet as an example. You add $2 to your bet after every losing race, dropping back to your original $2 after you win.

Progressive Betting

Race 1	Bet $2 to win	Lose
Race 2	Bet $4 to win	Lose
Race 3	Bet $6 to win	Lose
Race 4	Bet $8 to win	Win
Race 5	Bet $2 to win	?

The theory is this: Although you lose more races than you win when you bet on horses, you *do* eventually win. The concept of adding to your bet each time you lose assures you of having a big chunk of money on the winner when you do hit the correct horse.

The example was a straight bet, straight amount progression. You're dealing with only a $2 increase with each bet. But there are other ways to follow a progressive plan.

If you want to be in line for really big payoffs, you can double the amount of each bet after a loser. That system would look like this:

Race 1	Bet $2.00	Lose
Race 2	Bet $4.00	Lose
Race 3	Bet $8.00	Lose
Race 4	Bet $16.00	Win
Race 5	Bet $2.00	?

You can establish any kind of progression you want and can afford. You may, for example, square the bets and put $16 on the third race, $256 on the fourth race, and so forth.

Any kind of progressive system has certain inherent problems:

➤ While you'll eventually pick a winner, it could be a very long time coming. Everybody who has anything to do with racing has stories about extraordinarily long losing streaks. Great jockeys can lose 100 races in a row (just ask Triple Crown winner Steve Cauthen). Fifty favorites in a row can lose. The Kentucky Derby can be run for 20 straight years with no two-year-old champion ever winning the biggest race for three-year-olds. By the time your losing streak ends, your deficit can look like the national debt.

➤ Even if your win comes sooner than later, your win will probably be with a horse with fairly short odds. In the "Progressive Betting" table earlier in this chapter, if your fourth race winner has odds shorter than 3-2, you'll still be in the hole.

Is there a progression that's a little safer and won't require you to bring your betting money to the track in an armored car? Yes. Instead of progressing your bet after one loss, do it after two, three, or four. This way, your total investment at the time of your winning bet may be a little lower, as will be your payoff, but you won't run out of money so quickly.

It's safer and probably more sensible to follow a money management system that calls for bets based on a percentage of your bankroll, rather than specific dollar amounts. Most of these work in the opposite manner from progressions.

The Percentage System

Bring a specific amount of money to the racetrack or simulcasting center with which to bet. Choose a percentage to bet on each race. The figure should be no higher than 10 percent if you plan to bet on each race of a ten race card.

If you've brought $100 and have chosen 10 percent, bet $10 on Race 1. If you lose, bet $9 on Race 2, and so on. When you win, the payoff goes into the bankroll. If you've won Race 2 for a payoff of $30, your bankroll grows to $120, and you bet $12 on Race 3.

You're not going to tap out with this system, and you're going to get a chance to enjoy the entire day's race card. Besides, you may walk away with considerably more money than you brought.

The Parlay

A percentage system is actually a kind of parlay since you bet more as you win more, even though the percentage of your bet hasn't increased. *To parlay* means to put your winnings for one race, if any, directly into a bet in the next race.

From the Horse's Mouth

To **tap out** is to lose the money you set aside for betting.

Some tracks even permit you to make a five- or six-race parlay bet on a single ticket with one visit to the betting window. Here's how it works.

➤ Pick your choices to win in as many races (up to the track's limit for a parlay) as you want to parlay, beginning with the race you feel most confident about. You must make all your decisions in advance of the first race in your parlay, so you can worry only minimally about odds.

➤ Fill out a parlay slip (or remember the race and horses' numbers) and buy the ticket in the amount you want to risk. It can be the track's minimum bet—$1 or $2—if you want to be very conservative.

➤ If your choice in the first race wins, the payoff will go directly into a win bet on the second horse in your parlay, and so on. Just sit back and watch. The computers will figure it all out for you.

You may do your own parlays, of course. Put whatever you win in the first race you bet into the next race, and you've done it. It's less convenient than when you let the track do it for you, but it's worth sacrificing convenience in certain situations:

➤ If the weather is changeable, and you think the track may become wet for a later race.

➤ If you're not sure about track bias, and you want to see its tendencies for the day.

Hedging Your Bets

You can decrease your chances of losing money while increasing your chances of collecting bets by hedging with place or show wagers. You hedge by:

➤ Betting to win, but betting only 1/3 of what you want to put into the race, and then:

➤ Bet 2/3 to place *or*...

➤ Bet 2/3 to show on a different horse.

If you have chosen well, you stand a good chance of earning back your investment, and a fair chance of making a decent profit.

Betting the same horse to win, place, and show is an *across-the-board* bet. It's the most conservative hedge of all, but it's likely to pay for itself only if the horse in question has pretty long odds.

Dutching

It's theoretically possible to place a bet on every horse in a race and guarantee yourself a profit, no matter which horse wins the race. It used to be done in the days when bookmakers ruled the race betting world.

The system is called Dutching, and it's concept is simple, although the implementation is neither simple nor cheap. Decades ago, some bettor (or possibly a bookmaker, hoping to protect himself) spent quite a few cold winter nights figuring out a mathematical formula to tell him how much money he should bet on horses at different odds to make sure that the lowest minimum payoff would be more than the total investment in bets.

It worked.

He knew that he would, for example, have to bet $12 on a 3-1 shot, $8 on a 5-1 shot, $3 on a 15-1 shot, and so on to make sure that he'd have his profit, regardless of who won. It would still work, if you could buy tickets with set and unchangeable odds. Figure your table, buy your tickets, and wait for your profit.

Unfortunately, the pari-mutuel system sells you the ticket on the horse, not the odds, which change up to post time. Yes, you can wait until the last moment and hope that those odds you see while you're standing at the betting window will be the final ones. But you're more likely to be standing there trying to adjust to last minute changes and describe 10 different bets with wildly varying totals to the clerk as the machines lock up, and you're shut out of the race.

But you can still use some of the Dutching concept to good advantage in your money management betting. Eliminate from your betting equation the horses who have no chance. Even the serious Dutch bettors probably hated to put anything on some of the horses, no matter how strong the guarantee of profit.

Pick three or four most likely winners among those you haven't eliminated. Divide the amount of money you plan to bet on the race among those three or four like so: The horse with the shortest odds gets the most money, the one with the longest odds gets the least. As a rough estimate, put about 25 percent more on a horse with 1 point shorter odds. Here's what your bet might look like on three good horses.

Horse 1	4-1	$8.00
Horse 2	3-1	$10.00
Horse 3	2-1	$12.50

If Horse 3 wins, he'll pay the least, but you'll win more than $36 for an investment of just over $30. If none of the three wins, you're out your $30, but this partial Dutch should work in most cases. No guarantees, though.

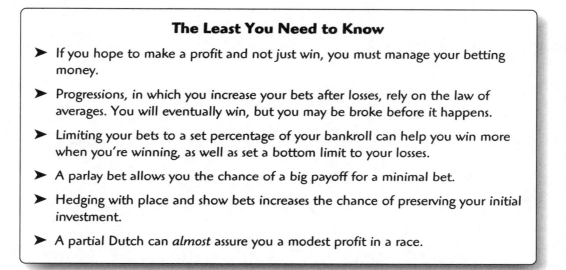

The Least You Need to Know

➤ If you hope to make a profit and not just win, you must manage your betting money.

➤ Progressions, in which you increase your bets after losses, rely on the law of averages. You will eventually win, but you may be broke before it happens.

➤ Limiting your bets to a set percentage of your bankroll can help you win more when you're winning, as well as set a bottom limit to your losses.

➤ A parlay bet allows you the chance of a big payoff for a minimal bet.

➤ Hedging with place and show bets increases the chance of preserving your initial investment.

➤ A partial Dutch can *almost* assure you a modest profit in a race.

Chapter 22

The Brave New World of Betting

In This Chapter

➤ Off-track betting

➤ Simulcasting

➤ Internet wagering

➤ Racetrack gaming

You don't have to go to the racetrack to place a bet. For a few hundred years now, you've been able to put money on a horse you've never seen, and you don't have to watch one second of the race after you do it. Nowadays, you don't even have to skulk through unmarked doors or whisper into pay phones to do it safely. In fact, many states license and a few operate off-track betting facilities, all in the name of revenue.

Thanks to Alexander Graham Bell, Thomas Edison, Bill Gates, and other techno adventurers, there's now more money bet away from the racetrack than at its pari-mutuel windows. Betting without a trip to the track is a growth industry, hugely popular and here to stay. It's usually not the best way to bet on a horse, but it can be done successfully.

Just-the-Facts OTB

Basic OTB is an old concept. The earliest facilitator of off-track betting was the book-maker who set up in the neighborhood rather than the grandstand. He's still there, although he and most of his colleagues might refuse your race bets in favor of action on the NFL, the NBA, and the NCAA finals.

Since betting on racing is legal in most states, illegal bookmakers and their customers nowadays prefer to avoid the chance of arrest on something everyone can do legally. But if you like the idea of non-pari-mutuel wagering on horses, there's still one place you can place legal bookmaker-style bets.

Las Vegas and Horses

Live horse racing has failed miserably in Las Vegas, but betting on horses has not. For 50 years, the casinos operated race books featuring odds that they set, just like old-time bookies. You picked your horses, and you waited for the results to be announced. Today, you can still do that for some races, including the Kentucky Derby and the Breeders' Cup.

Several casinos operate future books on big races, and bets placed with these books offer the advantages and disadvantages of all bookmaker betting:

➤ If you're a big bettor, you can wager on credit

➤ You get to lock in your odds, with no chance of seeing your potential payoff drop along with the odds as race time approaches.

➤ Your odds are locked, but you don't get to opt out if something occurs to your selection, and he doesn't look quite so good going to the post.

Early book betting, particularly the very early kind, can offer the opportunity for huge payoffs to people who are good at assessing a horse's potential for both improving his performance and remaining sound. If you want to place a future book bet on a horse, follow these rules:

➤ Don't bet any horse with anything that resembles short odds. It's not worth the risk because you can get short odds much closer to race time when it's clear whether they are deserved or not.

➤ Don't bet in the future book on any horse who already appears overraced. If it's February and you're looking at a horse for the Kentucky Derby in May, he'd better not have raced steadily since the previous summer. By May, he will be in his stall, munching hay, and resting up.

➤ Don't bet a horse with a history of unsoundness. Chances are he will be unsound again by race time.

For most races, the majority of Las Vegas race books commingle their pools with those of the racetrack, making a Las Vegas bet like a regular pari-mutuel off-track bet.

Here's what you miss with no picture: an unhappy horse with front bandages. He's probably not ready to do his best.

OTB Outlets

The simplest OTB outlet includes a betting window or two, a monitor that shows entries and odds, and a loudspeaker to transmit the call of the races. Some of them lack the loudspeakers, and you must look at the monitor to see if you've won or lost.

It's standard pari-mutuel wagering with your money going into a pool that's either exclusively made up of OTB bets or is commingled with on-track wagering. That can be good or bad:

➤ It's bad because most OTB operators add an extra little takeout, so your payoff for the same odds is less than it would be at the racetrack.

➤ It can be good if the serious, knowledgeable bettors all go to the track. You may get better odds on good horses at OTB than you do at the racetrack.

OTB outlets are usually more convenient to visit, but what you make up for in convenience is lost in other ways when you take your money to a bare-bones OTB outlet rather than take a trip to the track. You miss:

➤ A look at the horses being saddled and paraded to the start. You don't see who's using up his energy misbehaving or who looks especially healthy and sound.

➤ A look at the racing surface to see its true condition.

➤ A look at the early races on the card to judge the daily track bias.

Here's what you should do to make up for the weaknesses of no-picture OTB:

➤ Avoid betting on races where behavior is most likely to play a role, such as two-year-old events.

➤ Avoid races at the beginning of a race meet or early in the year, when many of the horses are coming off a layoff.

➤ Avoid races in inclement weather, since off tracks can be slow, fast, sticky, slippery, or anything in between. You can't judge it unless you can see it.

➤ Avoid a bet until you check the results of the first few races, noting past performances of the winners and placed horses. Try to figure out if the successful horses were early speed animals, if they prefer to stalk the leaders, or if they are in the habit of coming from behind. If you heard the race calls, see if the successful horses were able to run their typical races and if the track helped or hindered their preferred racing styles.

Simulcasting

Simulcasting was designed to cure the ills of OTB, and it has proved to be an easy pill to swallow for the racing industry. It emerged in a limited form during the late 1970s, and then exploded in the early 1990s as the primary forum for betting on horse racing. Most tracks now enjoy a larger handle from off the track than from on, and the percentage of the wagered money they collect in exchange for providing the racing program keeps some of them operating.

Simulcast races are transmitted by satellite from the racetrack to other locations where betting is accepted on them. The signals go to OTB outlets, to other racetracks where they're shown between live races, to greyhound tracks, to jai alai frontons, and to other facilities that are permitted to accept pari-mutuel wagering.

From the Horse's Mouth

Handle is the amount of money bet on a race or races.

Some simulcasting facilities take the word "simulcast" seriously, importing pictures from half a dozen or more racetracks at the same time. Others may show races from only a track or two. Simulcast races allow you to see the horses, judge the track surface, and look at the running of early races, overcoming many of the problems faced by people who have to bet blind at the other OTB parlors. But keep the following in mind:

➤ Some simulcast facilities don't show you pictures of the horses until they're being loaded into the starting gate, far too late to make any betting decisions based on appearance.

➤ Those who show post parade or even paddock pictures can't show every horse all the time. You're more likely to miss a horse acting up than actually see it.

➤ If signals are being imported from more than one racetrack, you must be very careful to make sure that you're watching the right horse. Horse 4 who's unloading his rider may not be the Horse 4 you're hoping to bet on in the next race.

➤ The betting cutoff at post time is usually extremely strict at simulcast facilities. You may find yourself watching the horses in the paddock but unable to bet on a race because the distant track is running late. Your chance to bet may end at the published post time, not the real start.

➤ Don't use betting systems or money management methods that rely on keeping track of last-minute odds and betting pool changes. That information may not be displayed in time because the monitors are being used for other races.

In-Home Wagering

As soon as they had computer systems that could handle it, most off-track betting enterprises began to offer telephone betting. Customers established accounts, usually through advance deposits, and called in their bets as the mood struck them. Among the negatives of telephone betting:

➤ You know even less about the horses than you do at the non-simulcast OTB outlet.

➤ You can't watch odds and pool changes, often finding yourself basing your bet on morning line odds and hoping that they'll hold.

The next step was to link telephone wagering and television broadcasts of races, thereby solving the most serious shortcomings of telephone wagering: the inability to see the horses and the difficulty in determining odds. The technology then moved quickly from telephone/television to interactive television.

Several tracks have begun experiments with equipment that allows bettors to watch races and place bets by pointing a device at the screen. They've been popular, but it's unlikely that either television or racing will want to invest any time soon in the expensive equipment that large-scale interactive systems will require.

Technology invariably explodes on several fronts at once. At the same time that computers became sophisticated enough to handle telephone betting, satellite time became both available and cheap. Racetrack signals could be sent anywhere in the world, and the concept of sending out a signal only locally became old-fashioned almost as soon as it began.

It's easiest to get legislative approval for bets placed by in-state residents on in-state races, but races in another state are another matter; and the linking of gambling, the telephone, and television broadcasts potentially runs afoul of several federal laws. Some states and tracks do offer telephone or television betting across state lines, but its legal future is hardly secure.

It's a rapidly evolving area, made even more complicated by the technology explosion on a third front: the home computer and the Internet. There are hundreds of companies that would like to get your betting dollars through your computer, and a couple dozen of them are already in operation. A few more will probably have opened by the time you finish reading this paragraph.

At the moment, most home computer-based wagering is of doubtful legality. This is almost certainly legal:

➤ An operation in which people in one state bet on races that take place in their own state via a state-regulated system.

➤ An interstate internet wagering system with the approval of all states involved.

These are possibly legal but may not be:

➤ Offshore operations which are run outside the United States but solicit bets from inside the U.S.

➤ Operations run from Indian reservations that do the same.

This is probably not legal:

➤ A U.S.-based, privately run system that solicits bets within the U.S., but who knows?

The law, as well as the number of potential betting sites, will change over the next few years (or even the next few minutes). In the meantime, follow these rules if you plan to try and hope to succeed at betting via computer:

➤ Keep track of the law. Some lawmakers want bettors to be prosecuted as vigorously as bet-takers.

➤ If you're convinced it's legal, bet by deposit rather than credit card. Otherwise, you may find yourself losing more than you ever intended or expected.

➤ Unless the law and the betting system provide prerace pictures of horses and track surface, follow the rules for betting on non-simulcast OTB races.

The Racetrack as Casino

In an inevitable effort to maximize profits, some racetracks now offer other ways to risk your money. More would do it if their state legislatures would allow them to.

Some tracks offer card rooms, others prefer video poker, but most would like to have slot machines, those voracious and mindless revenue generators favored by bettors who'd rather deposit money than think about their bet.

Racetracks, whether they own the slot machines or not, get a percentage of what's bet. This they direct towards purses, track maintenance, or profits.

When alternative gaming was first proposed for racetracks, the traditionalists predicted dire consequences for their beloved sport. Fans, they argued, come to the track with limited funds. Why let it be deposited in machines rather than bet on horses? Supporters argued that it didn't much matter where the money was put, as long as the revenue stream to the track kept flowing.

So far, the pro-slots people seem to be winning. Tracks that have installed them have seen less money bet on horses but more money coming into the tracks' coffers. Most of the tracks with slot machines have done well, and some have saved themselves from financial ruin. Financial ruin may still occur at these tracks, but it will happen to the people who deposit their money in the machines.

From the Horse's Mouth

Gambling proponents usually use the word **gaming** to describe non-racetrack wagering. A bet placed under any name is still money risked, and it doesn't seem like a game when you've lost it.

Most serious horse players stay away from alternative gaming at the track, particularly slot machines, for these reasons:

➤ You can't handicap machines like you can races, and you're trusting your money to chance.

➤ Time spent playing games is time lost for handicapping races.

➤ Money spent on games is money unavailable for betting on horses.

The Least You Need to Know

➤ Off-track betting is convenient but risky: You can't form an opinion about horses' physical condition, you can't judge the track surface, and you have trouble keeping track of odds and pools.

➤ Simulcasting cures some of the ills of OTB, but the plethora of racing at many facilities requires close attention to the odds and post time.

➤ In-home wagering may be the wave of the betting future, but at the moment its legality is suspect.

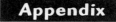

From the Horse's Mouth— The Glossary

Apprentice jockey   A rider with less than a year's experience. His mounts get a break in the weights. Since he has an asterisk next to his name in the program, he's also called a bug boy.

Backstretch   It's the long straightaway on the opposite side of the oval from the grandstand. The word also refers to the barn area, sometimes called the backside instead.

Bar shoe   A supportive shoe needed by horses with hoof problems.

Barn   They're really stables, but around the racetrack you must refer to horse housing as barns.

Bay   A horse with a red or brown coat and a black mane and tail. It's the most common color of Thoroughbreds and Standardbreds.

Bias   The tendency of every racetrack to favor one style of running over another.

Boots   Jockeys wear them, but so do harness horses to protect ankles, knees, and elbows from being cut by their own hooves.

Box   When you pick candidates for an exacta or trifecta but aren't sure of the order of finish, you box them. You choose your two or three horses and bet them in any order. That's two bets in an exacta and six in a trifecta.

Breakage   The few cents on each payoff for a winning bet that's averaged down from the nearest 10 cents. It goes into a special fund to pay off the bettors in minus pools.

Bridge jumper   Someone who puts a huge wager on a supposedly sure thing. He bets the horse to show, even though the guaranteed profit is only 5 percent. The bridge figures in if the horse finishes fourth.

Bullet   The fastest workout of the day, noted by a bullet sign or asterisk in past performance charts.

Bute   The common name for the pain-killing drug phenylbutazone, commonly given to American racehorses.

Cannon bone   The primary bone between knee and ankle in the horse.

Catch driver   A driver who concentrates on driving, rather than driving horses he trains himself.

Chart caller   He makes a simultaneous written record of how individual races are run and how each horse performs.

Chestnut   A reddish brown horse. He's likely to be called sorrel if he's a Quarter Horse.

Claiming race   A race in which any horse can be bought for a set price. It's the most common kind of race in North America.

Colt   A young male horse. Thoroughbreds remain colts until the age of five, while Quarter Horses and Standardbreds turn into stallions at four.

Condition books   A listing of scheduled races issued by racing secretaries several weeks in advance.

Conformation   A horse's physical structure, both overall shape and individual body parts.

Connections   Owner, trainer, and other people involved with the horse.

Crossfiring   A Standardbred gait flaw that occurs when one hoof strikes the hoof or leg on the oppposite corner.

Cushion   The amount of loose material, whether sand, dirt, or petrochemical particles, on top of the racing surface. It's usually two to three inches deep on a running track.

Dam   A horse calls his mother this.

Dark bay or brown   This common color of Thoroughbreds looks black to everyone except the official identifier.

Dark day   A day on which no racing is conducted at a particular racetrack.

Dash   A single race in which the first place finisher is the winner of the overall event.

Dead Heat   When two horses finish in a tie for any of the placings.

Entry   If two or more horses owned and/or trained by the same people are entered in the same race, they're called an entry and are considered one horse for betting purposes.

Exacta   A bet in which you must pick the first two finishers in exact order.

Exotic wagering   Anything other than straight win, place, or show betting.

Figs Not fruit, but figures. These are the results of complex mathematical equations developed by people who think that quantifying speed shown in previous races is the best way to pick winners.

Filly A young female horse. Thoroughbreds are fillies through four, while Quarter Horses and Standardbreds become mares at that age.

Flat Three definitions for the price of one: A Standardbred who doesn't break into a gallop from his trot or pace stays flat. A race that doesn't involve fences is a flat race. A horse who doesn't quite perform up to snuff is flat.

Foal A baby horse. You're most likely to hear it in reference to a stallion's or mare's offspring: Secretariat sired 653 foals.

Furlong One-eighth of a mile. It's the primary unit of race measurement in North America and Britain.

Gallop The horse's fastest gait. It's prized in every race horse except the Standardbred, who has to be pulled out of contention if he breaks into one.

Game A horse who's brave, determined, or hard-working.

Gaming If you want a more genteel word for gambling, use this one.

Gelding A castrated male horse. Geldings are usually more consistent and better-mannered than stallions, but horses with outstanding breeding are rarely gelded.

Get The offspring of a stallion. Get also refers to a horse's ability to race a certain distance. If he can do it successfully, he can get the distance.

Hand The basic unit of horse measurement, equaling four inches. Horse height is measured from the ground to the high point of the withers, the top of the shoulder just in front of the saddle.

Handle The amount of money bet on a race or on a race card. It's more important to racetracks than attendance, since the figure usually includes off-track wagering.

Heat racing To win this kind of Standardbred event, a horse must win two or more individual races before being declared the winner of the event.

Hindquarters What we'd call the hips and buttocks in the human being.

Hock The rear leg equivalent of the knee in four-legged animals.

Hot box A steam room for jockeys. It's not a luxury but rather a necessary device to help them make their assigned weights.

In the money This usually applies to a horse who finishes first, second, or third, providing a payoff to his bettors. Some people consider a horse who earns a portion of the purse to be in the money, so fourth- and sometimes fifth-place finishers may be included.

Jockey's colony This refers to the jockeys who ride regularly at a given racetrack.

Journeyman   Once a jockey loses his apprentice allowance, he becomes a journeyman.

Length   The body length of a horse. This unit of measurement is used to compare positions of horses at various points in a race.

Lines   Harness racing uses this term instead of reins, but it means the same thing.

Maiden special   This race is limited to horses who've never won but who have too much potential to risk in claiming races.

Mare   An adult female horse.

Morning line   The odds set by the track oddsmaker, attempting to predict how the public will bet.

Off track   Any track that isn't fast and dry. It can range from sloppy but very fast to wet, deep, and slow.

Out   A start.

Pace   This Standardbred gait features legs on the same side moving backward and forward at the same time. Pacers are sometimes called amblers or sidewheelers.

Paint or pinto   A horse with splotches of white and solid color. If you see one racing, you're not watching Thoroughbred, Standardbred, or Quarter Horse racing.

Parked   When a harness horse is parked, he's still moving. But he has been forced to race wide.

Past performances   How the horses performed in their previous races. The charts of past races hold the key to the present race.

Payoff   The amount of money you get back on a winning ticket. It's also called the payout.

Pool   The total amount of money bet in each wagering category. In the average race, you'll see separate pools for win, place, show, and any exotic bets being offered. A minus pool is one in which there's not enough money to pay back the minimum payoff to every winner.

Post parade   This is the first time most of the crowd sees the horses before a race. They walk in front of the grandstand before beginning their warmups.

Post position   The place in the starting gate for each horse, with the lowest number nearest the rail. They're usually drawn, but they are assigned in some Standardbred races.

Profit   The amount of money returned to the winning bettors, minus the money they put into their bets.

Provisional driver   In harness racing, a driver who's not fully licensed. It's the equivalent of an apprentice jockey without the weight advantage.

Purse   The prize money offered for the race.

Quarter Horse   The racing breed that specializes in races of 220 to 660 yards.

Quinella   A bet in which you pick the first two horses. If they finish 1-2 in either order, you win.

Race card   The entire day's race lineup makes up the race card.

Rating   This is what the jockey or driver does when he asks his horse to save energy for a run later in the race.

Rigging   A Standardbred's harness, protective equipment, and other gadgets designed to make him perform better, plus the manner in which it's fastened to him.

Ringer   A horse who's entered in a race under a name not his own. When it's intentional, it's to make a killing at the betting windows. Nowadays, it's usually accidental and discovered before post time.

Roan   This is a horse whose body is a dark solid color with white hairs intermixed. He'll probably look gray to you.

Route   A race that's longer than 1 1/8 mile.

Scratch   The withdrawal of a horse after the entries are announced but before race time.

Shafts   The two long pieces that attach the sulky to the horse's harness.

Shipper   A horse who travels from where he's trained to race at another track. A shipper is an unknown quantity and often enjoys long odds.

Simulcasting   Televised transmission of a race for betting purposes.

Sire   A horse's father goes by this name.

Sound   Some people use this word to describe only a horse whose legs are healthy and painless. Others consider a horse to be sound only if his legs are strong, his breathing is adequate, and his general health is good.

Spavin   A swelling in the rear leg on or near the hock. You're more likely to see it in a Standardbred rather than in a Thoroughbred.

Spot play   A race that offers a particularly good bet, such as one with a healthy horse dropping down in class. A sensible bettor usually concentrates his money on spot plays.

Sprint   A race shorter than one mile.

Stakes race   It also goes by the name of added money race. Horses are either invited by the track or staked to the race by a fee paid by their owners. The fees are added to the purse.

Stallion   An adult male horse.

Stamina   The endurance needed by a horse who hopes to win any race longer than a sprint.

Standardbred   The racing breed that competes under harness, either at the trot or pace.

Stewards   The officials who act as judge and jury in the interpretation of the rules of racing, including placements, disqualifications, and suspensions.

Stoopers   People who scour the floors after races, looking for mistakenly discarded winning tickets.

Stud fee   The amount of money the owner of a mare must pay to have her bred to a stallion. The highest at the moment is about $150,000, enjoyed by half a dozen Kentucky Thoroughbreds.

Sucked along   A Standardbred who races directly behind another, benefiting from less wind resistance. If he were a race car, he'd be slipstreaming.

Sulky   The vehicle pulled by the Standardbred during a race. He usually trains with a jog cart.

Tack   Horse equipment, including bridle, saddle, harness, and miscellaneous accouterments.

Tag   A horse who competes in claming races is running for a tag. The tag is his claiming price.

Taken down   A horse who's disqualified is taken down. In reality, it's his number that's taken down. He remains upright.

Takeout   The money in each betting pool not returned to the bettors. It goes to the racetrack for operating expenses and to the state for taxes.

Tap out   This is what happens when you don't follow the advice in this book and lose all the money you brought to the racetrack.

Thoroughbred   The racing breed that specializes in 3/4-mile to two-mile dashes.

Tote board   This is short for Totalisator board, named for the company that first produced it. It's the computerized display board that tells you what you need to know about odds, payoffs, time, and other details of the race.

Track superintendent   He's responsible for maintaining the racing surface. He always plays a role in who wins, and he often has something to do with who survives to race another day.

Train   In a broad sense, horses who are being conditioned are being trained. More specifically, to train is to work out at something approaching race speed.

Trifecta   Also known as the triple. This bet requires you to pick the first three finishers in exact order.

Triple Crown   The most famous Triple Crown is Thoroughbred racing's Kentucky Derby, Preakness, and Belmont Stakes for three-year-olds. If one horse wins all three, he earns the crown. In harness racing, both trotters and pacers have their own Triple Crowns.

Trot   The normal midspeed gait of four-legged animals. It features legs on opposite corners moving at the same time.

Turf   Grass. It's the most common racing surface in most of the world, but not in North America.

Vet's list   A list of horses temporarily prohibited from racing for medical reasons.

Walking ring   In flat racing, you first see the horses here, as they're saddled, mounted, and walked around before heading to the racetrack. At some tracks, proceeding saddled in a paddock before proceeding to the walking ring.

Wheel   To pick one horse, then bet every possible combination with that horse in an exotic wager.

Wire   The finish line. There's no actual wire involved. It's an imaginary line running between poles.

Yearling   A young horse between his first and second birthdays.

Index

Y